Acing the Interview

How to Ask and Answer the Questions That Will Get You the Job

Tony Beshara

AMACOM

New York • Atlanta • Brussels • Chicago • Mexico City • San Francisco
Shanghai • Toyko • Toronto • Washington, D.C.

Special discounts on bulk quantities of AMACOM books are available to corporations, professional associations, and other organizations. For details, contact Special Sales Department, AMACOM, a division of American Management Association, 1601 Broadway, New York, NY 10019.
Tel: 212-903-8316. Fax: 212-903-8083.
E-mail: specialsls@amanet.org
Website: www.amacombooks.org/go/specialsales
To view all AMACOM titles go to: www.amacombooks.org

This publication is designed to provide accurate and authoritative information in regard to the subject matter covered. It is sold with the understanding that the publisher is not engaged in rendering legal, accounting, or other professional service. If legal advice or other expert assistance is required, the services of a competent professional person should be sought.

Beshara, Tony, 1948–
  Acing the interview : how to ask and answer the questions that will get you the job / Tony Beshara.
      p. cm.
  Includes index.
  ISBN 978-0-8144-0161-3 (pbk.)
  1. Employment interviewing.   2. Job hunting—Handbooks, manuals, etc.   I. Title.

  HF5549.5.I6B4715 2008
  650.14'4—dc22

                                                            2007033582

Printing number

10 9 8 7 6 5 4

*To my beautiful soulmate
for 38 years, Chrissy*

Contents

···

Prologue

··

'm often amazed at how many people think that answering job interview
questions is straightforward and easy. "Just be yourself," they say, "answer
every question truthfully to the best of your ability, and you'll be fine." It
would be great if things were that simple, but there's a lot more to job interviews than that.

Answering questions in today's interviewing environment is much harder
than most people realize. Tough or unexpected questions can be thrown your
way at any stage of the interview process. Some questions are not even designed to elicit a right or wrong answer, but just to see *how* you answer them.
You won't succeed if you try to "wing it" through an interview. You must be
ready for every question; the wrong answers can cost you a wonderful career
opportunity.

Maintaining a successful business today is more challenging than it has
ever been. The global economy has increased competition across the board.
Technology has leveled the playing field for efficiency and productivity. Employers are taking extra care to see that they hire the right people, and they use
a wide range of questions to get the information they need. While job opportunities have increased, so has the possibility of making the kind of crucial mistake that immediately weeds you out of the competition for a specific opening.

I have been finding people jobs since 1973. I have personally placed more
than 6,500 people on a one-on-one basis. I have interviewed more than 22,000
people, and I have interacted with more than 25,000 hiring authorities. I have

experienced just about every conceivable question and heard just about every answer to questions used in the interviewing process. In this book, I share with you the surefire answers to those questions—the answers that will get you hired.

Getting a job offer is one challenge, but finding out about the company and the people you are going to work for is just as important. With the rapid changes in business today, a job seeker must not only be able to answer a variety of interview questions, but also be able to ask the right questions before accepting a job. This book also will show you what questions to ask to protect yourself so that you don't wind up working for the wrong company. It will teach you how to "check the references" of your potential employer.

My goal in writing *Acing the Interview* is to enable you to take charge of the interview process, to give you the confidence to answer any and all questions, and to provide you with the questions to ask in order to land the right job for you.

Tony Beshara
Dallas, Texas

PART

1

Today's Hiring Authority and You

Chapter

1

What Today's Job Seekers Need to Know About Themselves and Their Competition

....

This book is about how to answer and ask questions in the interviewing process so that you, the candidate, can get the best job possible. In order to answer questions correctly so that you can get a job offer, as well as ask questions so that you can evaluate a job offer, you need to be aware of your condition, so to speak, as a job candidate.

The emphasis of this book is not just to know how to answer and ask questions skillfully, but to put into context those answers and questions so that you can not only get a job offer, but choose the right one. Over the last few years, the context—that is, the market, the rules, the situation, etc.—of being a job applicant has drastically changed. The job search market is always erratic and highly volatile, and the past few years have been no exception.

There is a phenomenal amount of paradox in the context of being a job candidate today. On one hand, the U.S. economy has been adding over 110,000 new jobs every month for about the past two years. Unemployment has held at about 4.5% of the working population—close to a six-year low and a far cry from 6% to 6.3% in the early 2000s. But, even though the economy, on paper, is expanding, there is a phenomenal amount of erraticism with businesses in the United States.

We will discuss the context of the average U.S. company (if there is such a thing as "average" in today's markeplace) and the hiring authorities in those firms in the next chapter. In this chapter, I'm going to describe the context of today's job seeker. If you understand this context, answering and asking questions in the interviewing process is going to be a lot easier. You will understand better how to get the best possible job.

Gone are the days of looking for a job and at the same time seeking a "career path" within that same firm. If, as a job candidate today, you ask a hiring authority what the career path with the company will be, you will either get a big lie or, if the hiring authority is honest, you'll get a blank stare, a pregnant pause, and a truthful answer of, "I really don't know."

Keep in mind that my perspective comes from personally working with thousands of hiring managers since 1973. I am personally on the front lines of dealing with hiring on a daily basis and have been since I began in this profession. Our firm deals with hundreds of companies on a monthly basis and thousands on a yearly basis.

This book is going to relate to you the context of *real*, in the trenches, frontline U.S. businesses and hiring in this country. Keep in mind that the vast majority of businesses in the United States employ fewer than 100 people. I will get into it further in the next chapter, but suffice it to say, most businesses do not, contrary to popular belief, operate with common sense and distinct business acumen. The sad truth is that many businesses in this country lack common sense and can be greedy and ignorant (often reflecting the people who run them). In spite of these negative factors, the U.S. business climate is still the most successful in the world and it will continue to be.

As a candidate, however, when you go to answer or ask questions in the interviewing process, you need to be aware that the vast majority of U.S. businesses and U.S. business people do not operate with pristine theory or foolproof business acumen. Complaining about it won't do any good. You just have to deal with it.

Putting Yourself in Context

In order to perform well in the questioning of the interviewing process, you need to recognize a little bit about yourself and your peers looking for a job in today's market. If you understand your own context, as well as the context of the people you are interviewing with, successful interviewing will be easy.

As mentioned above, the idea of going to work for an organization and building a career path for any reasonable length of time simply isn't realistic. This is the reality of the context of today's job candidate.

Highlights from a recent study published by the Bureau of Labor Statistics of the U.S. Department of Labor showed that:

- Persons born from 1957 to 1964 held an average of 10.2 jobs from the ages of 18 to 38. These baby boomers held an average of 4.4 jobs while ages 18 to 22. The average fell to 3.3 jobs while ages 23 to 27, 2.6 jobs while ages 28 to 32, and 2.5 jobs from ages 33 to 38.

- These baby boomers continue to have large numbers of short duration jobs even as they approach middle age. Among jobs started by workers when they were ages 33 to 38, 39% ended the job in less than a year and 70% ended in fewer than five years.

- The average person was employed 76% of the weeks from age 18 to 38. Generally, men spent a larger percent of weeks employed than did women (84% vs. 69%). Women spent much more time out of the labor force (26% of weeks) than did men (11% of weeks).

- This group also experienced an average of 4.8 spells of unemployment. Business Briefings recently reported that a 40-year-old average U.S. worker has changed jobs ten times.

The average 40-year-old worker in the United States changes jobs every two years. Although the Bureau of Labor Statistics has never attempted to estimate the number of times people change careers in the course of their working lives, my sense is that the older we get, the more stable we become in our jobs. In fact, a Department of Labor statistic bears this out. The DOL showed that the median tenure of workers aged 55 to 64 was 9.6 years—more than three times that of the younger workers. The worker at age 55 to 64, however, as we will analyze, sees the world differently then the 28- or 29-year-old worker. My sense is that the stability factor of these older workers isn't as much a reflection of today's business as it is a reflection of the values that were established when they first entered the work force thirty-five or forty-five years ago.

One challenge to compiling labor statistics is that there is no consensus as to what, exactly, constitutes a career change. For instance, if a person is promoted in an organization from a sales position to a sales manager's position or from an accounting position to an accounting manager's position, has his or her career changed from sales and accounting to a career of management? It would depend on how you define it as a career change. If a web designer was laid off and then took a job as a production supervisor for six months, then went back into web design, has he or she changed careers? There is no way of having a consistent definition of what "changing careers" means.

As a friend of mine, Paul Hawkinson, who is the editor of *The Fordyce Letter* (February 2007, p. 6), the foremost U.S. publication for the recruiting industry, writes that:

> It seems that we're becoming a nation of "itinerant fruit pickers" where almost *all* jobs are impermanent. When CEOs are playing "musical chairs" with increasing frequency and most other senior executive level jobs are just transitory in nature, it's no wonder that America's work force has adopted a similar mindset. Especially since employers are no longer keeping "retirement watches" in their inventory because so few of their employees are kept on board long enough to get them. Loyalty is a two-way street and that street is full of potholes these days.

Let's face it; life on this earth is temporary, anyhow!

With this in mind, your approach to the interviewing process is going to be different. Your "career" will likely be a string of two-and-a-half- to three-year stints for at least the first 75% of your working life.

The Uncertain Attitude of the U.S. Worker

Although the economy is expanding and unemployment is lower than it's been since the late 1990s, the perceptions of risk and insecurity on the part of the U.S. worker do not match this reality. Although people think the economy is better, they aren't sure if they are actually better off as individuals. The average U.S. worker feels insecure about both job and future employment.

As stated above, the United States added an average of about 175,000 new jobs every month in 2006, and more than 110,000 every month in 2007, and we've gone from 6.3% unemployment in 2003 to between 4.7% and 4.5% today. The average income in the United States was up 6.5% in 2006 over 2005. Salaries were up 6.9% in 2006 over 2005. U.S. households' net worth recently hit $52 trillion, which is a record high, and corporate profits also are up. As a country and as individuals, we should be encouraged if not elated.

But in spite of all of the positive signs, we as individuals are pessimistic, uncertain, and, to say the least, vulnerable. Countless corporate restructurings and layoffs have destroyed the concept of career-long employment that for too long sustained the U.S. workers' confidence.

Lifelong employment is a thing of the past. Louis Uchitelle, who wrote *The Disposable American* (New York: Alfred A. Knopf, 2006), notes that, between 1981 and 2003, some 30 million U.S. workers were displaced due to layoffs, according to the Bureau of Labor Statistics. A modern form of contracting the workforce began with "layoffs."

Quite a number of surveys confirm that the percentage of individuals "somewhat likely" or "likely" to be laid off or fired has steadily risen over the past decade. Layoffs are not going to go away, but they don't have to be as numerous as they have been since the late 1990s. Uchitelle asks, "Are we going to once again be a community of people who feel obligated to take care of one another, or are we going to continue as a collection of individuals each increasingly concerned only with his or her well being? If we can band together again, as we did during the 40-year stretch that started in the Depression and ended with the Vietnam War, job security will gradually return to the United States," according to Uchitelle. His hope couldn't be further from the truth.

Even on the CEO level, stability is treacherous. In 2006, a U.S. company CEO departed either voluntarily or by force every six hours, double the number of CEOs who left their jobs in 2004.

Political commentator Ruy Teixeira* observed that the United States is a "nation of unhappy campers." He cited a Hart Research Associates/AFL-CIO poll that found 54% of Americans are "worried and concerned about reaching their economic goals." The majority of these people felt that their real wages were declining, felt that their earnings were not keeping up with prices, and worried "very or somewhat often" about the cost of living rising faster than their income. In spite of the reality of things like low unemployment and high household net worth, over 75% of Americans are both dissatisfied with the country's economic situation and worried about achieving their economic and financial goals. The concrete facts don't support our fearful attitude.

This fearful attitude reaches all strata of employees. Traditionally, the least educated are far more economically insecure than their better-educated peers.

---

*Ruy Teixeira is a Senior Fellow at The Century Foundation and The Center for American Progress and author or coauthor of five books. Quotes are from *What the Public Really Wants on Jobs and the Economy*, Ruy Teixeira, Center for American Progress, October 2006.

Workers with less than a high school education are the group most likely to report significant employment and financial anxiety. However, recent studies indicate that college-educated U.S. workers, with perceived "comfortable" earnings, are experiencing the same significant levels of anxiety.

In addition, the percentage of U.S. managers, mostly degreed, who felt they were doing worse financially in a given year than in the previous one has increased over the last three decades. In fact, the rate of job losses among the most educated, those with a college degree, has increased more steeply than the rate of job loss among the less educated. In one study that included proportionate samples of all education and economic levels, close to 50% of the individuals surveyed reported that they would be very fearful of finding a job with the equivalent pay and benefits to their current job if they lost their current job.

Rising levels of insecurity, even among those who have traditionally been in the highest and most secure levels of employment, suggests that the U.S. dream is under a lot of pressure. It appears that the most advantaged among us are lying awake at night, thinking about job and economic issues. National disasters like 9/11 and extended war, as well as regional "recessions" caused by things like Hurricane Katrina and the subprime housing bust don't help. They reinforce economic and job fears.

Generational DNA

Know who were the most exciting players of the 2006 Super Bowl were, don't you? Well, it wasn't the football players. The high point of the Super Bowl was the four players who entertained everyone at halftime. Mick Jagger and the Rolling Stones, whose average age is 62.8 years, entertained and transcended generations of workers. Their energy was fantastic. Their product is at least thirty years old, but they give a great original delivery every time they perform. Baby boomers in the work force!

Soon, there will be four generations of people in the work force and therefore four generations of people competing as job candidates. The "traditionalists" born between 1922 and 1943, the "boomers" born between 1943 and 1960, the "Gen-Xers" born between 1960 and 1980, and the "Millennials" or "Gen-Y" born after 1980. Each generation has a different perspective of a work role.

It is important to know where you personally fit in the "generational DNA" because you're going to be competing with different people from different generations as well as interviewing with different hiring authorities of different generations. We'll look at the need to be aware of this regarding hiring authorities in the next chapter, but here I will discuss how this reality affects you as a candidate regarding your competition—other candidates.

Traditionally, U.S. business has had to deal with, at most, two working generations at a time. Even then, the values of those generations were not drastically different. Primarily because of technology, there is a much greater difference between all of the generations that are now and will be in the work force. Their differences have come faster and are greater than ever before. These differences are going to be revealed in the interviewing process. They can work for you or against you, depending upon your recognition of them.

The "traditionalists" are known for their loyalty, hard work, and faith in their institutions, i.e., employment, government, and social (e.g., churches, schools, etc). They remember World War II and, if they didn't experience it, felt the immediate impact of the Great Depression. They're fiscally responsible. Work/life balance is very important to them, and if they haven't retired yet, they're likely to just "redirect" their careers.

"Boomers" have a tendency to identify themselves with their career achievements. They invented the 60-hour or more workweek and the getting-ahead-through-hard work ethic. There are 80 million of them in the work force. They have a tendency to be optimistic but see themselves as "change agents." They are idealistic, but not as trusting in their government as their predecessors as a result of Vietnam and Watergate.

"Gen-Xers" grew up with the advancement of technology. They are adept and comfortable with change in their resources, hard working but want an individual balance of work and play in their lives. They're the first generation of latchkey kids and the first generation of techies. They have a tendency to trust themselves more than the group and are independent but flexible with change. Their job security is to be constantly learning. Their attitude is that "If I know enough, and am getting new skills, no matter what happens, I can always find a job." They have experienced scandals in business as their predecessors experienced scandals in government. The drastic and erratic changes in business don't bother them at all. They like to be in control and want fast feedback.

The "Millennials" (Gen-Y) grew up with technology. Everything can or should move fast with them, they're eager to learn, and they enjoy questioning. They grew up with customized iPods, 24-hour media, 180 TV channels, the Internet, a global marketplace, and September 11th. They have a tendency to be pragmatic, collaborative, and really understand a worldwide global perspective. They like teamwork, are flexible, have a keen sense of time management, and are the ultimate multitaskers.

So, how does this affect you? Well, if you were 25 years old and had three jobs in three years after you got out of college or five jobs in five years since you entered the work force and you're interviewing with a 62-year-old traditionalist who has been with the same company for thirty-five years, or started it, for that matter, you're going to have to interview differently than you think!

If you are a 60-year-old "boomer" interviewing with a two-year-old company founded by three 25-year-old "Millennials" who are high risk takers, you are going to have to alter your interviewing style.

These cultural differences also will have an impact on how the hiring authority views his or her company. We will discuss that in the next chapter. Just be ready for the generational DNA differences in today's economy. This awareness will impact your questions and answers in the interviewing process.

Your Emotional State

On top of these new issues in the interviewing and hiring workplace, you, as a candidate, still have to confront the age-old issue that looking for a job is an emotionally difficult thing to do. Having to find a job, whether you have one or you are looking full-time, is an emotional strain. Next to death of a spouse, death of a parent, death of a child, coupled with divorce, looking for a job is the fourth most emotionally stressful thing we do. Today, more so than in any other time in our history, even though the economy is on healthy recovery, research shows that you as an individual are very insecure about keeping your present job. If you have a job, you are scared that if you lost it, you couldn't replace it at the same level.

No matter how often a person looks for a job, it is still emotionally stressful. People are usually scared and frightened. I discuss this state in detail in my book *The Job Search Solution*, but suffice it to say here that when people are frightened, scared, and emotionally distressed, they won't interview well unless they are prepared for the shock.

When it comes to answering interview questions in this state, unless a candidate thoroughly prepares and practices, there is a great likelihood that this emotional unease will be revealed and thereby destroy any chance at a good interviewing process. When people are in such an emotional state, they have a tendency to focus on their own needs and forget that their goal in the interviewing process is to sell themselves to a perspective employer. They have to focus on what they can do for the potential employer rather than what the employer can do for them.

When people are emotionally stressed, they usually want to focus on their own needs, rather than on the needs of someone else. They often forget that, in order to get a job offer, they have to focus on how they can solve the hiring authority's problem—his or her needs, not those of the candidate.

I would emphasize that one of the purposes of this book is to prepare you for the emotional strain of looking for a job that is reflected in the interviewing process, especially in answering and asking questions. If a candidate answers and asks questions in a nervous, self-centered, fearful manner, he or she simply won't get hired.

There are many ways to deal with the emotional strain of interviewing, but one of the most important things that an individual can do will be emphasized in this book and that is to practice for the interviewing process so well that fear is minimized, if not eliminated. If you practice the answers to the questions in this book and understand the real reason that certain questions are being asked, the emotional strain of the interviewing will be minimized.

Likewise, if you are prepared to ask the right kind of questions about an opportunity, at the right time, the probabilities of making a mistake in taking a job will be minimized. Again, asking these kinds of questions takes practice. Candidates are so often anxious about getting a job offer and possibly losing or taking one that they often forget to ask the right questions, even if they know them. This book will keep that from happening to you.

Paradox of Interviewing

There is a great paradox of interviewing that has become even more prominent over the last few years. Just recognizing this paradox is going to put you one step ahead of your competition. The paradox is simply this: You are going to interview and are being interviewed for a position as though the position was one you are going to be at for the rest of your career.

It is very rare for any hiring authority or hiring organization to admit that it's going to hire you or anyone else for a two-and-a-half- or three-year period of time. Most organizations would be better off to admit the average tenure of the individuals in the particular groups in their organization—i.e., accounting, engineering, sales, and so on—and interview people with that kind of time span in mind. In other words, they should be asking themselves, "What could this person contribute within the two-and-a-half- to three-year period of time she will be here?" But I've run into very few hiring authorities or hiring organizations that will interview in this manner.

So, you are going to interview for each position as though it is going to be for a "forever" relationship. But you know and I know and your hiring authority knows that's not very likely. This is one of the illusions to the interviewing process and one of the reasons that it is a staged-contrived event, which I will discuss a little more in another chapter.

The importance of the transiency of the new position that you might take is this: Since you are probably not going to build a "career" at your next job, you'd better view your next position as a "building block" for your career. In other words, you have to be asking yourself in the interviewing process, to the best of your ability, "Does this job build upon the experience that I have had before? Is it going to enhance the experience that I've had before? If I get two and a half years of this kind of experience, can I leverage it in the future?"

Now, these kinds of questions, especially the one about leveraging the new job in the future, are going to be very hard to answer. The business environment, as I will explain in the next chapter, is more erratic than it is ever been and it isn't going to change. So, knowing what you can do to leverage the experience of a new job may be very difficult to predict. But you need to be asking yourself that question.

If you've been out of work for the last six months and you manage to get a job offer, this issue may not be as important to you. But, with the expansion of the job market, you will hopefully have more than one or two potential job offers. So one of the questions that you have ask yourself (a question that people have not had to ask in previous generations) is, "Is the job that I have been offered a positive continuation of the experience that I've had, and will I be able to leverage it for a better opportunity for to build my career two and a half to three years from now?"

The answer to this question may make the difference in the job offer that you may take. No one is ever going to be able to predict the future accurately, but you need to get some sense of "where can I go with this experience later on when I change jobs again?" There will be some job opportunities that you may get that will be better for you in this regard.

So, the paradox of the interviewing has a great implication on your career. Simply take it into account and be mindful of it.

How These Things Affect You

What all this means to you is very simple. You need a job or you need to change jobs. But the process and decision making used during your job search and interviewing processes is a lot more complicated than it is ever been.

Even though the job market is expanding and there are more job opportunities than there have been in the past few years, it is likely that you will change jobs more often than you ever imagined. You are more afraid of losing the job you have, if you have one. You are insecure about being able to replace the one you have if you have to leave it or you lose it. Your competition over the next few years will be people from four different generations of workers. You're going have to try to build your career on a number of different jobs with a number of different companies. And, on top of all of this, you still have to deal with the emotional distress and dis-ease of finding a job . . . again and more often than you like.

You need to be better prepared for every interview. Knowing how to deal with the toughest interview questions as well as asking the most important interview questions for your own protection are crucial to your job search success.

Chapter

2

What Today's Job Seekers Need to Know About Today's Hiring Authorities and Their Companies

··

n order to be successful in the interviewing process, especially when it comes to answering and/or asking questions, a candidate has to understand the audience with whom he or she is interviewing. In the pages to follow, we'll look at a snapshot of how the hiring authorities you will be interviewing with see the world.

Unfortunately, most books on interviewing and the job search don't address at all the nature of the companies you'll be talking to and the people who will be interviewing you. In order to answer questions more effectively and to understand what questions are asked in the interviewing process, you need to appreciate the "world" the way your potential boss does.

This is really important because, as mentioned in Chapter 1, when you are looking for a job, you have a tendency to focus on what you want and what you need. When we are stressed and emotionally uneasy, we have a tendency to be more self-centered than normal. This leads us to focus on our own needs in an interview, when we should be focusing on how we can fill the needs of the employer. So, it is even more important to be conscious of how your prospective employer sees the world because there is a tendency to focus on your needs (i.e., getting the job) instead of his or hers.

This is easy to forget. In fact, one of the most interesting observations I have discovered in my profession is that the vast majority of the individuals I have worked with as hiring authorities forget all about these issues when they themselves become a job seeker. It amazes me that I can work with an individual hiring authority who sees the world from the point of view that I will describe here, but when he or she becomes a candidate of mine and starts looking for a job, the hiring authority who is now interviewing for a job him- or herself totally forgets all about how he or she saw the world as the hiring authority and morphs into a scared, self-centered "applicant." It is one of the mysteries of my profession.

So, even if you think you know this or think that since you've been a hiring authority in the past, you don't need to review this, read it anyhow. You need to be reminded, just like everyone else does—even HR pros. Here is a quick overview of how your perspective employer sees the world and how it affects you.

The Nature of Companies

The vast majority of companies in the United States employ fewer than a hundred people. Small businesses create 75% of the new jobs in our economy and make up more than 97.7% of all employers. Contrary to the myths that companies are run with great business acumen, that's not always the case.

Most of the companies in the United States are run like the people who own them or manage them. They focus on what they do as a business, rather than who does it. They think that if they do what they do well enough, they will have a model business. In general, though, they can be unfocused, disorganized, and ambitious beyond their abilities. Many do not have any real system or set of procedures for doing business and operate with a seat-of-the-pants mentality.

When a recession comes along and globalized competition becomes a reality, things become even more complicated. Competition affects every company, and it has become more and more intense. Businesses come and go more than they ever have, and they expand and contract and move faster than any time in history. This erraticism affects the hiring process.

If you are interviewing for a job with a firm ten years old or less, here are its chances of survival:

First year, 85%
Second, 70%

Third, 62%

Fourth 55%

Fifth, 50%

Sixth, 47%

Seventh, 44%

Eighth, 41%

Ninth, 38%

Tenth, 35%

The Department of Labor estimates that 3,000 businesses start each day, 2,500 fail each day, and 2,000 change their addresses each day. Erratic or what?

Even if a company has survived beyond its start-up phase, fears of recession often still linger. Today's economy might be rebounding, but business is as difficult as it ever was. Globalization has led to worldwide competition. Technology has made it necessary for companies to expand and contract more rapidly than ever before. Consolidation often leads to layoffs for "redundant" positions. All of these factors affect not just you, but the hiring authority and how a prospective firm views you and your potential as an employee.

Contraction and expansion of U.S. businesses is a lot more erratic than it has ever been. Simply looking at the number of job changes employees of today make would lead one to believe that if employees are changing jobs every two and a half to three years, the companies they are working for are expanding and contracting in the same way.

For example, globalization has dramatically affected the manufacturing sector. Longitudinal studies of building and closing of manufacturing plants have probably the longest history of analysis than any other U.S. industry. The conclusion of a study by Andrew B. Barnard and J. Bradford Jensen, published in May 2007, concludes that "ownership by a multinational firm significantly *increases* the shut down probability of manufacturing plants." These studies also prove that new ownerships were significantly likely to close more plants. Multiunit, multinational firms have greater flexibility in adjusting to changing market conditions by opening and closing plants often.

Technology has affected most service industries and professions. Competition for most businesses doesn't come from just down the street any more;

it comes from all over the world, especially as technology booms outside the United States. Technology comes to my home or place of business from anywhere in the world. The automation of the supply chain has revolutionized manufacturing and assembly. Rarely is anything manufactured by a "self-contained" organization. Subcontractors (or outsourcers) are the predominant "makers" of most parts of the manufactured goods we buy, and these goods often are assembled or even distributed by someone other than the firm or company we actually think we're buying from.

Technology has allowed service subcontractors and outsourcers to be more efficient. Your bank or insurance company, for example, may have dozens of independent service firms providing them services and information that may be transparent to you. Customer service, payroll, accounting, benefit administration, portfolio management, and a host of other services are efficiently contracted out to independent organizations on the part of the "company" you think you're doing business with.

For instance, as of this writing, the Heinz company has thirty-four different subcontractors for the manufacture of plastic tops for its ketchup bottles. These subcontractors and outsourcers will be constantly competing for other business with technology, innovation, and dependability. The people who work for these contractors will be constantly competing with technology, innovation, and dependability. These firms will be hired and fired on a moment's notice if they don't produce results. And so will the individuals who work for them.

The nature of subcontractors or outsourcers to any business is that they can be replaced by other subcontractors relatively easily. So, if your insurance company or credit card company can get better customer service in Bangalore, India, than they can in Bangor, Maine, they "move" customer service. If that program doesn't work very well, then they fire the firm in India and "move" customer service to somewhere else, maybe back to the United States.

Tom Friedman, in his book *The World Is Flat* (New York: Farrar, Straus, Giroux, 2005), talks about his computer being "manufactured" and delivered to him by hundreds of different subcontractors. It is pretty easy to see that subcontractors, no matter what size they are, will expand and contract depending on their ability to perform and their ability to sell their services to needy companies.

The world is becoming privatized with subcontractors. In the early 1980s China allowed peasant farmers to grow and sell their own crops. China is now a food exporter. Two-thirds of China's state-owned enterprises are partly or mostly private.

A 2005 World Bank report found that from 1990 to 2003, governments around the world generated $410 billion in privatization proceeds. Even state and local governments are turning over garbage collection, payroll processing, and parks operations to private subcontracting firms.

If we are becoming a nation of individual "itinerant fruit pickers," we're also becoming a *world* of subcontracting/outsourcing "itinerant" organizations. So, as the world becomes more global, competition becomes swifter and businesses become more erratic in their hiring processes.

Your Next (Possible) Employer's Generational DNA

We discussed in the previous chapter how candidates from four different generations are competing for different positions and how it might affect you. Well, hiring authorities are affected as never before by the different generations in the employment marketplace. And it makes hiring much more difficult.

When boomers were younger, there were, for the most part, only two or, maybe once in a while, three generations of workers available to hire. Now there are at least four, and they are, as we have seen, very different in what they are influenced by, their general attitudes, and how they might be managed. This poses a challenge for most hiring authorities.

A company, for instance, interviews a traditionalist with a loyal, strong work ethic who doesn't want to retire but merely redirect his or her efforts. This person's main motivator in life may be to be involved with grandchildren and those grandchildren require a lot of time. If grandpa is working, the role of work in his life is different than it is for the Gen X'er or the Millennial.

A boomer who hires a Millennial who expects the same sort of idealistic, optimistic, 60-hour week might just get a different type of employee. The latter may very well complain about the antiquated technology the company has and communicate a confident, pragmatic "I was looking for a job when this one came along, and I can find one just like it at any time" attitude. Throw more people like this together and you have a real workplace environment challenge.

Most hiring authorities and employers, in general, are just getting used to this kind of environment. If there will be fewer potential job applicants available, then hiring authorities are going to have to figure out how to create an environment that can accommodate the attitudes and approaches to work that most, if not all, generations might have.

To give you an idea of just how differently employers and employees see the world, a survey reported in *Business Briefing,* 2006, asked employees to rank these traits as most important in their job:

1. Appreciation
2. Feeling informed
3. An understanding attitude on the part of management
4. Job security
5. Need for good wages

Amazingly enough, employers in this same study—that is, the people who actually employed the workers who were surveyed—ranked these traits on behalf of their employees *totally opposite* and in reverse as the employees ranked them. In other words, management didn't see the world the same way their employees did.

Here is another snapshot: A 2005 Conference Board survey stated that 57% of the employees polled didn't like their jobs and were planning to leave them. And management thinks everyone is happy!

Personality Styles and the Individuals You Will Meet

Understanding the different personality traits in business will help you answer tough questions and ask better ones in the interviewing process, so let's briefly review them.

Hippocrates in 370 BC defined four basic types of personalities. Since then, literally thousands of philosophers, theologians, and psychologists as well as business teachers have recognized the same defining elements of people's personalities.

If you recognize the differences and/or likenesses in personalities in the interviewing process, your answering and asking questions will be much more successful. The four basic personalities are analytical, driver, amiable, and expressive. (Hippocrates called them, respectively, melancholy, choleric, phlegmatic, and sanguine.)

Like the name denotes, the analytical type of professional has a tendency to see things in very analytical ways. He likes facts, details, and numbers and is oriented to the "bottom line." Analyticals have a tendency to be well organized; they stick to specific schedules, and they are sticklers for detail and are usually not risk takers. Their personality traits tend to be trusting, patient, not assertive (even somewhat passive), easy going, even tempered, motivated by their own internal recognition, and calculating. Professionally, they have a tendency to be engineers, mathematicians, accountants, scientists, chemists, and other technically oriented people, and work in positions that require high degrees of exactness and patience.

The driver-type professional likes to be blunt, right to the point, is mostly limited on time, is always busy, looks for immediate results, makes decisions very quickly, likes to be in the power position, is very independent and forceful, and is usually a really "can-do" person. She has a tendency to be assertive, distrusting, impatient, energetic, high energy, motivated mostly by an external recognition, impulsive, and fast-paced. Drivers are plant managers, CEOs, CFOs, and managers in general. Driver types of personalities who also have an analytical style would more likely be engineering managers, CFOs, controllers, accounting managers, etc. Drivers coupled with an expressive personality (discussed below) would more likely be presidents, vice presidents of sales, sales managers, etc.

The amiable-type professional likes relationships, likes to be liked, is easygoing, is not a big risk taker, looks for the support of others, makes careful decisions, and can appear to many to be "wishy-washy." Amiables also, as with many analyticals, have a tendency to be trusting, patient, somewhat passive, easy going, even-keeled, and motivated by their own internal recognition. They have a tendency to be involved in low-pressure sales, sales support, customer support, customer service, etc. If they are amiable, along with the expressive style, they can be great ombudsmen, as they are the type of people who understand everyone in the organization and have a tendency to "bridge" between people and departments.

The expressive-type professional has a tendency to be a dreamer, use hunches to make decisions, is gregarious and outgoing, "follows his gut," makes quick "feeling" decisions, takes risks regularly, focuses on the big picture, and has a tendency to be relationship oriented. If an expressive is also somewhat of a driver, he probably likes sales, sales management, leadership in the sales type of organization, and leadership positions that require a lot of interaction with other people. If an expressive also has amiable traits, then she would have a tendency to excel in customer service management, sales support management, and human-resources director types of positions.

The major reason that you want to know all of this is that you had better have a good idea of what your own personality traits are and how they're going to mesh with the people who will interview you. If you are an outgoing expressive type of salesperson who, as part of the process of being hired, is interviewing with an analytical/driver CFO, you'd better be ready to come across a little more driven and bottom-line oriented than you normally would.

If you are an analytical type (systems programmer, accountant, controller, etc.), and, as part of the interviewing process, you have to interview with a V.P. of sales or sales manager who is expecting support from you in the way of reports, etc., or will interface with you in any way, you'd better be ready for an aggressive interview. To get that person's support, you need to know that she sees the world differently than you do.

This whole thought process is really simple, but lack of awareness of it blows more interviews than you can imagine. So, as you practice the questions and answers to the toughest questions you will be asked, think about the different ways you might answer them depending on your personality and the ones you will be interviewing with.

It isn't that difficult to assess the personality type of the person you might be interviewing with. If you are in sales and are interviewing with the sales manager, V.P. of sales, or anyone in that department, you are likely interviewing with a driver or expressive type. If he or she has been successful in sales, he or she almost has to be one, if not both, of these. If the expressive person has a leadership personality, like a V.P. of sales, likely he or she has a driver personality as well.

An accountant or controller is obviously an analytical-type person as would be anyone in the information technology department of a company. Customer service managers, marketing directors, and H.R. directors are usually amiably oriented.

The interviewing process, fortunately, involves managers who have probably been in their position or profession for some time. A controller doesn't get the job if he or she isn't very analytical.

Where most candidates fail is when, in the interviewing process, they have to interview with someone who has a totally different personality than theirs. They don't recognize the difference and blow the interview. It is not uncommon for companies to have candidates interview with different managers in different departments (speading the risk). If candidates don't watch what they say to those "different" personalities, they can get eliminated from contention by the opposite personality type manager.

For instance, I had a very aggressive sales candidate who was in the interviewing process with a $150 million software distributor. The director of customer service was one of the people that he had to interview with. Now, keep in mind that this was a very aggressive, but very successful person. Admittedly, the candidate had a bit of a strong ego, but he was a top performer. He didn't do very well with the director of customer service because she was left with the idea that he was way too aggressive for her customers and she didn't feel he demonstrated enough care and concern for the customers that he was to sell to.

This person had a fifteen-year track record of phenomenal sales success. If he hadn't been sincerely interested in the success of his customers with his products, he would never have performed very well. But in the interview with the director of customer service he neglected to take into account her amiable nature and came across as too much of a driver. He apparently didn't communicate enough empathy and compassion for the customer.

He got the job, but he had to go back and interview with her again, and for a week or so it looked like she would stand in the way of his being hired. The vice president of sales, who was directly hiring my candidate, was so convinced of my candidate's ability to do job, he "negotiated" another interview with the customer service manager.

My candidate toned down his aggressiveness and became more amiable in the second interview. All of this could have been avoided if my candidate had recognized that customer service managers are probably more "amiable" than he was. Now he didn't have to change his personality, he just needed to recognize that with a more amiable person he needed to soften his approach.

A candidate can usually detect the kind of personality the interviewing authorities may have by the kinds of positions that they hold. No one should try to change his or her personality for an interview. But candidates should take into account how the interviewing authority sees the world and communicate with them in a way that makes sense to them.

Fear of Making a Hiring Mistake

One of the biggest concerns relating to the nature of a hiring authority is the fear of making a mistake. Next to losing money or customers, the biggest fear that most hiring authorities in companies have is the fear of making a hiring mistake. No one likes to make mistakes, but making a mistake in hiring is one of the greatest fears that businesses have. Mistakes cost money and time—and can affect the credibility of the hiring authority. All of this can add up to a lot of anxiety on the part of the hiring authority.

Most hiring authorities will never outright admit to the fear of making a hiring mistake. This is a great driver in the decision-making process. Face it: No matter how sophisticated the interviewing process might be in hiring someone, hiring someone is still something of a crap-shoot. No matter how calculated the interview process and subsequent decision-making process might be, it is a very big risk.

You don't have to be around business or in business or have worked for someone very long to realize what a disaster a hiring mistake can be. Hiring authority egos and reputations are on the line whenever they hire anyone.

The four, foundational, gut-level questions that any hiring authority or company is trying to get answered when he or she interviews you are:

- "Can you do the job?"
- "Do I/we like you?"
- "Are you a risk?"
- "Can we work the money out?"

We will discuss the impact these four questions have in subsequent chapters, but after "Can you do the job?" the most crucial question in any hiring authority's mind is, "Do we like you?" No one is going to hire someone he or she doesn't generally like as a person. After you are "liked," the hiring authority will ask, "Are you a risk?" (i.e., Am I going to regret hiring you? Are you going to quit soon after I hire you? Will I have to fire you? Are you going to embarrass me? Am I going to look bad to my colleagues after you have been here six months?)

So, you need to realize that since the hiring authority is trying to minimize risk, your liabilities are going to be analyzed (and you thought you didn't have any!). Your job in the interviewing process is to assure the hiring authority that he or she is not making a mistake and that he is going to look good to the rest of the world by hiring you.

How These Things Affect You

You need to realize the nature of the companies that you are interviewing with as well as the individuals within. Many often are unorganized, illogical, and don't operate with great business acumen. Their expansion and contraction is more erratic than it has ever been because their cycles of business are shorter and their competition is worldwide. These organizations have to try to attract and retain four different generations of people in the workplace. And often, sadly, companies and the individuals who run them apparently don't understand their employees.

This may sound harsh or disappointing, but recognizing all of this will help you better understand the kinds of answers you're going to have to give in the interviewing process in order to be successful. You'll also need to be aware of the different personality styles that you might interview with as well as recognize that part of your goal in the interviewing process is to mitigate the fear associated with hiring either you or anyone else.

Simply understanding and recognizing that most all of these are traits of the organizations and the people with whom you were going to interview will empower you to answer questions more effectively. The organizations you are interviewing with don't care about you as a candidate. They care about what they need and only what you need to an extent that you could help them get what they want. This mindset also will empower you to ask better questions.

Chapter

3 How and with Whom to Get an Interview

···

Nothing is more important in the interviewing process than face-to-face interviews. All of the preparation, pristine resumes, excellent interviewing skills, a great track record, etc. don't matter unless you can actually get in front of somebody who has "pain." i.e., the need to hire someone. This is where the rubber meets the road.

The kind of in-depth questions and answers you are going to learn in this book won't mean anything unless you can get interviews. Inertia and lack of activity are the two biggest mistakes that most people make when they go look for a job. Fear causes inertia, and not knowing what to do causes lack of activity. An initial interview with just about anybody that really has a need to hire someone, if you are successful, will lead to second, third, and fourth interviews.

Getting a job is a numbers game. Numbers of interviews are crucial to your getting good offers. In the coming market you may very well be able to get multiple offers. If you do your job right, and sell yourself well in *enough* quality interviews, getting great job offers will not be hard.

You want to sit down and brainstorm all, and I mean all, of the people that you can think of who might be looking for a good employee. Here are some of the people you need to think about calling:

- **Previous employers, peers, and subordinates.** These are people that you've worked for before moving on to other companies. You may not even be in contact with these people any more, but they very well might be able to help you. However, I don't recommend going back to work at a company that you have worked for before unless the company has totally changed management or it is a relatively new company.

- **Family.** The bigger your family and extended family, the better off you are. Don't be embarrassed to call these people, even distant relatives, and let them know that you are looking for a job. The stigma of looking for a job or being unemployed is nowhere near as great as it was a generation ago. Let's face it—these people are going to be calling you in a short period of time asking for the same advice or information.

- **Friends.** Call your friends; call friends of friends; call friends of friends of friends. Every time you ask somebody if he or she knows of any opportunities, ask if he or she knows of anybody else who might know of some opportunities. You would be amazed at the number of people you will think of that you might call to help you get an interview.

- **Acquaintances.** These are little different from friends. They're people you know, but not that well. A study back in the 1970s found that people looking for jobs were more likely to find opportunities from acquaintances than friends. The study concluded that often people make friends with people they work with or who occupy the same world. So when a large organization has a layoff, it is likely that a person's friend will be laid off too. But acquaintances may operate in completely different worlds. People in your church, athletic club, social club, volunteer organizations, and parents of children who were friends with your children are all people you should make aware of your looking for new job. Even acquaintances of your spouse are good.

- **Competitors.** Most of us know who our business competitors are. If they're in the same business that we are in, we know something about what they do. You may be of greater value to these people than most anyone else you can talk to.

- **Suppliers and distributors.** These are organizations that currently supply goods and services to your firm or the organizations and people that receive your goods and services. The knowledge you have is probably applicable to these people.

- **Customers.** If you are presently employed and your looking for a job is confidential, you *don't* want to call these people. Don't even think about it if you are employed. It will get back to your employer, and you cannot afford to be discovered and fired. But if your looking for a job is known by all or you are not working, customers are great people to call.

- **Trade and professional associations.** Some are more active than others, but they are a good source of information.

- **Alumni associations, fraternity and sorority members.** Even if you haven't kept up with some of these people, it is a great introduction to be able to make a personal connection and ask them if they know of any job openings.

- **College and university placement offices.** Even if you have been out of school more than a year, it doesn't hurt to find out what firms might be hiring people from your school. Graduate school placement offices often get requests for people with lots of experience.

- **Job fairs.** As employment markets ease and more jobs become available, more hiring organizations come to these. It can hurt to attend them. Don't do this if you presently have a job, as you might be embarrassed if you run into people with whom you work.

- **Religious, community, and social organizations.** Common values are one of the major criteria that people use in the hiring of others. Fellow church members, community, or social organization members love to try to help each other. Let them know.

- **Bankers, loan officers, lawyers, CPAs, business brokers, commercial real estate agents.** Anybody you might know who is in the business of helping other businesses in any way often know about what businesses are expanding or what businesses might be coming to town. For instance, attorneys who specialize in business law or certain kinds of legal specialties often know of organizations that are expanding because they represent them or give them advice. The same might be true for venture capital firms, CPAs, and bankers.

Think, think, think! Get with your spouse or coach and come up with other kinds of people that you may know whom you can call.

Keep Records

You really need to remember to make good records of the date you call people, their numbers, and what they might have told you. If you don't find a job, you may be calling these people back in 30, 60, or 90 days. Many people will not respond to you positively for a month for two. You want to remind them that you need a job!

Most of the time it will take two or three *reminders* for people to really remember that you need a job. You could talk to them today about your need, and a week from now they become aware of a job opportunity and totally forget to associate it with you. After you've talked to them two or three times and reminded them of your need for a job, those kind of connections will be made. They will think, "Oh, yeah, _____ called me a couple of times and mentioned he needed a job . . . I forgot!" So, keep good records, and don't hesitate to call people back.

A simple white sheet of paper with dates, names, phone numbers, and the place to record the results of your calls will be sufficient to keep records. Some people use a calendar so they know to call people back. Keep your records simple, but keep them.

What to Say

Previous Employers, Peers, Subordinates, and Acquaintances.

Name _____ Phone # _____ Date _____

Date to call again _____

Script: "Hello, _____, this is ___ (your name) ___, and I am presently looking for new job. We know each other from _____. I am calling to ask if you might know of any job opportunities available either with a firm you work for or any others that you might know about. For the past _____ (period of time) I have been working at __ (name of the company or what you have been doing) _____. Can you think of anyone who might need what I can offer? long pause . . .

(If "no") then say: "I really appreciate your time. I'd like to send you my resume, and if you can think of anyone who might be interested, please pass it along to them. By the way, I'm not sure how long my search will take; I'd like to call you back in a month or so to see if you might have thought of anyone who might be interested. Would that be all right?"

Results _____

_____

Family

Name _____ Phone # _____ Date _____

Date to call again _____

Script: "Hello, _____. This is _____ (your cousin, brother-in-law, etc.), and I am presently looking for a new job. I called to ask if you might know of any job opportunities that might be available. For the past ___ (period of time) I've been working at _____ (name of company or what you been doing) ____. Can you think of anyone who might need what I can offer? long pause . . .

(If "no") then say: "I really appreciate your time. I'd like to send you my resume, and if you can think of anyone who might be interested, please pass it along to them. By the way, I'm not sure how long my search will take; I'd like to call you back in a month or so to see if you might have thought of anyone that might be interested. Would that be all right?"

Results _____

_____

The Internet

The Internet is tremendously popular for posting resumes. The last count I read, there were close to 65,000 different "job boards." The range of people that these job boards cater to is immense.

Posting your resume on a job board—any job board—can be risky. If you're presently employed, you certainly don't want to do it. No matter what anybody tells you, even though these sites are supposed to represent you confidentially, you can't afford to be "discovered" by your present employer. You're likely to be fired.

On top of that, you never know who might get ahold of your confidential information and how it might be used. We hear complaints all the time from people who say they're approached with scams because their resume was posted on the Internet. And to make matters even more interesting, your resume can "float" around in cyberspace long after you found a job. I personally had a candidate, who, six months after I had found her a job, was called in by her employer and asked if she was looking for a job. She was startled and after explaining that she wasn't, asked what led her employer to ask that question. Well, her resume was still floating around in cyberspace even though she had posted it eight months earlier. She had "removed" it from the primary job board where she had posted it, but some of the secondary job boards that pick up resumes from the primary boards still had it posted.

I know that if you need a job, you'll probably post a resume on the Internet. Even though it is popular, the nearest estimates that I found range anywhere from 2 to 6% of the people who post their resumes on the Internet find a job *directly* as a result of their posting. There is no way to verify these estimates. I read a source that stated that 90% of the people who post their resumes on the Internet never get a response. How can one measure that? The study had no documentation to it. Often professional recruiters will find potential candidates on the Internet. I'm not talking about that kind of "secondary" success. Of course, you don't care how you find a job, or who finds it for you. That's fair.

One of the primary reasons people post their resumes on the Internet is because it is an easy thing to do. But most of the time, it is one of those activities that is confused with productivity. It probably isn't going to get you very far except maybe for some come-ons and scams. The big mistake is to expect any kind of positive response, including an interview or even a job. Just don't expect very much from this effort.

How the Internet Can Help You

All of the above being said, there is no doubt that the Internet can help you look for a job. But it is going to require work in a different way than you might think: a very simple technique that will get you face-to-face interviews.

When you find a company that has posted a job on the Internet that you think you might fit, make a note of it. If you respond to the posting on the Internet and send a resume to most of the places the advertisement says to respond to, I guarantee you will be lost in cyberspace. Most organizations that post jobs on the Internet appoint some lower-level administrative person who really doesn't have any knowledge of the job being posted to review and to sort through the hordes of resumes they're going to receive. These "screeners" are instructed to look for certain things on a resume. If they don't recognize them, they will probably pass on the candidate. The probability of anyone's getting an interview with this process in place is very slim.

The wonderful thing about the Internet is that it is loaded with information—especially information about the companies you might want to interview with. So, if you find a posting for a job that fits the description of what you are looking for, go to the website of the company that has run the ad and research who would likely be a hiring authority for the job. Whatever you do, don't call and ask for the human resources department. That is going to be as productive as hitting the "send" button on your computer.

Call the company that you've chosen and ask for the person who would likely hire for the kind of position you would fill. I will discuss in a moment exactly what to say. This process is very simple. Think about it. If you are in customer service, you will call the customer service manager. If you work in accounting, call the accounting manager. The idea is to call a hiring authority with "pain" . . . the *personal* need to hire someone.

Frequently, the names of these people are actually on the website of the company itself. Also, many times their direct phone number is on the website, as well as their e-mail address. I recommend actually picking up the phone and calling the probable hiring authority. Don't send an e-mail or your resume without a phone call, or you will be wasting your time.

You can believe me now, or you can believe me later, but this is the only way to use the Internet effectively to help you find a job. Most people will e-mail their resume to a destination posted on the Internet then whine and moan that they never got a call to interview for a job that they fit absolutely "perfectly." Well, 434 other people are feeling exactly the same way. *Pick up the phone and go to work!*

Businesses That Can Help You Get an Interview

When I first got into the placement and recruitment business in 1973, only 2 to 5% of the professional hires that were made in business had some kind of placement fee associated with them. Today that figure is closer to 35%, maybe even 40%. The section on recruiters follows; here is a list of other kinds of firms that might be able to help you find a job:

- **Temporary staffing firms.** They used to be called "temporary agencies." Traditionally, they were only oriented toward secretaries and administrative workers. Today, these organizations staff all kinds of professional positions on a temporary basis. There are some staffing firms that place doctors, CEOs, CFOs, accountants, lawyers, technical writers, nurses, and all kinds of healthcare professionals from phlebotomists to X-ray technicians to medical insurance clerks, and human-resources professionals, drafters, designers, and engineers.

- **Staffing/consulting firms.** There firms are usually oriented to information technology or engineering services. In recent years, consulting firms have grown to take on significant amounts of information technology development. These firms hire out their technical expertise, from very narrow and specific types of software development to general software applications. Most of these firms do not see themselves as staffing companies. They see themselves and present themselves more as consultants. They often work on specific projects for their clients, and often these projects can last for many years. The clients pay a high price for this kind of expertise and, as with general staffing, do not have the burden of long-term employees.

- **Employee leasing firms, outsourcing services, and outplacement services.** These provide employment services to employers, but they normally cannot help a candidate actually get an interview.

- **Newspaper and Internet advertisements.** I covered this above, but it certainly doesn't hurt to know who is hiring. This can be valuable. It is good to know if a company is expanding, even though it may not be advertising the kind of job that you do. Those in motion tend to stay in motion. The company that is hiring a number of customer service people may very well be hiring in accounting or the sales department. Read the want ads and call the prospective hiring authorities.

Working with Recruiters

As the employment market expands and there are more jobs with fewer people to fill them, the use of recruiters on behalf of hiring organizations will increase. The vast majority of people have no idea about the variety of recruiters and professional placement firms there are in business. It is likely that in the future you are going to be contacted by a professional recruiter or have the need to solicit the help of a professional recruiter. It is important for you to understand the differences in the kinds of organizations there are.

I'm going to present to you the number of different kinds of recruiting organizations and professional placement people there are, as well as what they can and cannot do for you. It is important for you to understand not only the different kinds of firms there are, but also what you should expect of them. Your expectations of each type you run into will have a real bearing on your ability to gain employment through recruiters.

Perspective on What Recruiters Can and Can't Do for You

The *Fordyce Letter*, the country's foremost authority on the placement and recruitment profession, maintains a database of some 33,000 firms in the United States that are, in one form or another, involved in the business of direct personnel placement. (This would include even the "casual" placers of people, temporary staffing firms or companies who, as a part of their business, do some sort of placement.) For the past ten years or so, according to Kennedy Information, Inc. who publishes *The Directory of Executive Recruiters*, there are approximately 5,500 permanent recruiting firms of all types in the United States. Over 35 to 45% of this number went out of business over the past three or four years and will be replaced by the same number. Twenty new recruiting firms open in the United States every week. It is estimated that one-third of these firms work on a retainer basis and the rest on some form of contingency basis. The average recruiting firm, according to *The Fordyce Letter*, has 3.1 "consultants" in it who average successfully recruiting and placing 1.5 people a month. The average tenure of these firms is seven years, and the average "consultant" has been in the business for three years. In the early 1970s it was estimated that 5 to 10% of the professional people who were hired in business were hired through the help of a third-party recruiter of some sort. That estimate today is closer to 30 or 35%. As the job market expands, good candidates are harder to find, and third-party recruiters will be used even more.

Traditionally, recruiters have been defined in two broad camps. The *retained recruiter* is paid partly in advance to find an employee. The *contingency group* receives its compensation only if it is responsible for causing a candidate to be hired. There is, however, a broad range of contingency firms that you need to be aware of so that you can decide if they can actually help you find a job.

We will discuss, in general terms, the reasons why you should use a recruiter and what the recruiter can do for you, as well as what a recruiter cannot do for you. The most important aspect of this topic is for you to know how all of the different kinds of recruiters can help you, based on that type of recruiter's relationship with the employer. What you should expect from and how you should deal with a recruiter depends on your understanding of the kind of recruiter that you're dealing with.

In general, here is what a recruiter, **can do for you:**

- A recruiter has access to and knowledge of opportunities with firms before they are "broadcast" to the world.

- For the most part (and we will see the exceptions to this below), recruiters have a much more in-depth knowledge about an opportunity than an individual could gain on his or her own.

- Recruiters will coach you and sell you and your attributes, as well as sell around your shortcomings, better than you can for yourself.

- Recruiters know how you compare with your competition for a position and provide information about your strengths and weaknesses. Recruiters know their market.

- Recruiters will help you manage the process of interviewing and negotiating. Because a recruiter deals with this process daily, it knows how to do it better than an individual even if he or she changes jobs often.

- Recruiters are going to help a candidate maximize his or her compensation possibilities. Most of the time the recruiter is compensated based on the salary package the candidate receives. It is in our best interest, therefore, to help you reach your compensation potential.

- Recruiters can provide you more job interview opportunities faster than you can do it for yourself. Most people don't deal with the job opportunities, career moves, etc. on a daily basis. A recruiter does.

- The help of a recruiter implies **confidentiality.** Most top professionals don't want their job search to be "floating around" the Internet, or anywhere else for that matter.

- A recruiter, many times, has an intimate but objective view of the hiring company, the hiring authorities, and the "politics" of the specific hiring process.

- Recruiters are comfortable with all of the steps in the process of getting hired.

- Recruiters know what to do when things "go wrong" in the hiring process.

Here are some things that a recruiter **cannot do for you:**

- Recruiters cannot **get** you a job. They can open the door, coach, teach, advise, strategize, and help. But the candidate still has to be to the primary force in getting the job.

- A top recruiter might give career advice, but recruiters are not counselors. They are information brokers and hiring process managers. Unless the information or process is of current and immediate importance to the company or hiring authority the recruiter represents, he or she doesn't have the time to "counsel"—i.e., deal with other aspects of your life.

- Recruiters are not "miracle workers" . . . they can't get you the "job of your dreams" . . . find you an interviewing opportunity that you are not qualified for . . . help you change careers when the economy won't bear it . . . help you negotiate compensation plans on deals they are not involved in. They cannot do a lot of handholding or immediately respond every time you call or blindly e-mail a resume.

- Recruiters don't analyze and peruse every single resume that is sent to us. Unless we are a "boutique" search firm, we receive hundreds of resumes. Each one will get ten to fifteen seconds of attention, and, unless what is on it is so obviously stellar and **needed by their hiring companies,** it will be stored in a database.

- Recruiters don't have time to give you advice about the "market" or if it's time to "stick your toe in the water" to see if your skills or experience might be "more valuable" to someone else.

- Unless they are involved in the process of securing **you** a new opportunity, they're going to be fairly short on advice about "what you should do" regarding your changing jobs down the line.

- For the most part, recruiters are not going to give you advice about a job or career change that they are not involved in **unless** they have a longstanding relationship with you.

Recruiters' Biggest Challenge with Candidates

The biggest challenge recruiters all have regarding candidates is the candidates' misperception of the marketplace and how their skills, abilities, and experience stack up with what is available to the recruiters' clients. The biggest complaints recruiters hear about themselves is that a candidate states, "Well, I can do that job—why won't you get me the interview? I sent you my resume; I am the most qualified that you can find, and I can't understand why you can't get me an interview. . . . and so on.

The recruiter's best candidates come from referrals or networking or actually calling a presently employed, well-qualified person and presenting a possible better opportunity (recruiting). Some recruiters will respond to a resume for a specific opportunity that they might advertise (if they do that) or respond to your phone call. Some recruiters will find your resume on the Internet and call you.

Most candidates, even qualified candidates, have no idea how many excellent people there are available for most opportunities. Candidates, as you know, if you learn from this book, have a tendency to "see the world" through their own eyes and their perceived **ability to do a job.** A good recruiter, even with a narrow search assignment, can usually begin with at least 100 to 200 "qualified" candidates or resumes. Even the top retained search firms, according to Kennedy Information, Inc., start out with 100 to 300 candidates in the database for each search they do. They then qualify and phone screen those down to twenty to fifty candidates, in-depth interview ten candidates and present a final panel of three to six candidates.

Candidates are often surprised and enlightened (or shocked) when they understand the number of quality candidates available for most positions and that their being successful in even getting an interview isn't based so much on their **ability to do a job,** as it is **their ability to get the job.** Most candidates do not see themselves in the light of how they compare with other viable candidates. Most candidates evaluate themselves based on their own perception, and unfortunately they don't have the perspective of comparing themselves to 100 or even fifty other people at their same level of professionalism.

Recruiters' Biggest Challenge with Hiring Organizations

If you absorb most of the information in this book, it won't come as a surprise to you that the biggest challenge recruiters have with hiring organizations is they are "spiritual beings acting human." Just because the organizations might need to hire a professional on any level doesn't mean that they're going to do it all the time, or that they will change their minds about the kind of person they need a number of times in the process of a search. Also in play are corporate politics, unrealistic expectations of what the candidate market will provide, mergers and acquisitions, buyouts, unexpected changes in the business climate, stock prices, product failures, and so on. Non-human events like 9/11 and Hurricane Katrina can postpone or shut down the best of intentions to hire someone.

Like most professions, the recruiting business is one that is full of uncertainty. They deal with human beings on both sides of the equation. They are one of the few professions whose "product" can say "no " and walk away and whose "client" is just as unpredictable.

These two primary challenges are what make this profession so exciting and gratifying. The service of recruiters can change the lives of the individuals they are involved with as well as the course of their companies. But the downside of this kind of gratification is lots of emotional and business risk.

Perspective

Keep in mind that on average, recruiters individually only place 1.5 people a month. Even the top recruiters in the most recognized search firms, according to Kennedy Information, only manage ten to eleven "searches" at a time (the author averages twelve). If the 5,500 recruiting firms in the United States have an average of three consultants, and each one of them averages 1.5 people a month, that's only 24,750 people a month.

By itself that number may appear to be large, but when you put it in perspective of all of the professional job changes that go on in the course of the year, it is not that many.

What This Means to You

What this all means to you is simply this: A recruiter might be able to help you. But you need to manage your expectations of what a recruiter can do for you and help him or her help you. **And what a recruiter can do for you depends on the nature of the recruiter and the relationship with the hiring authority or hiring company he or she is working for or representing.**

There are a number of types of different recruiters and their relationship with the hiring authority or hiring company varies. The types are summarized in the following table, along with each one's advantages and disadvantages as well as how to deal with this type of firm.

Type of Recruiter	Description	Advantages	Disadvantages	How to Deal with
Retained Search Consultant	• Hired by company, paid 33-35% of salary obtained	• Wants to find best quality candidates • Has strong knowledge of opportunity • Can provide excellent information to candidates	• Loyalty is to company, both for information given out and candidates promoted • Relationship with candidates fleeting	• Don't contact directly—recruiter lets candidate know what is needed
Contingency Search Consultant	• Paid when candidate successfully placed	• Since paid only for success, sense of urgency high to place candidates • Loyalty balanced between hiring organization and candidates	• Hiring authority may be working with other recruiters • Hit-and-run service—loyalty of hiring organization only as good as last person placed	• Ask lots of questions to qualify firm's experience and history with hiring organization, as well as how many other people the firm represents • Be honest and forthright • Approach for ideas for possible opportunities
Employment Agent	• Paid when candidate successfully hired • Oriented toward marketing candidate to potential employers; candidate-oriented	• Oriented to finding candidate a job • Works with many of the same employers over and over • Tries to get candidates as many interviews as possible	• Not a lot of in-depth knowledge of employers • A lot of interviews generated by cold calling • Not a lot of time spent working for individual candidates, unless someone is interviewing for an immediate opening	• Realize that agent will get interviews if employer will talk to candidate • Ask lots of questions about the opportunity • Know that most of these companies need to fill jobs quickly • Go on every interview or agent will stop getting them • Candidate will get help in selling self, but agent may not know enough about company to provide valuable insights

(continued)

Type of Recruiter	Description	Advantages	Disadvantages	How to Deal with
Placer	• A "one-man band" • Scours Internet for resumes that might fit jobs also found on Internet, then sends out resume • If an employer bites, contacts client to see if interested • Narrow experience, e.g., copier sales, long distance service calls	• If candidate is found, means one opportunity with one company • If candidate follows instructions, can be effective with one or two organizations that placer works with	• Only presented to one organization • Presented with five or six other candidates • Not many placements because no real rapport with companies	• Sell yourself stronger than other candidates, since this agent places same kind of people with same kind of firm all around country • Ask what hiring authority likes and why other people have been hired through this agent
Contract Recruiter, Internal & External	• Hired by companies on a contract when candidates needed over short period of time • Paid on hourly basis with a possible bonus for each person hired • Contract to one organization at a time for specified period	• Since pay based on performance, want to get people through the hiring process as quickly as possible • Has a lot of useful information about the company • May have database for future jobs with other companies • Needs to get people hired quickly	• Only representing one firm at a time • Often between contracts, i.e., looking for work	• Realize that this is an independent contractor, so don't expect in-depth knowledge of company • Don't expect a lot of hand-holding; focus is on quick placement

Internal Recruiter	• Permanent employees of company, dedicated to the company • Recruit for company aggressively • Find people quickly to avoid paying third-party recruiter fees	• Pretty aggressive with ego wrapped up in being successful, good at knowing kind of person company likes to hire, so a little more aggressive with hiring authorities to gain interviews • Will push for whomever seems to be a good candidate	• If you don't seem to be a good candidate, will not push at all • Doesn't like "thinking outside the box"	• Ask about role and responsibilities • Get this person to like you a lot and see you as a viable candidate; impress with your abilities • Help recruiter to "look good"
Staffing/ Consulting Firm Recruiter	• Is close to hiring managers of client firms • Hires candidates as employees of staffing firm then contracts to companies, on "assignments" • Firms cover broad range of staffing and consulting needs, e.g., IT, technical, engineering • Moves quickly	• Opportunity is "hot"— be ready to go right to work	• Opportunity is "hot"— be ready to go right to work, or someone else will	• Keep in close touch • Be ready to move NOW
Management Consultant	• Recruiting not primary business but often asked to do it • Consulting service more important than recruiting	• Really know the company consulting for • Will push for client to hire you, if a match that makes consultant look good	• Primary job consulting, recruiting secondary • Will not let process of recruiting jeopardize primary relationship	• Once you are in the door, don't rely on consultant to help you get hired • If not "perfect," consultant may distance self

(continued)

Type of Recruiter	Description	Advantages	Disadvantages	How to Deal with
Research Consultant	• Paid to find individuals with very specific skills that relate only to narrow professions or businesses • Can use passive techniques to get into company websites to find employees • Activates candidates from databases; lists bought and sold • Paid salary and small bonus			• Reply as if speaking to potential employer • No sloppy e-mails, voicemails, or could cause elimination

Features, Advantages, and Benefits

Before we get to calling individuals whom you do not know who might be interested hiring you, let me briefly discuss the idea of *features, advantages, and benefits*. As a first exercise, I want you to write a features, advantages, and benefits statement about yourself that you are going to use with a prospective employer.

A *feature* is an aspect of your career that makes you unique. It can be the number of years of experience. It can be grades in school. It can be things like hard work, determination, persistence, and dedication. A feature, in a job-seeking situation, is simply a unique fact about you that will be translated into being a good employee.

An *advantage* is something that this feature does to set you apart from the average. So, if you graduated cum laude from college and worked your way through college with two jobs (features), you demonstrated hard work and commitment above the average person (advantage). If you have been promoted three times in the last seven years (feature), you have demonstrated upward mobility, performance, and leadership (advantages).

A *benefit* would be gained by a company from hiring a person who brings unique features and advantages. So, the features of graduating at the top of your class, as well as working two jobs demonstrating your advantage to perform on a higher level than average, would show the company that you will perform in the same way for whomever you work for, and the company will benefit from your work.

So, now, write your:

Features _____

Advantages _____

Benefits _____

You're going to integrate these features, advantages, and benefits in your presentation of yourself to a prospective employer.

Warm Calls

By most sales standards, calling prospective employers you don't know is a "cold" call. Personally, I would rather name this kind of calls "warm" calls. That's because, for the most part, neither you nor the potential employer are really "cold." Both of you are warm people just trying to do your jobs. The call itself has been called "cold" simply because the person receiving it is not expecting to get it. The purpose of this call is to get you in front of a prospective employer who needs to hire someone. You are trying to get an interview *regardless* of whether there is a position opening. You are selling an interview, not necessarily selling the idea of getting a job. You are selling a "date" . . . not marriage. Don't confuse getting hired with an initial interview. All you're trying to do is to sell an audience with that person.

Close to 33% of the people whom we find jobs for are interviewed by hiring authority when they *don't* have an opening. As professional recruiters, our clients rely on us to inform them of top talent when the talent becomes available. Clients will interview them based upon our say-so, regardless of whether they have "open" headcount.

I do not recommend calling the H.R. departments unless you are seeking a job in the H.R. department. Most of the first-line screeners in an organization are taught to send anyone who is inquiring about a job to the H.R. department. H.R. employees are usually midlevel record keepers in 97% of the companies in the United States. The H.R. department is not going to help you find a job in the company. Its responsibility is to screen out most every candidate, unless he or she is perfect . . . and who is perfect? So, don't get relegated to the H.R. department.

So, pick up the phone and simply ask the name of the manager of the department you would normally work for. If you're in sales, call the sales manager. If you're in marketing, call the VP of marketing. Get the picture? Here is what you say.

Warm Call Script

"Hello, who is your ____(controller, vice-president of sales, IT director, CEO, etc.? Please let me speak with _____.

"Hello, _____ my name is _____ and I am a ____(kind of professional you are)____ with ___(some kind of feature)___, and I have a great track record of ___(advantages and benefits)_____.

"I would like to meet with you to discuss my potential with your firm. Would tomorrow morning at 9:00 AM be good for you, or would tomorrow afternoon at 3:00 PM be better?"

If you get a response like, "I really don't have any openings," your response will be:

"I understand, and the kind of people whom I want to work for probably do not presently have an opening.

"I would just like to take 15 to 20 minutes of your time because I'm a top-notch performer. I'm the kind of person whom you would want to know to either replace your 'weakest me' or to know of my availability when the next opening does occur. Now, would tomorrow morning be good for you or is tomorrow afternoon better?"

You will either get the appointment or a more consistent response of, "I really don't have any openings. There's no reason for us to meet."

Your response: "I understand that you don't have any immediate openings, but I've a great track record of ____(features, advantages, and benefits)____.

"Mr. or Ms. _____, I'm the kind of professional who is better than 90% of the employees that you might have now. It is in your and your company's best interest that you would at least talk to me and be aware of my availability. If not for now, then maybe in the future. My experience has taught me that, often, great talent comes along when you don't need it. It is always a good idea to be aware of the talents on a face-to-face basis. I will only take a few moments of your time, and it may wind up being beneficial for all of us. Would tomorrow morning or tomorrow afternoon be better?"

If the response is, "Well, you can e-mail me a resume," your response is:

"I can, but my resume is only one-dimensional, and it is of value for both of us to associate a face and a personality with a resume. I'd like to bring it by, hand deliver it to you, and spend maybe 15 minutes of your time to let you know what my accomplishments are and how they can benefit you and your company. Is tomorrow morning good or would tomorrow afternoon be better?"

If the response is an emphatic, "Just e-mail me the resume!" (which is just a nice way of saying "NO.") Then, your response is:

"I will, right now. I will call you back tomorrow to be sure you have received it, and then we can set up a visit."

If you get a very emphatic "no," and it is clear that you're not going to get any kind of face-to-face interview, you then need to pause for two or three seconds and say:

. . . pause . . . "Do you know of any other opportunities that might exist in your firm with any other manager?"

If you get a person's name, ask: "May I use your name as a reference?"

If you get the name of another manager, also ask for his or her phone number. If the answer is "no," then ask, after a two- or three-second pause:

. . . pause . . . "Do you know of any other organization that you might have heard of through the grapevine that might need someone with my experience?"

If you get the name of an organization or a person's name, ask: "May I use your name as a reference?"

If you get a reference to a particular person or organization and the person who referred you said you could use his or her name (this is an indication of how strong the ties are that people might have . . . after all, we all really want to help our friends . . .), here is the script:

"Hello, Mr./Ms. _____. I was referred to you by _____. I am _____ with _____ and I have a great track record of _____.

"I would like to meet with you to discuss my potential with your firm. Would tomorrow morning at 9 AM be good for you or would tomorrow afternoon at 3 PM be better?"

You will be amazed at the number of opportunities you will uncover this way. Controllers know other controllers, VPs of sales know other VPs of sales, and so on. It is not uncommon for one type of manager to know a number of other types of managers both within and outside of his or her own company. These managers are often asked by their counterparts in other organizations if they indeed know somebody to fill vacant positions. You might only get a productive response maybe one out of every forty times. The one interview you get as a result of asking that question is worth the forty or fifty times of asking.

Regardless of whether you get a referral, it is a very good idea to end the conversation with the following:

"Thank you for your time, I would at least like to e-mail you my resume in case something might change with you or someone you know."

Nine out of ten times, the person on the other end of the phone will be willing to receive the resume. No matter what the response, whether it be positive or not, end the conversation by saying:

"I'd like to give you a call back in 30 days or so to see if there might be any openings there or if you might know of any with friends of yours."

Again, nine out of ten people will agree to your doing that. To a certain extent, that lets them off the hook for the moment; but they know, in the back of their minds, that they could easily have a position open up at any time.

This whole process of warm calling is a "numbers" thing. Just like everything else in this process, the more calls you make, the more likely you are to get an interview. There are numerous hiring managers out there who consider, and rightfully so, that part of their job is to be constantly interviewing to know the talent that might be available on the market. These kinds of managers won't spend every opportune moment interviewing, but they will do it from time to time. Again, it's a numbers thing.

If the hiring manager just plain dismisses you or insists that you deal with the H.R. department, then you can say:

"My experience with company H.R. departments (as far as identifying top talent when there isn't an immediate need) just hasn't been good. I am sure they are wonderful people; but I need to be talking to decisive managers who can make immediate decisions. Is there any other decisive manager in your firm who has an opening?"

Analysis of the Script

This is very simple but very strong stuff. The idea is to "sell" a face-to-face interview regardless of whether the hiring manager has a position opening. You are not asking if there is a job opening or asking to get hired, you're simply getting a face-to-face interview. Face-to-face interviews are all that matter. They are the quintessential way that you will get a job. The script is meant to be forceful and to the point.

There are a few very crucial aspects of this script. First of all, you do not ask the person answering the phone who might be doing the hiring. If you ask who does the hiring, nine out ten times you'll be relegated to the H.R. department, and that, for the most part, is a dead-end.

Once you get a hiring authority on the phone, you have to provide features, advantages, and benefits as to why you should be interviewed. This is very important! If you simply call and ask for an interview without giving specific features, advantages, and benefits to the prospective employer, you won't get to first base. This is, again, simple stuff and easy to do if you are aware of what you are doing. Here are some examples:

"Hello, Mr. or Ms. _____. My name is
_____, and I am a (*features*) engineer. I am registered, and I have sixteen years of very stable engineering experience. I have worked my way up in two organizations from the ground floor to engineering manager positions. The *advantage* that I bring is stability and performance. The *benefit* to you and your organization is that you would have a long-term employee with a great track record."

"I would like to meet with you to discuss my potential with your firm. Would tomorrow morning at 10:00 AM or tomorrow afternoon at 2:00 PM the best for you?"

Or, another example would be:

"Hello, Mr. or Ms. _____. My name is _____ and I am a (*features*) salesperson. I have eight solid years of experience with two of your competitors and have never sold less than 110% of quota. I continually (*advantage*) perform in the top 1% of the sales organizations that I've been with. I would like to (*benefit*) continue this kind of a performance with an organization like yours."

"I would like to meet with you to discuss my potential with your firm. Would Tuesday morning at 9:00 AM or Wednesday afternoon at 3:00 PM work the best for you?"

The purpose of this script is to briefly and succinctly tell a hiring authority your personal features and advantages so that they can be perceived as benefits to the hiring authority's company. The question is, and always will be, on the part of that a hiring authority, "Why should I hire you?" The whole interviewing process centers around this one question. The process begins with a feature, advantage, and benefit statement.

Now, remembering that you are selling yourself and that you are briefly giving a prospective employer a reason of why he or she ought to interview you, write a features, advantage, and benefits statement about yourself:

"Hello, Mr. or Ms. _____. My name is _____.
I am a _____. I (features) _____
_____
_____,
which are (advantages) _____
_____
_____ and, therefore (benefits) _____
_____
to you and your firm."

Practice writing this and in just a few minutes you can write three or four features, advantages, and benefits statements on yourself to fit just about any occasion. Remember, the purpose of this statement is to intrigue a hiring authority enough to want to interview you. Do not try to "sell" the whole idea of hiring you in one phone call. The purpose is to get the interview by a giving a hiring authority a brief statement about what you can do for him or her.

The closing question of, "Could I see you tomorrow morning or would tomorrow afternoon be better?" is a simple minor choice resulting in major decision that most salespeople learn in their first training class. This concept is so simple it's almost too good, and yet a phenomenal number of people will avoid using it because it appears to be obviously manipulative. It definitely is simple, but it definitely works! Please do yourself a favor and don't try to change what works. At the end of your feature, advantage, and benefit statement, ask the minor choice and major decision question. It works. Do not ask things like: "Would you be interested in talking with me?" "Could I come by and see you?" "Can we set a date for an interview?" etc. None of these questions are anywhere near as effective as: "Could I see you tomorrow morning at _____ AM or would tomorrow afternoon at _____ PM be better?"

Please, please don't try to be coy or cutesy by making this more complicated than it needs to be. Simply make the features, advantages, and benefits statement and ask the alternative choice question. Then, SHUT UP! Don't say another word until you have a response.

Now, most people who are not in sales, and even some that are, will have a difficult time using this statement and question, especially, in the beginning of their job search. I have been using this format for finding other people jobs for more than thirty-one years. It works better than anything you can imagine. A number of years ago I altered this statement and question, thinking that I would be perceived as more sophisticated and intelligent. I really don't know how I appeared, but I do know that when I altered the script to this process, my results were disastrous. So please, you need to change jobs as fast you can. If you want to experiment with some crazy alternative to this script, you are welcome to. But when what you do isn't as effective as this is, you'll come back to it. Is your goal to find a job or to come up with revolutionary ideas on how to get an interview? It works . . . don't fix it!

So, there you have it. A features, advantages, and benefits statement followed by an alternative choice question that will get you the results that you need. Now all you need to do is to: Practice, practice, practice! *You have nothing to lose but your anonymity.*

Leaving Voicemails

Somewhere along the line you're going to be faced with leaving a voicemail. You practice, practice, and practice a warm-call presentation, and then you get voicemail! Oh, brother! Well, there is a lot of debate as to whether you should leave a message on a hiring authority's voicemail. Try your own experiment and see what works. I recommend doing it. I would, however, call a hiring manager two or three times, trying to make a presentation, before I would leave a voicemail. If I come to the conclusion, after even the second time, that I'm not likely to catch this hiring authority answering the phone, I would leave a voicemail. The script for the voicemail message isn't much different from the script used when a live person answers the phone. The ending, however, is slightly different. It goes like this:

"Mr./Ms. _____. My name is _____. I am a _____. I have (features) _____ _____ that are (advantages) _____ _____, which would be (benefits) _____ to you and your firm.

"I would like a chance to meet with you. My phone number is _____. Again, that is _____(your name)_____ and my phone number is _____."

Be sure to repeat your phone number at the end at least once, and repeat it very s-l-o-w-l-y so the person can write it down and as you record it the second time. It is just too hard for people to go back and listen to your voicemail a second time to get your phone number. If you say your name and number slowly, and repeat even more slowly at the end of the message, people are more likely to write down the information and return your call.

If you don't get response the first time that you leave a message on a voicemail, I wouldn't hesitate to record a similar message two or three times for the same person. This sounds a bit excessive, but my experience has been that if there is even the slightest "pain" of needing someone now or in the near future, this kind of message will get the attention of a hiring authority. After all, you have nothing to lose but your anonymity.

After leaving four or five messages similar to this and not getting a response, I would stop calling, at least for now. If my experience had been with a similar kind of organization where my value might be greater than the average candidate looking for a job, I would certainly call back a number of times down the road. But, for now, I would stop calling after three or four messages.

If you do get the courtesy of that callback from a hiring authority, you would deal with it in the same manner that I have written about above. Just don't take it personally when people don't return your voicemail.

How These Things Affect You

The only way you're going to get a job offer is to interview. Getting interviews is *the most important activity* you can do in order to get a job. Performing well on an interview can be perfected with practice, but getting an interview is an ongoing activity.

Get them any way you can. Through your own efforts, recruiters . . . any way you can. I know it has dawned on you that in looking at the manner in which I suggest you get interviews there is going to be a high degree of refusal. Do not accept this refusal as a rejection. When a company does not have an opening or does not wish to interview you for any reason, you were not being personally rejected. It is simply refusal, and it means that you have to keep calling and getting appointments.

But, if the pain of not having a job or the need for a job change is greater than the pain of the refusal that you will experience, you'll get used to it very rapidly. In fact, after a while, you will be encouraged by each refusal, realizing that it is just one more refusal that is going to lead to a positive response.

Getting interviews and performing well on them are actual things you can control in the job search process. The more calls you make, the more opportunities you are going to uncover.

Chapter

4

Important Reminders About Interviews

· ·

Interviewing is a staged, contrived event. It is like what Winston Churchill said about democracy: "Indeed it has been said that democracy is the worst form of government except all those other forms that have been tried from time to time." Interviewing (and any amount of the sophisticated testing, screening, etc.) is still the best employee selection process free enterprise has been able to come up with.

But it's important to realize that interviewing is not a total reflection of either you or the company that you are interviewing with. Although the concept purports the idea that the job interview is a mutual evaluation of your record, talents, and a prediction of how you're going to perform in the future, as well as your personal evaluation of the organization, it is rarely any of these.

Each party in the process of interviewing is putting his or her best foot forward—and rightfully so. Candidates are responsible for selling themselves to the employer, trying to convince the employer that they're the best person for the job. The company, or the individuals representing it, is trying to find the best person to do the job and, at the same time, both selling the company and screening out the candidates they do not think will be capable of doing the job or fitting in.

If you think about it hard enough, this fact will dawn on you. But when people don't change jobs very often, they forget this and are "reminded" about it four or five interviews too late. Take notice: Interviewing is a staged, contrived event.

As we learn more (or remind ourselves) about the interview process, let's take a look at some of the key factors about interviewing.

- **You are selling yourself. It isn't a "two way-street."** You have to sell yourself harder than you think in the interview process. Don't think interviewing is a mutual "give and take." While you are expecting some "giving," your competition is selling themselves hard to get an offer. You need to be selling yourself, just like your competition is. Don't waste time in an interview trying to figure out what the company can do for you. Get the offer, and then you can evaluate everything.

- **You need to sell your particular "features, advantages, and benefits."** You need to be able to quickly and efficiently "sell" to an employer what you can do for him or her that the other candidates can't. If you don't know the unique aspects of you and your experience and communicate them clearly and concisely, you will lose the opportunity.

- **The most qualified candidate does not always get the job.** It is usually the most qualified candidate who sells him- or herself the best in the interviewing process who gets the job. The first "threshold" to cross is to be qualified. But that doesn't matter unless you sell yourself well and interview better than everyone else.

- **Prepare by researching for interviews.** This means doing extensive research into the company that you're interviewing with and the specific opportunity. With access to the Internet, doing this kind of research should be very easy. The more you demonstrate that you know about a company and the person doing the interviewing, the better you look in the interview. Digging deeply into a company's website, reading white papers published by the firm, knowing about the competition, even knowing the background of the hiring authority you might be speaking to, are all easy tasks to do.

- **Have prepared questions.** You may not need them. In fact, you will rarely have to use all of them. By having prepared questions, ones that you will learn in this book, you will set yourself apart from other candidates.

- **Who should you get an interview with?** Anybody who is willing to listen! Within reason, you want to talk to anyone you can about getting a job. Social interviews, informational interviews . . . any kind of interview will do. Most people make the mistake of not talking to enough people about going to work. You never know who might hire you or know someone who will.

• **Interview with a non-hiring authority is different.** Any "intermediary" who interviews you but who is not the hiring authority with "pain" (needing to hire someone) is going to be more interested in being careful not to take risk on any candidate than a hiring authority is. This person is going to be more concerned about what he looks like in passing you "up" the interviewing process than he's concerned about your ability to do the job. If you interview with one of these people, your objective is to move beyond him in the interviewing process.

• **Time is your enemy.** The longer the period of time between interviews, the less likely you are to get hired. Time kills deals! Your job as part of the interviewing process is to keep the interviews going as rapidly and with the sense of urgency as possible. Strategic e-mails and the right phone calls, even voice-mails can move a "hire" along. See Chapter 3 for some guidelines.

• **Take notes.** If you don't take notes during the interviewing process, you don't look very bright, and your competition will "clean your clock." You won't remember the important points of an interview, because you will be pretty focused on selling yourself. When you go back over the notes you take during the interview, you will have "ammunition" for follow-up letters, e-mails, and, especially, subsequent interviews.

• **First impressions are critical.** Whether you like it or not—and most folks don't—study after study proves that interviewers adopt an opinion about a candidate in the first 15 to 20 seconds of the interview. My experience is that these studies are about right. Now, a candidate may very well be able to overcome a marginal or poor initial "opinion" by interviewing well. But you need to have it reinforced by what mamma said, "you don't get a second chance at a first impression." Make sure your first impression is a good one.

• **Dress professionally.** Always, especially on an initial interview, wear a dark suit and white shirt, conservative tie for a man and a light-colored blouse for a woman. Don't let anybody kid you: Casual dress in an interview is not to your best interest. You just look more like a businessperson with the appropriate dress. If, after the initial interview, you discover a very casual organization, you can dress "down" on subsequent interviews.

- **Watch your body language**. Keep your feet planted flat on the floor, your arms open or at your side or on the arms of the chair. You want to sit up straight and lean forward enough to make good eye contact with the interviewing authority. You should communicate openness and just a bit of intensity. Never come across as laid back. Practice!

- **Delivery is important.** Your voice delivery should be enthusiastic, focused with a high degree of confidence. In the beginning most candidates are scared and come across as meek, sometimes in mumbling monotones. You must communicate decisiveness, confidence, enthusiasm, and conviction. Practice!

- **Don't talk too much or too little.** The two biggest mistakes in interviews themselves are to talk too much or not say enough. Answering questions in the interviewing process takes practice. You want to answer questions or explain things clearly so the interviewing authority understands. But it does take practice.

- **Give clear explanations.** You need to make sure that all of the explanations that you give about your background and your experience are precise and clear. If a high school senior can't understand exactly what you're talking about, you're probably making things too complicated. Remember, interviewers or hiring authorities don't have much reference to what you've done. If your answers are too complicated, too detailed, and unclear, it is too easy for the hiring authority to simply pass on you because she doesn't understand your explanations. Ask, "Did that answer your question?" if the interviewer appears to have not understood.

- **Close for the next interview.** Always, always, always "close" the interviewing authority for the next interview. You simply state, "Based on what we've talked about here, I am a great match for this job. What do I need to do to get it? " Never leave an interview without asking for the support of the person you have just interviewed with. Even if he says something like, "well, it's really not my decision," you need to come back and say, "Mr. or Ms. _____, I wouldn't be speaking with you if you didn't have influence or you couldn't say 'no.' So, it is very important that you give me your promise that you will support me and promote me to the next interview."

- **Focus on the process of interviewing and don't worry about the result.** The interviewing process is to successfully go from the first, to the second, to the third, etc., interview, becoming, eventually, the choice of the hiring authority and getting an offer. Don't worry or focus on the result of getting a job offer—just focus on the next step. If you focus on the process, the result will take care of itself. You don't have to be concerned about offers if you do well on every interview. You can't control offers as much as you can control your interviewing process.

• **It's a numbers game.** Most people don't realize the massive number of interviews it may take to get a job. People start out like gangbusters and imagine they can get a job in the short period of time as a result of two or three interviews. It takes a lot of phone calls to get an interview and a lot of interviews to get a job. Get ready to work the numbers.

• **Be aggressive.** The vast majority of people have a tendency not to be aggressive enough in the interviewing process. Since you're already at emotional dis-ease, there's a tendency to fear more emotional pain by experiencing rejection, so people are way too "soft" when it comes to asking for a job. They will destroy an interview by saying weak things like, "Well, where do we go from here?" or something like, "What is the next step?" instead of simply asking the cold, aggressive question of "What do I need to do to get the job?" or "When can I go to work?" If you're going to get refused (not rejected), you want to get it sooner than later so you can move on to the next situation.

• **"No" is the second best answer you can get.** Most job seekers are so afraid of rejection that they will worry and fret needlessly about their status during the interviewing process. After they interview, they wait, hope, worry, pray, and wonder, how they are doing. Do what you can to interview well, follow up well, and sell yourself as hard as you can. But don't be afraid of "no." The goal is to sell yourself to get as many "yeses" as you can, but if you get "no," that, too, is part of the process. It is the second best answer you can get. Quit worrying about getting "no" and spend your energy getting interviews and selling yourself well. You are going to get more "nos" than "yeses" anyhow, so keep track of the nos, knowing that they lead to yeses.

• **All you can do is all you can do.** Remember, you can control the process more than you can the results. When it comes down to the final decision to offer you a job, it is really up to someone else. All you can really control is getting as many interviews as you can, performing well on the interviews, and selling yourself hard to get an offer. Twenty-five percent of the time companies say they are going to hire someone, but they don't hire anyone at all. So, do all you can do, and don't worry about what you can't control.

- **Taking on the same style as the interviewer doesn't work.** Since interviewing is a staged contrived event and since the initial opinion of you is going to be established in the first 15 or 20 seconds of the interview, it is important for you to realize that you should not necessarily take on the demeanor of the person you were interviewing with. In the initial parts of the interview you must come across as energetic, assertive, and confident. So, no matter how laid back and relaxed a hiring authority might seem, you have to be energetic and enthusiastic in the initial part of the interview.

I can't tell you how many candidates over the years have performed poorly in an initial interview, and I've had my client, the hiring authority, say something like, "Well, Tony, the lady just didn't show any energy or enthusiasm. She was just way too laid back." And when I ended up checking with the candidate, she would say something like, "Tony, that was the most laid-back, low-keyed, unimpressive, slow-moving person that I ever interviewed with. So, I simply mirrored and matched his personality. I can't believe that he said I was laid back with no energy. I took on the same personality that he communicated."

The initial moments of the interview have to be performed on your part, with energy, aggressiveness, and confidence. Even if you think that you were being much more aggressive and assertive than the person doing the interviewing, you have to be this way. The interviewing authority is comparing you with the dozens of others that she might be interviewing. You have to set the tone of energy and confidence.

- **Sometimes taking on the style of the interviewer *does* work.** As mentioned above, since interviewing is staged, you want be the first one to be aggressive and get the attention of the hiring authority. A forceful, enthusiastic presentation of yourself does that initially. However, after you have the interviewing authority's attention and rapport, you may begin to establish deeper rapport by taking on the style of the interviewing authority. The purpose of building that kind of rapport is to "lead" the interviewing authority into being more "like" you.

So, after you have gotten the interviewing authority's attention and interest, you may build rapport by "mirroring" his or her style. So, if she leaned back in her chair and crossed her arms, you do the same. If he talks in low tones, you would do the same. However, you would only do this long enough to *build rapport.* Once you have built that rapport, you can "lead" the hiring authority to take on your style. The ultimate compliment of building rapport is that a person mirrors your style.

• **Tell stories.** Telling stories bypasses conscious resistance to hearing the point that is being made. Stories are powerful. They remove people from their personal prejudice and get them to mentally and emotionally focus on what you are saying.

Have stories about yourself. They need to be relevant and specific to issues about your being a good employee. Keep them short and relative to the topic.

The ideal use of a story is to answer a question, then add a little story. For instance, you are asked, "How do we know you are a good worker?" Answer, "I have worked hard all my life. While in college, I held three jobs. I was a resident assistant in the dorm, I sold life insurance, and delivered pizza on the weekends. All this while maintaining a 3.2 grade point average."

There will be resistance to and fear of you as a candidate. When you tell stories in the interviewing process to support your features, advantages, and benefits, you remove the natural fear to hiring you. For example, Jesus Christ, and every great teacher, led people to believe by telling stories and parables. Don't go overboard here, but three or four stories that prove you are a good employee, that bolster what you're saying in the interview, will always set you apart from your competition. Remember: Stories sell!

• **Recognize and use metaphors and analogies to your advantage.** I want to give metaphors and analogies a bit of attention. I've never found, in all of the research on interviewing and finding a job, any author who addresses the importance of these "keys" to expert interviewing. Along with the use of stories, you will notice that I refer to metaphors and analogies often.

Recognizing the metaphors and analogies that your interviewing authorities use during the interviewing process will give you an almost magical insight that you can use to land a job. Remember the sales adage, "if you see the world through John's eyes, you know what John buys"? Translated into the interviewing process, we would say that if you see the world the way the interviewing authority sees the world, you know how to communicate and sell yourself better than your competition.

It is very important to listen to interviewing and hiring authorities' metaphors about themselves, their company, and the job that they are interviewing you for. People are emotionally motivated by the metaphors and analogies they use in describing themselves, their lives, their company, and their jobs. If you master this concept, your interviewing will be more successful than you ever imagined. In fact, as I will show you, not only listening to the metaphors and analogies the interviewing or hiring authority uses, but also asking questions on your part to elicit these metaphors and analogies will really catapult you to the top of the candidate list.

Recognizing the metaphors and analogies used by a person, a company, or a job is very easy to do. The goal is to listen, to elicit metaphors and analogies from the interviewing or hiring authorities, and then present yourself to them with the same metaphors and analogies that they use. You sell yourself using the same "way they see the world," and therefore you will be identified as a person who sees the world they way they do. You will therefore be liked and looked upon as a great candidate that "fits" into the company.

Metaphors are figures of speech that communicate comparisons. An analogy is a concept that draws our relationship between two things that may not have a prior relationship. All of us don't see the world or experience reality as it really is. We experience our perception of reality. We represent reality in feelings and thoughts as an emotional response to those perceptions.

A quick way to measure and quantify a person's perception—i.e., his or her reality—is to listen to the metaphors and analogies. Complete these metaphors:

Life is _____.

I am _____.

My job is _____.

My profession is _____.

This company is _____.

The people that work here are _____.

The candidates we have interviewed are _____.

Working here is like _____.

My management style is _____.

After you have completed these metaphors and analogies, I want you think for a moment about how you might respond to an interviewing or hiring authority if he represented himself, his company, and his job with these types of metaphors and analogies:

Life is *a bitch and then you die.*
Life is *an exciting, everyday challenge, lots of fun.*

I am *a real tough manager who will push you to the limit.*
I am *a mentor rather than a boss.*

My job *is the toughest one in the company, and everybody knows it.*
My job *is wonderful, I work with wonderful people . . . I can't believe they pay me to do it.*

My profession *is an elite group of the top 1% of the top 1% and everyone recognizes it.*
My profession is *an honorable one with a high degree of integrity.*

This company is *demanding and very hard working.*
This company *prides itself in retaining employees who work together in a family atmosphere.*

The people that work here *take no prisoners, do whatever it takes; they are drivers.*
The people that work here are *totally involved in making sure the whole company reaches its goals and objectives by putting the customer first.*

The candidates we have interviewed *are all "slugs"—not one of them is worth a damn.*
The candidates we have interviewed *have been really great; we just haven't found the right match.*

Working here is like *working for the Marines, it's tough, disciplined, and demanding.*
Working here is *a great challenge . . . we all work at our own pace . . . a lot is expected, but it is all appreciated. . . . Each one of us feels like we grow personally.*

My management style is *real clear . . . I'm great to work with, but hell to work for . . . if you do your job you get to keep it.*

My management style is *very hands-off . . . I expect you to do your job and ask me when you need help . . . I'm here for you.*

You don't have to have a Ph.D. in psychology to figure out what these metaphors and analogies tell you about a person, his or her company, or the job you are being interviewed for. Don't make the mistake that many people do, because an organization might be " . . . like the Marines, it's tough, disciplined, and demanding" of thinking that it may not be a really good place to work. I have worked with many organizations whose style was "take no prisoners," but they still were excellent organizations and a perfect fit for the right candidates.

There are two things that you want to be aware of when you hear these kinds of metaphors and analogies. The first is that you need to be sure that your personality and style is compatible with the person and/or the company that you are interviewing with. You may be a rather meek, humble, nonthreatening type of person but can easily work for the manager who is "great to work with, but hell to work for." Even if your style is not the same as this type of person, you still may be able to work for her and be very compatible. You just need to know what you're getting into.

I can't tell you the number of placements that I've made over the years where the candidate, a few weeks after starting the job, has called me complaining that the hiring authority was a totally different personality in the hiring process then he or she really was. Remember I said that interviewing was a staged contrived event? Well, it works both ways. Ninety-nine out of 100 times the candidate simply didn't listen to the metaphors and analogies that the hiring authorities made about themselves and the working environment during the interviewing process.

The second reason that you really want to pay attention to these metaphors and analogies is that you can better sell yourself to the hiring authority. If the hiring authority communicates that "the company prides itself in retaining employees who work together as a family," you will want to communicate a co-operative, consultative, and collaborative style about yourself. If the hiring authority communicates that "life is a bitch and then you die," you might want to communicate that you are a "survivor" and discuss all of the difficult business situations that you have survived.

Again, this is not to say that any of these metaphors or analogies communicate anything intrinsically good or bad about a company. I've known some rather harsh, blustery, "in-your-face" egomaniacs who were very successful leaders. You just have to know what you're dealing with.

Listening to analogies, metaphors, and stories can help you figure that out. Pay attention to all the people that you interview with and listen for their metaphors and analogies. I recommend that, somewhere along the line, and especially with the hiring authority that might be your potential boss, ask things like, "What's it like to work here? What is the company like? What are you like to work for?" and so on.

Listening to and absorbing the metaphors and analogies that a hiring authority provides you in the interviewing process not only tells you what you might be getting into, but also give you keys to selling the perspective employer on hiring you.

• **You don't have anything until you have an offer.** This is the bottom line. While the interview process may be complicated, the goal result is simple. Your purpose in the interviewing process is to get to the next step so you can get an offer. Nothing else matters. You have nothing to evaluate until you have an offer. If you follow these guidelines, you'll be in a better position to get to the next interview, and, ultimately, to the offer.

Chapter

5   Acing the Initial Interview

···

I'm going to offer you a format and script that I have developed. It is a tried-and-true technique that can be used to make your initial interviews successful 95% of the time. This is a bold statement, but it is true. If done correctly, you will be successful in at least the initial interview, if not beyond. Remember, you're trying to sell yourself through to the next interview. That's all you're trying to do, so that you can be in the final group of people who are considered for the job.

There are two variations on this format. The second one is not quite as effective as the first one, but in some instances it might work. Always begin your interviewing process with the first one. It's going to get you to subsequent interviews 95% of the time. But, you have to execute this technique exactly the way I demonstrate. Practice with your coach.

Successful Technique No. 1

You walk into the interviewer's office or interviewing environment. You are rested, refreshed, prepared. You sit down, lean a bit forward, and after you share a few "break the ice" comments, you hand the hiring or interviewing authority your resume (even if he or she already has it) and state:

Phase 1: "Mr. or Ms. _____, I'm here to share with you why you should hire me."

"First of all, I am (ten or twelve descriptive adjectives to explain your work ethic):

_____

_____

_____

_____

(transition phrase 1) "And here in my background is where these *features have been benefits* to the people that I have worked for:

_____

_____

_____

_____

Phase 2: "I am presently (. . . or most recently have been) at _____ company. I function for them in the capacity of _____

_____

_____

_____

_____ (a thorough description of exactly what you do, how you do it, who you do it for, and how successful you are—in terms a high-school senior could understand) (you then emphasize *how much you love the job and the company, the reason you have to leave, or why you left* . . . in very positive terms).

"And before that, I was at _____ company. There, I functioned in the capacity of _____ (a thorough description of exactly what you did, how you did it, who you did it for, and how successful you were . . . in terms a high-school senior could understand)

_____

_____

_____

(you then emphasize *how much you loved that job and why you had to leave it* . . . in very positive terms).

"And before that, I was at _____ company. There I functioned in the capacity of _____ (a thorough description of exactly what you did, how you did it, who you did it for, and how successful you were . . . in terms a high-school senior could understand) _____

_____

_____

_____

(you then emphasize *how much you loved that job and why you had to leave it* . . . in very positive terms)."

"And before that, I was at _____ company. There I functioned in the capacity of _____

_____

_____

(a thorough description of exactly what you did, how you did it, who you did it for, and how successful you were . . . in terms a high-school senior could understand _____

_____

(you then emphasize *how much you loved that job and why you had to leave it* . . . in very positive terms)."

Continue in this manner for at least three jobs, if you have that many. If you've had a series of short stints at jobs, like one year or less, you may want to go back further than three jobs.

(transition phrase 2) "Now, tell me, Mr. or Ms. _____, how does what I have to offer stack-up with what you are looking for?"

Phase 3 : (You now pull out a legal pad, unless of course you have one in front of you already. Start asking questions of the interviewer and start taking notes. If you do this correctly, one question will lead to another question, which will lead to another question, which *will lead to a conversation* . . . , which is exactly what you want).

It is in this part of the interview that you are going to get the questions that I have outlined in subsequent chapters.

You need to practice these with your coach. Practice the whole interview technique every time you go to answer different questions. You have to practice a lot—it doesn't come naturally.

(As the conversation progresses, the hiring or interviewing authority is going to tell you more of what he or she is looking for in an individual. As this unfolds, you weave into the conversation any of the important information that *pertains* to the job that you extract and expand upon the information about where you have been, what you have done, and how you did it in the second portion of your presentation).

As the conversation/interview winds down, when you feel the time is appropriate, you say:

Phase 4: "Based on what we have discussed here, Mr. or Ms. _____, my _____ (background, experience, or potential) _____ makes this a good fit for both of us. What do I need to do to get the job?"

(Then be quiet and don't say a word).

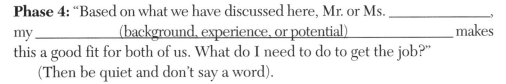

Now, the conversation may evolve into a number of different directions. If you have to repeat your enthusiasm and interest in the position, you may have to push harder and repeat the fact that you are an ideal candidate for the job and you have to know what you need to do to get it.

Script Analysis

I will analyze this technique and tell you why it works so well. Then I'll present three specific scripts that have worked in a recent practical application.

Phase 1. What you say in Phase 1 is really simple. It is ten or fifteen basic intangible traits of a hard-working, successful, committed worker that you possess. In the final analysis, all hiring or interviewing authorities want to see is somebody who is going to possess the traits of a committed, hard-working employee. It is that simple.

What you're doing in this phase is simply communicating that you understand what hard work is. You would be shocked and amazed at the number of people who go into an interviewing situation and just assume that the interviewing or hiring authority already knows that he or she is a committed worker. Remember that your hiring or interviewing authority is scared of making a mistake. He's afraid of a risk. When you communicate the ten or fifteen intangible traits of a hard worker that you possess, it provides assurance in the interviewer's frightened state that you not only know what the traits of a hard worker are, but that you possess them. What I recommend here are traits like hard worker, determined to go the extra mile, early riser, staying late, accomplished, passionate about your work, committed to the customer, going the extra mile, loving what you do, intelligent, great work ethic, quick learner, etc.

I can't emphasize it enough that prospective employers hardly ever hear these words from the typical candidate. You are simply communicating basic attributes that every employer wishes he or she saw in every employee.

Transition phrase 1. The transition phrase to Phase 2 of your presentation is, "Now, here in my background is where these features have been benefits to the people I have worked for." This is a powerful phrase. You are using the terms *features* and *benefits*. It is implied that these features will be benefits to the hiring authority and his or her firm. This transition phrase allows you to lead into an explanation of every job you have had, what you've done, how you've done it and how successful you were.

You are doing the hiring authority's thinking for him or her! No one has to ask that stupid question, "well, tell me about yourself."

Phase 2. Here is where you are going to work backwards and give a short, but very thorough description about exactly what job functions you had, how you did, who you did it for, and how successful you, were, as well as, and this is very important, that you *loved* the job, and why, in very positive terms, you're looking to leave or why you left. The execution of this phase of your presentation is so very important.

First of all, you have to be sure that you explain exactly what your job function is now or was in the past so that the hiring or interviewing authority understands exactly what you have done before. I can't tell you the number of times over the years that candidates have walked away from interviews thinking that they had done a really good job on the interview—only to have the hiring authority, in giving us feedback, explain that he really didn't understand what the candidate did (either in his present job or the jobs he had before). Here is why that happens.

In the interviewing process, a hiring authority is just as nervous as you are. He or she feels the need to get a deeper understanding about you and your background in order to evaluate you. This process takes place with, usually, quite a number of people. Most of the time in the interviewing process, when a hiring or interviewing authority asks a question, part way through your answer that person is thinking about the next question, and then part way through that answer, thinking about the next question, etc.

On top of that, most hiring or interviewing authorities don't want to look stupid or ignorant. Most of them, like most people, are uncomfortable with saying, "I don't understand, could you explain it to me in layman's terms so that I really get it?" After all, they are the "hiring authority" . . . got it? "authority." They are supposed to "know" and "understand" everything, since they are the "authority." So, they will act like they know exactly what the candidate is talking about, and nod their head in complete agreement and understanding as the candidate speaks in terms foreign to everyone but himself. Then, after the candidate leaves, rather than admitting they had no idea what the candidate was talking about, they will claim that the candidate's skills, experience, background, personality, etc. aren't what they were looking for.

You then need to be sure to explain, in very positive ways, why you are looking to leave the firm you're with now and why you left other jobs. I can't overemphasize this enough. You are going to weave into your explanation, along with what you've done, how you have done it, etc., all of the *positive reasons* that you left the companies and the jobs that you had or the one that you are leaving now. If you bring up why you left in positive terms—even if it wasn't under the most positive circumstances, i.e., you were fired—the whole scenario has a tendency to be more palatable to a hiring authority.

The reason(s) that you are looking to leave, and the reason(s) that you have left other positions, have to be very specific and almost detailed. Saying things like, "it was a mutual understanding; it was just time to go; we grew tired of each other; management changed; the company was bought; the company was sold"—or any broad generalization—*will not* help you be successful in the interview. Remember that the interviewing or hiring authority is very concerned about taking a risk. Nebulous, unclear, broad generalizations have "risk" written all over them.

This is one of the many situations in the job-finding process where you absolutely have to see what you are communicating through the eyes of the interviewing or hiring authority. There is a tendency for all candidates to see the reasons that they're looking to leave, or the reason that they left other opportunities, from their own point of view. What matters is how the hiring or interviewing authority is going to react to the reasons you give. If those reasons communicate risk, you're doomed.

This is going to take much thought and practice on your part. You always want to tell the truth, but you might have to put a "spin" on it, that, if nothing else, neutralizes any negative connotations. Do not think that an interviewing or hiring authority is going to see things from *your personal point of view.* He or she isn't.

The third idea that you are going to communicate in the second phase is that you just "loved" every job you ever had. You don't have to use the word "love" in every instance. But you do have to communicate that you had a very positive experience with every job that you have ever had . . . , that you learned a lot from each one, and that you really appreciated the people you worked for. You can communicate this by saying things like, "you know I really love the organization that I work for now, but unfortunately. . . ."

The point is that you talk positively in every way you can about the organization that you're presently with and every organization that you ever worked for. No matter how difficult the circumstances are or were, you have to put your present or previous employers in a positive light. Even if they laid you off or fired you, you have to say something along the line of, "although I'm disappointed by not being there (. . . or having to leave), I do understand what took place from their point of view. . . ." Remember, employers identify with employers.

Both the second and third points in this phase of your presentation must never communicate an adversarial relationship between you and your present or previous employers. No matter how difficult the experience was or is with your past or present employer, you have to communicate a "we're all in this together" type of attitude.

In this phase of your presentation you only need to go back three, maybe at the most four, jobs and go through what I have suggested here. If you had jobs before that, unless they are germane to the position that you are presently applying for, you can "lump-sum" them altogether by just saying something like, "before that (. . . meaning the third or fourth position back) I was in sales . . . or accounting . . . or engineering, etc. for a number of different firms."

In this phase of the interview, you want to make sure that you don't go on and on so long that the interviewing or hiring authority gets bored. Stick to the high points in your background that are applicable to the job for which you are interviewing. It should not take more than five to seven minutes.

It is also advisable in this phase of the structured interview that you weave as many stories about what you have done as you can throw into the presentation of yourself. People love stories. People remember stories. People remember *you* when you tell them stories about your past. Stories, analogies and metaphors about you that pertain to the hiring authority's need are absolutely the best way to be remembered. The stories, analogies, and metaphors about you need to be short, to the point and, above all, pertinent to the opportunity for which you are interviewing.

Transition phrase 2. This is a transition phrase to the third phase of your technique. You simply ask, "Now, tell me Mr. or Ms. _____, how does what I have to offer stack up with what you are looking for?" *The person who asks the questions, controls the interview.*

Phase 3. When the interviewing or hiring authority starts answering your question of how you stack up with what he or she is looking for, you take notes. When he or she stops answering that question, you want to have a relatively prepared set of questions that you can even have written out. Some questions that you may ask are:

What are the most important qualities that a successful person in this position should possess?

How would you measure the success of the last person that was in this job?

Why was he or she successful? or Why was that person not successful?

In your opinion, Mr. or Ms. _____, what is the most difficult part of the job?

Mr. or Ms. _____, how long have you been with the company?

Why do you like working here? What is the most difficult part of your job?

Where do you see the company going in the next five to ten years?

As I was doing my research on the company, I found that _____ _____. Could you give me your opinion about that?

What is the biggest challenge that the company is going to face in the next five to ten years?

I believe your competitors are doing _____. How does your firm respond to that?

How do you know when you have found the "right" person for this job I'm interviewing for?

How would you describe the culture of the company?

What do you, Mr. or Ms. _____, like most about working here?

How many people have you interviewed for this position? Have you seen anybody whom you felt was qualified to do it? Have you offered the job to anyone before my interviewing here?

Well, I could go on and on but you get the idea. Ask enough questions to engage the employer or hiring authority in the conversation. You want this person to open up to you as much as she possibly can about what she wants in the person that she's going to hire. You then have a better idea of how to sell yourself into the job. You will also answer the questions that you will be asked.

Now, the following is very important. As the conversation progresses and you write down some of the highlights of what the employer is looking for, you will reinforce the fact that you are a qualified, excellent candidate by going back to some of the jobs that you had or the job you presently have and talk about it in even more specific terms than before. As the interviewing or hiring authority is sharing with you his or her exact needs, you need to be able to relate exact experience, responsibilities, duties, and successes that you have had *that specifically address* the particular issues being discussed. In the presentation you made (in Phase 2 of this technique), you talked about each job that you either presently have or have had, your duties and responsibilities, and your successes. But you did it in a very broad, descriptive way. Now you are going to use the information that the interviewing or hiring authority is giving you and bring up examples in the job that you have now or the jobs that you had before that specifically demonstrate your ability to do the job. Whereas your initial presentation about your experience and background was detailed enough for the interviewing or hiring authority to understand what you have done, you now get real specific about particular things that would be of value to the interviewing or hiring authority—based on the conversation that results from the questions you ask.

Phase 4. After the conversation has begun to wind down and you can see that the interview is almost over, you *close* the interviewer or hiring authority by stating that your background and experience fit what the employer is looking for and you need to ask, "What do I need to do to get the job?" This is the *hardball* part of the interview. You are either a candidate or you are not, and you need to know right now!

More often than not, candidates at this point in the interview will get afraid of being outright rejected. So they will say stupid things like, "Well, what's the next step?" Where do we go from here?" When should I hear from you?" etc. Weak, weak, weak, weak! These kind of weak questions are the ones that most interviewing and hiring authorities expect. They get them from 98% of the candidates they interview.

Interviewing and hiring authorities want to hire an individual who wants the job. I can't tell you the number of candidates over the years who fail to ask this essential question in the interview and end up being dismissed by the interviewing or hiring authority. I do know that this is terribly unfair. But life is unfair. This is a special part of the interview that truly is a contrived event. The truth this, there is no real way of knowing whether you really want this job right now. But, unless you ask for the job, you're never going to get beyond first base.

Whatever you do, don't fall into the trap of thinking, "Well, I'm not really sure that I want the job so, before I commit, I better think about it." Remember, while you are "thinking about it" somebody else is getting an offer. Remember, *you don't have anything to decide about until you have an offer.*

The question: "What do I need to do to get the job?" is gutsy and takes courage. That's OK. But if you're serious about finding a job, you will use this question at the end of every interview, especially the initial one.

Customization

This whole process and presentation of yourself in an initial interview is very simple. A lot goes into the presentation, though, and once you get the hang of it, it's very easy to keep doing. After all, you're going to give the same basic presentation to just about everybody you interview with. As you do your research for particular organizations, you will end up customizing your presentation when you know there are certain things that might be of value to the particular employer.

It's important to remember to try to find specific "differentiators" that you might have for a prospective employer that might put you ahead of the other candidates. This is one of the things you want to do when you ask questions after your presentation of yourself. If you ask the right kinds of questions, you will be able to get even more detailed information about what the employer might need. Then you can go back over your previous positions and emphasize your relevant experience.

Successful Technique No. 2

This technique is for those people who feel more comfortable with trying to find out what an interviewing or hiring authority might be interested in *before* they talk about their experience. I offer this technique because it does work in some situations. I really don't like it as well and never have. But it has been successful for lots of candidates over the years. So I will offer it.

It isn't much different than the first technique. It asks the question: "What would you like to find in the ideal candidate?" before the candidate talks about his or her intangible attributes and experiences and background. It works like this:

You sit down in the interviewing or hiring authority's office, take a deep breath and say:

Phase 1: (as you put the legal pad down in front of you) "Tell me, Mr. or Ms _____, what kind of candidate would you ideally like to find?" (As the hiring or interviewing authority speaks, you take notes about what he's looking for in an ideal candidate. You may ask a number of questions, but the idea is to find out, in the employer's words, what he's looking for.)

Phase 2: "If you will allow me, Mr. or Ms. _____, I would like to explain why I would fit what you are looking for and how I could do the job. First of all, I am _____ (ten or twelve descriptive adjectives that describe your work ethic)."

Transition phrase 1. "Based on what you said you wanted in a candidate, I would like to demonstrate where these features have been benefits to the people that I've worked for, in the light of what you need."

Phase 3: "I am presently (or most recently have been) at _____ company. I function for them in the capacity of: _____

_____

_____

_____(a thorough description of a exactly what you do, how you do it, for whom you do it, and how successful you are—in terms a high-school senior could understand) _____ (you then emphasize *how much you love the job and the company and the reason you have to leave or why you left* . . . in very positive terms)." Tell a story, if appropriate.

"And before that, I was at _____ company. There, I functioned in the capacity of _____ (a thorough description of exactly what you did, how you did it, who you did it for, and how successful you were—in terms a high-school senior could understand) _____ (you then emphasize *how much you loved that job and why you had to leave it* . . . in very positive terms)." Tell a story, if appropriate.

"And before that, I was at _____ company. There I functioned in the capacity of _____ (a thorough description of exactly what you did, how you did it, who you did it for, and how successful you were—in terms a high-school senior could understand) _____ (you then emphasize *how much you loved that job and why you had to leave it* . . . in very positive terms)." Tell a story, if appropriate.

(Continue in this manner for at least three jobs, if you have that many. If you've had a series of short stints at jobs—like more than one in the last the year or less—you may want to go back further than three jobs.)

The only difference between this and the first technique that I mentioned, it is that you might be able to be more specific about the things that the employer wants in a candidate, in the descriptions of the jobs that you had. So you may have a little bit of an advantage over the first technique.

Phase 4: "Based on what you said you wanted, I'm excellent match. What do I need to do to get the job?"

The slight advantage that you might have in using this technique is that you will get a really good idea about what the employer is looking for. The advantage of this technique does not, I believe, offset the drawbacks. The *major drawback* to this technique is that once the interviewing or hiring authority starts talking about the position and starts asking you questions, you may not get the chance to "take control" by talking about your features, advantages, and benefits—and the successes that you had in your previous jobs. The technique does work, but I don't think it is as consistently successful as the first one. Do what you and your coach think is best.

Ending the Initial Interview

Once you and the hiring or interviewing authority have gotten to the end of the interview, you're probably going to get an idea of what the next steps might be. Don't be afraid to be very assertive about pushing yourself into the next steps.

You may wind up being surprised that a lot of interviewing or hiring authorities may not be sure of what the next steps might be. Most often, even though you have pushed for the next interview, a hiring or interviewing authority is going to say something like, "Well, we have a number of people to interview. We're going to complete that process and then we're going to set up second interviews."

This is a perfect time for you to, again ask, "Based on what our conversation has been here, I would think that I would be in that group, would I not? So let's set up that second interview now." And you pull out your note pad or calendar and ask, "When would be good for me to come back?"

You will probably still get from the interviewing or hiring authority the standard, "Well, we'll get in touch with you." Again, this is an excellent time for you to find out how you really stand, relative to the other candidates, by asking, "Well, Mr. or Ms. _____, you must have some idea how I stack up with your ideal candidate or the others that you have interviewed. Please tell me what you think."

This kind of questioning (and statements) will usually get you a very good idea of how you stand. It is relatively aggressive, and it does not necessarily come naturally or easily. But if you practice asking these kinds of "hardball" questions, they will wind up becoming very easy for you.

If you don't get the chance to set a date and time for the next interview at the end of this initial interview, you need to ask and get clarification of exactly what the next step might be. Most of the time the interviewing or hiring authority will give you an idea about what the next steps are, but most likely will not commit to your coming back, at least at this moment. Don't worry about this too much. Remember, I'm emphasizing process. Getting an answer to how you stack up relative to the others is merely part of the process.

The Follow-Up Activity

The very first thing you should do after the interview, when you get into your car, is take out the notes you took during the interview and write down a summary of the interview on the form I have provided. Write down the high points of the interview: the *major issues or topics* that you spoke with the interviewer about. Summarize it for yourself: where you think your strengths are and where you think your weaknesses are relative to the interview. Write down your interpretation of the things that seemed the most important to the hiring authority, and make sure that you understand them clearly. Often, in the initial interviewing situation, we think we completely understand what a hiring authority is looking for, and we actually do not! The major reason you want to collect your thoughts immediately after the interview is so that you remember the important points: *You cannot rely on your memory.* It may be a two-to-four week period of time before the second round of interviews. You need to be able to refresh your memory with very good notes.

The important issues and criteria for hiring may change as the interviewing or hiring authority interviews more and more people. It is not surprising that hiring/interviewing authorities get confused about the candidates whom they have interviewed. Likewise, I have had candidates get confused and supposedly "remember" the wrong issues and embarrass themselves during the second interview. So, take very detailed notes after every interview on the form that follows and use them. Keep them in the folder for that particular employer and refer to them with your e-mails and letters. Keep them handy for when you go back to the follow-up interviews: Use them wisely and to your advantage!

First Interview

Date _____ Interviewing Company _____

Interviewing/Hiring authority _____

Was this an interviewing or hiring authority? _____

How long was the interview? _____

Summary _____

_____

_____

What are the most important aspects of my background to the interviewing/hiring authority?

_____

_____

What were the major concerns about my candidacy?

_____

_____

How could I have "sold" myself better?

_____

_____

What do I need to do to get to the next step?

_____

_____

Follow-up activity: _____ e-mail?

_____

_____

Overall impressions and thoughts _____

_____

Next steps _____

The Immediate E-Mail

You have gotten the business card of the interviewing or hiring authority at the time of the interview. Immediately after the interview, or as soon as possible, you want to e-mail the interviewing or hiring authority. You don't just want to thank her for her time. You, more importantly, *want to reinforce all of the reasons that you should be hired.*

Every interviewing book in the world is going to tell you to send a thank-you letter. You'd probably be shocked at the number of candidates who don't. One out of every seven or eight, even when they're coached by a professional, either don't do it or do it so late after the interview that it is ineffective. Of course, thanking someone for the interview is obviously important. But what is most important is that you reinforce the high points of what the interviewing or hiring authority said he wanted and restate *where or how you address those issues better than anyone else.*

The letter needs to be short and very much to the point. Do not go on about how much you appreciated the interview, how much you like them, or how you appreciate the conversation, blah, blah, blah. This letter is going to be read, like the resume, in ten seconds. It should look like the letter on page 83 (remember to make it look like an actual letter).

When you reinforce what the interviewing or hiring authority said she wanted, you need to try to do it in quantifiable terms. State things that can be measured objectively like percentages of quota, longevity on the job, grades in school, stability, being promoted consistently—anything that can be actually measured in a quantitative manner. Make sure that you address *specific issues* that the interviewing or hiring authority stated was of value.

Follow-Up Phone Call

Once you have e-mailed the letter, you need to be aware that interviewing or hiring authorities, after initial interviews, have a tendency to move on to other things and don't think about the interviewing and hiring process as much as you think they do—unless of course their "pain" is extremely severe. Interviewing or hiring authorities will have a tendency to tell you things like, "Well, we'll get back to you in a couple of days," and then go on vacation for a week.

With this in mind, it is advisable for you to follow up with the interviewing or hiring authority two or three days after the interview with a phone call to "check in with him" and see how his process is coming along. Interviewing

Dear Mr. or Ms. _____,

Thank you for taking the time to speak with me today, regarding the position with _____. Your needs and my qualifications are compatible.

You stated that you wanted someone who was:

- (desired experience or attributes stated by the employer or interviewing authority)
- (another desired experience or attribute stated by the employer or interviewing authority)
- (another desired experience or attribute stated by the employer or interviewing authority)

I have given a lot of thought to what we spoke about. I would like to reinforce the confidence you can have in me to deliver what you need.

- When I was at _____ company last year, I _____ _____ (accomplished the first thing that you wrote above) _____.

- When I was at _____ company, I _____ (accomplished or proved the second thing you wrote above) _____ _____.

- And, when I was at _____ company, I _____ (accomplished or proved the third thing you wrote above) _____ _____.

I'm an excellent fit for you in your company. I would like to go to work for you and your firm. This is a win/win situation for both of us.

Sincerely,

Your name

and hiring authorities have to at least act like hiring is a top priority. And sometimes it is. Hiring is something that everybody knows should be done with decisiveness and real business acumen, but it isn't. So, your calling reminds the hiring authority of the task at hand. It is often a timing thing—and you may catch her and all of a sudden, since you have her on the phone, she will make an appointment with you for a second interview. This is also a great time to ask her about anything you might have discussed in the initial interview that you didn't fully understand or that you need further clarification of.

If you don't get him on the phone, and often you won't, you'll have to deal with voicemail. In spite of the fact that I have a ton of experience in this profession, I'm never really sure of how many times to call someone back when he never returns your call. My suggestion is to call until you get him or her. So, you say, "Well, Tony, don't I run the risk of irritating them and making them angry, and, therefore, they will not be interested in hiring me?" Well, my answer to that is: You have absolutely nothing to lose. After all, until you have a job offer, you really don't have anything to "decide" about.

Most hiring authorities don't intentionally think, "I'm not gonna call that sucker back. She's a schmuck and I'm not going to hire her anyhow." The truth is that their intentions to do what they are supposed to do are sincere, but the activity just doesn't get done. The process of hiring often just slips further behind in favor of other more pressing issues. So, a timely call, and many of them after that—if you have to—may put you on the top of the list of potential candidates.

Now, after ten or fifteen days of calling an interviewing or hiring authority, with no response at all, you might be led to the conclusion that you should pursue other people and other opportunities. *Never, never, never take this "result" personally* and do something stupid, like calling the hiring authority and leaving a mean, sarcastic voicemail about what he can do with his job and that you didn't want it anyhow. There's always a tendency to take perceived rejection personally. The reason I say "perceived" is that your not receiving a callback may have nothing to do with your candidacy. Now, the odds are that if you have not heard from a prospective employer in several weeks, you were probably not on his list of candidates to be considered. But you never really know. Always leave the door open, so that if a prospective employer wants to still consider you, even after weeks or months have gone by, you could "resurrect" the opportunity—even if you thought it was long gone.

6 Supporters: Great Assets or Your Worst Nightmare

....

I have not come across anybody writing or giving advice about changing jobs that has specifically addressed the people who need to support you when you're looking for a new job. These people can be your finest supporters or your worst nightmare. They can be a tremendous asset in your looking for a job and *performing well on an interview*, or they can be one of the greatest hindrances you will encounter. I've experienced many well-meaning supporters in the form of spouses, parents, ex-spouses, relatives, friends, and acquaintances who can totally destroy an otherwise perfectly good job search process.

It is very important that you get as many of the supporters that you might have to read at least this chapter of this book. Certainly, you are going to read it; but it is especially important for those closest to you, who are going to help you in your job search, to be ready for the same roller-coaster ride that you are going to experience. What's so treacherous about the involvement of the supporters is that they can screw up the process more than they can help, and they do it most of the time in the most well-meaning fashion.

If the supporters become very aware of their positive role in your job search, they will help you not only get interviews, but perform well on those interviews. One or two of your supporters should be helping you every day to prepare for interviews. They should be helping you practice your interviewing skills and answers to the questions in this book daily.

I would like to address your closest supporters; please have them read this.

An Open Letter to Supporters

Dear (spouse, son, daughter, relative, or close friend):

As you know, your (spouse, son, daughter, relative or close friend) _____ _____ is looking for a new job. I have been in the placement and recruitment business since 1973 and have been asked to pass along to you all of the things that I've learned that will be most beneficial in helping you to help him/her and support him/her in the job change.

One of the most important things that you can do to help _____ find a new job is to be aware of the fact that YOU can either be _____'s most important supporter or you can be the worst nightmare. You can make an already difficult and emotionally charged process a lot easier or you can complicate it and make it ten times more difficult than it has to be. The choice is yours. Since you love _____, you're probably going to want to help him or her as much as you possibly can. That's good. Your intentions to help have to be positive. But in my years of finding people jobs, I have seen a tremendous number of well-intentioned people make the matter of finding a job more difficult than it needs to be. I have known candidates that literally got divorces because the supposedly supporting spouse really didn't know how to help his or her mate in finding a job. Now, the job hunting process was probably not the cause of the divorce, and it probably culminated an already rocky relationship, but nonetheless, well-intentioned, sincere efforts can still screw up a job-finding process if the support is wrong. Hitler was sincere, but he was still wrong.

So, for the next few minutes, I'm going to talk to you about how you can best help _____ in his or her job search. Trust me; you can make all the positive difference in the world. Finding a job could and should be a team effort. It is a compliment to you that _____ wants you to help him or her in this endeavor, and I'm going to teach you how to be a very good coach. If you do it right and truly help, you will have a tremendous amount of personal satisfaction and share in his/her own personal gratification.

I want to start out by telling you that I really understand how difficult your job as a supporter and coach is going to be. Now, it may not have dawned on you yet that your role here might wind up being difficult. But here is what happens from a practical point of view. On the one hand, you're going to want to help _____ do his or her best in finding interviews, preparing for interviews, and eventually accepting a new job. On the surface, that looks really easy. But the difficulty is that *you* can't be the person actually getting the interviews, performing well on the interviews, and accepting the job. You're going to get emotionally wrapped up in all of this process, you're going to experience all of the ups and downs that _____ experiences, and yet you're not going to be able to do it for him/her. You are going to have a tremendous amount of input in the process, but you're also going to have to know when to draw the line and realize that _____ has to carry his or her own "ball" without you. There will be times when you will not only be frustrated *for* _____, but you will also be frustrated *with* _____ because he/she didn't do what you thought should be done. So, you're going to take on the difficult position of being in the game but only in being able to affect it from a removed position. Being a coach on the sidelines can be very frustrating, especially when your life is affected so drastically by what goes on.

On the one hand, you're going to want to be close enough to the "action" to be able to help _____. You are going to want to help him or her do research, prepare for interviews, role play, help him/her express thoughts, help overcome fears, and just be there for him/her. On the other hand, you can't be so close that you lose your objectivity and get frustrated with him/her when he/she gets frustrated with the situation. Or that you feel personally rejected when he/she gets personally rejected, and, because you love him/her, you get frustrated when he/she makes mistakes. Your role is very tricky. And on top of that, you haven't done this very often, and you don't really know the right things to do. I can help.

If there is one thing you need to be aware of before you begin to support and coach _____, it's that looking to change jobs is one of the most emotionally difficult things person can do. If _____ has been out of work for any length of time, the emotional strain is even greater. You, as a coach and supporter, can help alleviate the emotional strain—if you help in the right way.

Remember, the four biggest challenges facing you in this endeavor are:

1. You love this person and *don't* see him/her the way the rest of the world does.

2. You love this person and *see him/her the way you want to.*

3. You don't have any idea what the market will bear for him/her and him/her skills.

4. You *can't* find a job *for* him/her . . . you can help . . . but you *can't do it for him/her.*

Being the Nightmare

Let me address here how you can become _____ 's worst nightmare and literally destroy his or her effective process of finding a job. These are a number of things that you **shouldn't do.**

• **Don't** *not* get involved. This may sound strange, but I have seen a number of situations over the years where the spouse, parent, friend, or loved one simply didn't even acknowledge the fact that, in your case, _____ needs to change jobs. I've seen people who should have been helping, supporting, and coaching simply dismiss the whole challenge as, in your case, _____'s problem. These people usually have a career of their own that they are focused on, and since they're not the one who's out of work, they simply ignore the fact that _____ needs help. This person's attitude is, "Well, anybody can find a job. . . . It's no big deal. What do you want me to do about it? I've got my own job, career, problems, etc. figure it out yourself. Don't ask me for help, I'm busy."

Usually, the people close to you who don't want to get involved aren't really as selfish and self-centered as this may appear. Most of the time, they are overwhelmed with what they are already trying to do and have absolutely no idea how they can help. Since they don't really know what to do to help, they shrug the whole thing off by ignoring the situation.

• **Don't** get involved *too much.* You want to be involved to the point that you help, but again, you can't do this for somebody. You have to act as though you are **not** personally affected by what happens to _____ in the job-finding process. You know that you are too involved when you get mad or frustrated with _____ when he or she doesn't do it the way you would. You know that you're getting too involved when you get mad at _____ for not getting the interview or blowing the interview or not getting an offer, etc.

- **Don't** criticize. "Why don't you do this? Why don't you do that? Why did you say that? Why didn't you say this?" is not the way to help anyone, especially in the emotional strain of trying to find a job. Communicate the idea that, "We're all in this together" and "Where you go, I go." The interviewing process is going to have fifty times more negative events than positive ones. If you understand the job search process, you will realize that _____ is going to "miss" way more opportunities than he or she is going to get. If you really understand that all of us need to focus on the process, and not on the result, then you realize that there's no room for criticism.

The biggest difficulty with this concept is that _____ is going to receive what you perceive to be your most positive suggestions as criticisms. If the job-seeking process lasts for any length of time, don't be surprised if you have downright arguments about these positive suggestions. Please remember that you, _____, and anyone else who is economically tied to _____ 's going to work, are frustrated and emotionally distressed over his or her needing to find a job. Even constructive criticism can be totally blown out of proportion. Just recognizing this makes it easier to deal with.

- **Don't** think the rest of the world knows how wonderful _____ is. This is the "halo effect." Anybody who would not hire _____ would have to be crazy. This is primarily because *you know* _____. Part of your job as a supporter and coach will be to help _____ communicate what a wonderful employee he/she might be to prospective employers. But whatever you do, don't keep telling _____ how wonderful he or she is when he or she is having trouble getting an interview and not doing well on the interviews he or she gets. There is nothing more frustrating for any job hunter than to go out and get rejected by just about everybody and have you telling him how wonderful he is and how "crazy" everybody else is. Those "crazy" people are the ones that need to hire _____. So, in the hiring category, your loving opinion of _____ doesn't matter. In fact, and we will talk about it, you need to see _____ *through the eyes of a hiring manager*. That's not going to be easy.

- **Don't** commiserate. Don't "help" _____ bitch and moan that the job he or she has isn't good, or how badly he or she was treated in the job that he or she just left. Be empathetic but not sympathetic, then get on with the task at hand—no matter how difficult the task might be. Help _____ under-stand that there is nothing he/she can do about the past and the only way to deal with the circumstances of the present is to take action and change the con-ditions. In other words, "either shut up or do something about it!" Explain to _____ that you are more than happy to try to help, but dwelling on the past or the way things are presently doesn't help him or her take action to change. Understand _____'s issues and concerns, but help him or her be as objective about it as possible and help him or her take steps to do some-thing about it.

• **Don't** act like you know everything about getting a job. This is especially the case if you are a spouse and you are gainfully employed. There is a tendency for people who are presently employed to take for granted the difficulty that another person, who is either presently employed and looking for a new job or unemployed and looking for a job, is going through. Flippant advice not only doesn't help, but it creates a tremendous amount of resentment. Admit that since you personally are not in the job market, you really don't know anything about what he or she is going through—or what's available—but you would be more than happy to help him or her in any way you can.

• **Don't** work the process *for* _____. Don't pick up the phone for _____. Don't try to get interviews for _____ because you don't think he or she can get them. Don't take _____ to interviews. Don't wait for _____ in the lobby. Don't try to talk to a prospective employer about _____ after he/she has interviewed there, telling them what a wonderful employee _____ is. (Don't laugh at all of these things, be-cause we have seen many supporters over the years try to help in these ways.) You can support and coach, but you can't do it for him or her.

• **Don't** rub it in when things don't go well. Remember this is a "numbers" game. You may have to remind _____ this all the time. But you need to remember it, too. If you rub it in, you take away a person's dignity. There are going to be many times when _____ is not going to know why he or she didn't get an interview, how he or she didn't do well on the interview, or why he or she didn't get the job. Your questioning along these lines, even in a constructive manner, may be perceived in the wrong way. Again, you're going to get frustrated when things don't go well for _____. Just try to make sure that your "frustration" leads to positive reinforcement. Remember, I did tell you that this was not going to be easy.

• **Don't** become an enabler. This is that fine line again between being empathetic, which is good, and sympathetic, which may not be. On the one hand, you don't want be so sympathetic with _____ that every time he or she has an interview that doesn't go well or doesn't get a job, you comfort him or her so much so that you inadvertently reinforce his or her either staying out of work and looking for a job or keeping a job that _____ shouldn't. Your "comfort strokes" could enable the job search process to go on longer than it should.

Being a True, Supportive Coach

• **Do** recognize all of the emotional strain that _____ is going through. Recognize and appreciate his/her vulnerability. Appreciate _____ 's fears and frustrations.

• **Do** accept _____ for just exactly who he/she is and where he/she is in the job-seeking process. Try to objectively observe _____ in the process of looking for a job and be as *nonjudgmental* as you possibly can.

• **Do** play the role of good *coach* by helping _____ in the *process* of finding a job. Help him or her write out goals. Discuss with him/her how *you* can help with those goals. Help each other. You will help _____ feel better about him or herself if you are giving him/her chance to help you.

• **Do** help _____ with recognizing what kind of personality he/she is as I discussed in Chapter 1. The more you help _____ realize his or her own personality traits and how he or she will perform in interviewing situation, the better he/she will do in the interviews.

• **Do** help _____ *research* all of the potential organizations that he or she might contact in looking for a job. This can be a tremendous help to _____ because he/she won't feel alone doing this task. On top of that, two or even three of you can simply do more research and get more information so that _____ has more opportunities available. The Internet is a phenomenal tool for doing that kind of research. Not only will you find information about companies, but websites will often list the managers in organizations that _____ should be contacting.

In one of the previous chapters, I instructed _____, if he or she is out of work, to spend most of the day cold calling organizations in order to get appointments. You can facilitate his or her making those appointments by writing out a list of companies, names of managers, and phone numbers so he or she can spend more time on the phone getting appointments rather than researching. This kind of help can have a major impact on _____'s success in finding a job.

And another great help is to research all kinds of advertisements on the Internet, in the newspaper, and trade publications—frankly, anywhere. The research shouldn't be focused primarily on advertisements for only the kind of experience that _____ has. As I mentioned in a previous chapter, companies or industries that are expanding positions in one arena may very well be expanding them in another as well. So, just because a firm might be advertising for something that _____ isn't, doesn't mean that _____ shouldn't contact this firm to see if someone of his or her skill is needed. Again, this kind of research can have a major impact on _____'s success.

In fact, becoming _____'s *research manager* is a great help to him or her.

• **Do** help _____ practice interviewing. It would be an excellent idea for you to help _____ write out the script that I recommend for each activity, the telephone presentation, the telephone interview, and a face-to-face interview itself. Then you need to sit down with _____ and have him or her practice the scripts with you. *These scripts need to be practiced over and over and over* until _____ can perform them flawlessly.

Any job hunter thinks that he or she is going to interview flawlessly with very little practice. This idea couldn't be further from the truth. If you help _____ practice the interviewing techniques and the scripts that I provide, he or she is going to get a job that much faster. You need to reinforce that successful interviewing takes tons of practice and that, as a coach, that's part of your job.

I can't overemphasize the interviewing practice that _____ needs to do. You have to help him or her by *role-playing* over and over. *Interviewing, for most people, doesn't come naturally.* Most people blow their first three or four interviews before they really get into the "groove" of interviewing. _____ can't afford to blow any the interviews, because there are not going to be that many. So, you, as coach, need to help him/her practice until he/she can literally perform in interviewing situations in his/her sleep. Be sure to make _____ practice the questions in the subsequent chapters of this book. Help _____ formulate good answers.

• **Do,** especially if you are employed, talk to all of your friends, at work and socially, to see if you can find any job opportunities that _____ may be qualified for. Don't hesitate to ask your friends, business associates, social acquaintances—frankly, anybody—if they might know of a job opportunity that _____ may be qualified for.

_____ might be embarrassed about your doing this at first. But you need to remind _____ to "get over it." Which is more painful—needing a new job or worrying about how he or she is perceived by someone else? Being out of work or needing a new job has nowhere near the stigma that it did even a few years ago. Society is beginning to understand that the business climate, even for the world, is a lot more fluid than it has ever been. Remember, the average job lasts between two and a half and three years. Now, I'm not saying that we all need to be constantly looking for a job, but I am saying that the need to change jobs does not have the negative connotation that it used to. _____ needs to realize that he/she need to get interviews in any manner possible.

Once you discover an opportunity for _____ in this manner, make sure that he or she follows up on it. _____ has to make his or her own calls, appointments, etc. As I mentioned above, you should not do it for him/her.

• **Do** provide as much spiritual and emotional comfort for _____ while he or she is looking for a job. Praying for _____ is definitely in order, if that is in your tradition or spiritual arsenal. Little surprises for _____, like an ice-cream cone, a cheery note or card, fixing his/her favorite meal, etc. can be wonderful, positive reinforcements that will make him or her feel loved and accepted. After all of the rejection that is most likely happening, _____ needs all of the positive reinforcement he/she can get. Just being there for _____ will make all the difference in the world. Sometimes, the only thing that you will be able to do is to listen. Listening in a nonjudgmental way will give _____ an opportunity to hear him- or herself and help in "thinking things" out loud. Just knowing that you were there to help will keep _____'s job search from being as lonely as it can be.

- **Do** help _____ stay on task. As an objective coach, it may be easier for you to recognize when _____ loses focus on the things that are most important in a job search. Fear of rejection is one of the biggest hurdles that a person looking for a job has to overcome. Oftentimes people will confuse activity with productivity. They will do all kinds of things that are not really important in a job search but are easy to do and don't run the risk of rejection. The most important things that a person can do in a job search requires running the risk of being rejected. People will often avoid those kinds of activities and try to convince themselves that doing the nonrisky things are important. Playing golf with a group of buddies in the middle of the afternoon of any weekday or going to lunch with old girlfriends from previous employment can be rationalized as activities that could be beneficial in a job search. But compared to picking up the phone, calling a hiring authority, making a presentation of yourself, and trying to get in interview with that hiring authority—which are much more beneficial to finding a job—these activities are a lot less threatening, but easier to do. Part of your job as a coach is to help _____ do the "hard things" when it would be easier to do the less risky activities. So, help _____ make a plan. Even a little bit of objective coaching in this manner makes _____ more accountable, not just to him- or herself, but also to you.

- **Most of all, just be there for** _____. Let him or her know that you want to help as much as possible. You both can grow together.

Syndicated careers columnist Joyce Lain Kennedy agrees and summarizes the role of supporters.

> Shared experiences can get you through the loneliness and uncertainty of unemployed days—the ups and downs, the insecurities and fears, and the brilliant moves and belly flops. You need family and friends who aren't rendered comatose by the microdetails of the job search process and especially those at the finish line, the interview. . . . When you are trying to pull off a great job search, there will be others willing to help you. Keep asking until you build the support team you need.

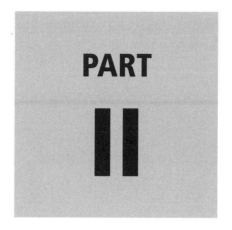

PART

II

The Four Types of Qualifying Questions

Chapter

7

Can You Do the Job?

···

As mentioned in Chapter 2, the very first question an employer is going to ask any candidate is "Can you do the job?" In my experience—and this may be surprising—your ability to do the job is only about 20% of the hiring decision. Now, it is the FIRST 20% "threshold" that a candidate has to cross before he or she can be considered, but it only accounts for about 20%.

Most candidates get really upset when they don't get hired but are told they are the most qualified candidate. Most candidates don't understand that any candidate who gets beyond the first two interviews is "qualified" to do the job (at least in someone's opinion).

But being qualified, even the most qualified, won't get you hired. In addition to being qualified, the candidates who get hired are the ones who sell themselves better than anyone else, as mentioned in previous chapters. The candidates who are liked better than the others, prove to be less risk than other candidates, and are the ones who are the most affordable are the ones that get the jobs.

Now, having said this, a candidate still has to establish his or her ability to do the job. It is the very first group of questions you will get. You have to answer them well to get to the other questions. But the essential step beyond that is selling yourself.

These are going to be factual, "What did you do"–type questions. The interviewing authority is trying to discover your skill level or potential. There are going to be only four or five factual aspects of your work history that will either get you to the second interviewing stage or eliminate you. Remember, just four or five facts, and it either supports or detracts from what you say you can do.

Some factual accomplishments might be:

- Graduated at the top of my class
- Got promoted three times in three years
- Was 130% of sales quota two years in a row
- Survived three layoffs
- Was recognized as _____ by my (company, superiors, peers, etc.)

Provide any facts that can be benefits to the employer. The further into the interviewing process you get, the more focused your facts might be. For instance, if you find that there has been a lot of turnover in the position you are interviewing for, you can emphasize your stability in previous positions.

So, let's look at some of the common questions interviewees are asked, and how you can best answer them so you can move to the next phase in the interview process on the way to getting a job offer.

How Do Your Skills and Experience Fit?

- **Tell me about yourself and your last few jobs.** Whatever you do to answer this question, don't start out with, "I was born and raised in . . ." The interviewing authority is trying to find out exactly what you have been doing professionally so he or she can assess your ability to do this job. He or she doesn't care where you were born or raised.

- **What kind of job are you looking for?** In other words, "Is what you're looking for the same thing that I'm looking for?" If you have done your research, you will know exactly what kind of position you are interviewing for. If not, then the answer is, "I'm looking for a position that is going to help make a company better and challenge me based on my experience and background."

- **Describe in detail your last two positions.** Even if you did a good job of your presentation on the last two or three jobs you had (what you did, how you did it, for whom you did it, and how successful you were), you still may get this question. Basically, give exactly the same description that you gave in the presentation of your professional background and expertise, but maybe with a little more detail. Be sure to precede your answer to this question with, "I really loved that job" or, "I really love the job that I'm on now" and then explain in fair detail what you do. Ask the question, "Did I make it clear?" One can "love a job" but still be laid off, downsized, fired, not make enough money, not get promoted, etc. There are lots of reasons to have to change jobs, even if people love what they do. In fact, any disparaging comments about a present or previous job can kill a person's chances of being hired.

• **Walk me through a day in your current or most recent job.** If you made your presentation correctly in the beginning, the interviewing authority will not have to ask this question. If he or she does, be sure you have concise 60- to 90-second answers. Emphasize the parts of the job that most correlate to the one you are interviewing for. Just be sure you have practiced this answer. It is amazing the number of times candidates hem and haw at answering this question, simply because they haven't practiced.

• **What was the most difficult part of your last two jobs?** Whatever your answer is, you need to say, "Even though that was the most difficult part of the job, I met the challenge every time." Then communicate in very appreciative, upbeat tones about the hardest part of the job. You can even add something like, "meeting that challenging part of the job made me a better person." Adding a short story as to how you overcame a difficult challenge in each one of your last jobs really works.

• **What are you looking for in a job?** Obviously, you need to answer this question with an answer that has something to do with the job or position that you were applying for. Make sure that you say something along the lines of, "I've enjoyed the challenge of learning in just about every job I've had" and, again, "I'm looking for a position that's going to help make a company better and challenge me."

• **What do you look for in a job?** Whenever you get a question like this, stay away from the simple, low-level inducements to work. Answers like "Well, I look for the most money in a job" will not get you very far. You always want to highlight a higher level of thinking by emphasizing concepts of personal growth and satisfaction. Something along the line of, "Well, I'd like the work to be challenging. I enjoy being challenged every day. By being challenged I'm going to grow personally and professionally, and I find if I'm growing personally and professionally, the economics, benefits and many things like that will always take care of themselves" would be a good answer.

• **Describe the best job that you've ever had and why was it so much better than other ones you have had.** Whatever you describe, make it similar to the position for which you are currently interviewing. Something along the lines of, "You know, there have been some wonderful aspects to just about every job I've had. I have really loved all of them, and they are all 'best' for different reasons" is a great way to precede the answer.

• **How do you define success?** Simple answer, "When I contribute to a successful organization, I am successful. We both grow." Then perhaps relate a story about how "successful" you were in your last one or two jobs. Remember, people love stories, and they remember them long after they remember most everything else.

• **What is your greatest accomplishment in each of your last three jobs?** Be sure to tell a story about each accomplishment you had in each job. Whatever attribute was associated with the accomplishment needs to be supported by a short, interesting story. This is an easy question to prepare answers for, and you are going to get asked this question by just about everyone you interview with, so prepare.

• **Are you creative?** Simply cite one or two instances where you were creative and tell the story. Keep all stories short and to the point.

• **What do you know about the position you are applying for?** What little you know about the position, you can voice. And if you don't know a lot about it, make sure you add a question at the end of what you do know, something like, "Can you enlighten me as to what you think the position entails?" This can be a bit of a Catch-22 question. A smart-aleck—and you will run into a few of them—can come back and say to you, "Well, if you don't know much about what you are applying for, how do you know you can do it?" And the answer to any smart-aleck question like that is, "I know your organization to be the kind that I would like to join, and from what I understand, my skills fit best in this position. Can you enlighten me as to exactly what this position entails?"

- **How do we know that you will be successful at this job?** Now, this is a good question. Whenever you are asked to predict the future, explain that you have been successful at everything you have ever done in the past, and there's no reason to believe that you won't be equally successful at this job. This kind of "predict the future" question will come up often. Just remember that the fallback answer is, "I've been successful before; therefore, I will be successful again." And if you have to shore up that statement, you can do it with success stories.

- **What is the most recent business lesson you have learned and how did you learn it?** You need to communicate that you are a life-long learner and demonstrate with what and how you have learned recently. Tell a story.

- **What specifically have you learned from the jobs that you held most recently?** Here, you talk about either a skill or a lesson that you learned. Intangible attributes like persistence, determination, earning respect, loyalty, etc., are great to bring out. Tell short, effective stories.

- **What made you choose to become a _____?** It doesn't matter what you fill in the blank. You need to be able to say that you always had an inclination or a passion for some aspect of your profession. For instance, if it is a sales position, you want to talk about passion for communicating ideas, helping people solve their problems, etc. If it is a position requiring math skills like accounting, engineering, etc., you want to communicate that you always had a passion and love for numbers, science, making things work, etc. Maybe you had a mentor, parent, teacher, etc., who modeled the kind of profession that you got into. Whatever you do, do not communicate that you "stumbled" into your profession, it "chose" you, you couldn't find anything better to do, or you figured it was as good as any profession. Anything that communicates lack of direction, passion, or willy-nilly career decisions will not fly.

- **What can you contribute most to our organization?** Simple answer: "Over and above my excellent professional performance, as I've documented in previous positions, I work harder and am more committed to work than most employees. Next to my relationship with God and my family comes my work." It doesn't get any better than this answer. If you communicated well in the presentation portion of the interview, you will just reinforce what you have done in the past.

• **What do you know about our business? What is our business's biggest challenge or problem? What trends do you see in our profession or industry? What do you know about our competition? What do you know about our company?** These are all questions whose answers you should have arrived at in the research you did on the company and the business it is in. Even if you don't get the answers exactly right, when you demonstrate that you did extensive research on the organization and the business it is in, you will have answered the question properly. Most interviewing authorities really don't expect you to know their business too intimately, but they do want to see if you have expended any effort in finding out as much about them and their business as you can.

• **What would be your ideal work group? How would you define a "good-fit" work environment? Do you work well with other people? Do you prefer to work alone or with other people? Do you require and appreciate lots of supervision? Do you work best with large groups or small groups?** The answer to any questions like these (relating to working alone or with others, in large or small groups, etc.) needs to be answered with something like, "Well, I've had the good fortune of being able to work in all kinds of different environments. I have worked well alone, with others, with relaxed work environments, in tension-riddled work environments, in big groups, and in small groups. I find that, fortunately, I am adaptable and work well in just about any environment." If the interviewing authority wants specific examples of any one of these conditions make sure you have one or two stories from different jobs that you had to demonstrate your points.

• **Why did you apply to our company?** Here's a chance to demonstrate the research you've done on the company and to communicate how your individual skills, experience, or background can contribute. Try to be as specific as you can about what you've learned about the company and how you, in particular, can help it.

• **I don't think with your experience and background you are capable of doing this job. What do you think?** Unless it is a relatively odd situation, it is not likely that you would even be interviewing with this person if you weren't capable of doing the job. This is more of a test to see how you respond rather than exactly what you say. But something along the lines of, "The people I have worked for in the last two jobs thought I was underqualified before they hired me. But I performed very well on both. I am an overachiever and have always been able to perform well beyond my apparent capabilities." Then tell a story if appropriate.

• **Why should I hire you?** "Because I can do the job, I'm a hard worker, people like me, I'm not a great risk, and we can come to a conclusion about money."

• **Why have you not been promoted sooner? If you're so good, why haven't you been promoted?** Don't let a question like this get "under your skin." You can never let a question like this make you mad, and it is best not to show irritation. Simply state that in the organizations that you had been in there was a "bottleneck" of very tenured people available for the few promotions that came up. Although you knew that the quality of your work deserved the opportunity to be promoted, the probability was very unlikely simply because there were too many other people looking to be promoted who had been with the company longer than you had. In fact, this is one of the very reasons that you were looking to change jobs.

• **How does our position compare with the other opportunities you are currently interviewing for?** Be honest and fairly brief. It is always a good idea to let an interviewer know that you were being considered by other organizations. If you feel comfortable in mentioning who the organizations are, that's fine. Always be sure to say something like, "Taking into consideration everything I know about the other opportunities that I am interviewing for, the position here with you seems to be a little bit better match." Just be sure that you have good reasons for saying that.

• **You really don't have as much experience as we would like; why should we hire you?** The answer to a question like it is simple. "You know, it's very interesting, and every job I've ever had I never went in to the job having all of the experience that my previous employers wanted. In fact, I went into three of them where I was hired simply because I had more potential than any other candidate. As you can see, I have been successful in every position that I've been in even though I had no experience before I started. Some people catch on to things more quickly than others and I happen to be one who is blessed that way. I'm a quick learner and I've been able to pick up the things that I didn't necessarily have any experience with and do extremely well."

- **Have you ever "failed" in a job?** Answer this serious question with a "light approach." Say something along the lines of, "Well, I'm like a ballplayer that never really lost—he just ran out of time. Even the very few things that I look back on and others might see as 'failures,' I really see as setbacks. Like most people, not everything that I've ever done has turned out as perfectly as I would have liked. But even when it didn't, I've learned from it."

- **If you could, what would you change about the position you're interviewing for?** You can begin the question here just something like, "Based on most everything that I know, it seems that what you are asking for in the function of the position is reasonable. I really don't know enough about the position to know what might or could be changed."

- **What do you like most about this position? And what you like least about this position?** Be prepared to address a particular aspect about the job that is going to be a positive challenge for you. The answer is something like, "I'm very anxious to take on the responsibility of this job. (This) and (that) about the job are most exhilarating. The right manager with experience will give me the chance to expand on what I've learned. I don't really think that there's anything about the job that I've heard so far that I going to dislike. I'm sure there are going to be some things that I will like more than others, but that's to be expected in any job."

- **Do you prefer to delegate or be a "hands-on" employee?** Simple answer: "I feel comfortable in delegating those things that should be delegated and personally doing the things that I do best. I know that even when work is delegated, not everyone is going to do the job just exactly the way I would. But I'm comfortable with that."

- **If you could start your career over again, what would you do differently?** Answer this question very carefully. If you answer this question in any negative way, you're going to shoot yourself in the foot. Being dismissive about it by saying something like, "Well, I'd rather have become golf pro" won't get you very far. Instead, communicate that you have made some mistakes in your career path but they were minor ones, that you learned from them and, looking back on them, there is not anything in the overall sense that you would do much differently.

• **If you could choose any organization to work for, whom would you go to?** This can be a trick question. If you enthusiastically say with a big smile on your face, "Unequivocally, this company is absolutely the one I would go to work for," you don't seem genuine. So you might say something along the lines of, "All of the organizations that I am talking to are quality firms with quality people just like this one. All of the positions that I am interviewing for have their strengths and weaknesses. A job is pretty much what you make it once you show up and start working. I see the opportunity to work here in your firm as one of the best opportunities available to me."

• **What is the most recent skill you have learned?** Try to keep the answer to a business skill. Learning to roller blade or play golf may really motivate you, but most hiring authorities aren't interested in hearing about it. Talk about one of the business skills that you've recently acquired or business seminar that you attended. Tell a story.

• **How do you keep updated and informed in a professional sense?** This is like a question, "What professional books have you read?" You better have a really good answer for it. Being a member of a professional organization does help. Simply subscribing to professional journals is not a good answer. You may get this question quite often, but once you have the answer you could give the same one to everyone.

• **What is the most important professional lesson that you have learned from the jobs that you have had?** Pick out one or two "important" lessons that you learned from each job that you held and relate them briefly.

• **Do you want to move into management?** This can be a loaded question. If you are not interviewing for a management position and you answer that you would love to get into management, you may be eliminated. The hiring authority may feel that since you are not being hired into a management position, and he or she doesn't know if a management position would ever materialize, you would leave as soon as you found out a management position was not available. On the other hand, if you say something like, "Well, I would never consider a management position," you may come across as not ambitious. So, the answer is something like, "I do believe I have management potential, but I know that good 'chiefs' are also good 'Indians.' If I prove myself in whatever role I am in, if there are opportunities to advance, I'm sure that I will be considered.

I will try to do those jobs equally well. If I do the task at hand, tomorrow and future positions will take care of themselves."

• **Have you ever had to fire someone? Describe the circumstances?** The answer to this question has to be made in an emotional and empathetic manner. If you answer the question in an authoritarian, domineering, "the-SOBs-deserved-it" fashion, you won't be respected. A confident but empathetic answer along the line of, "Firing people is one of the most difficult tasks that a manager has. But I've found that if one does it in a very careful, well documented, reasonable, businesslike manner, although uncomfortable for both parties, it could be done very gracefully." You then might add a short story of a circumstance where you had to fire someone. Basically, you ought to communicate that it was unfortunate but it had to be done and you did in a very graceful manner.

• **What kind of people have you hired and what you look for in those people?** If you have been involved in the hiring process, you want to describe the kind of people that you've hired. You want to be sure that you lay out a thoughtful, reasonable business approach to hiring someone. Describe a process as well as a description of how the process had been successful.

• **Describe a major project that you have worked on and how it contributed to the overall good of your employer.** If you have been involved in doing a major project, simply be ready to describe that project in relative detail. Describe your role, how it interfaced with the roles of other people, and how successful the project turned out.

• **Have you ever been involved in long-range planning?** If you have, simply explain how you were involved. Do not claim that you were involved in long-range planning unless you really were because you may very well be asked about your contribution, and your credibility will be questioned if you can't speak about what you did.

• **What percentage of your week or month was devoted to the different functions of your job?** You won't get this question very often, but it doesn't hurt to have an idea of the percentage of time devoted to all of the activities of your job. If you answer this broad statement like "I did it until it got done," you won't seem like a disciplined person.

- **Can you work overtime or on weekends?** On the one hand, you have to appear to be the kind who will do what ever it takes to get the job done. On the other hand, you don't want to be the kind of employee who has to work nights and weekends simply to get all work done at the minimal level. So, the answer to this question is, "I'll do whatever it takes to get to work done. I have found over my career that since I am a diligent worker, focused on the task at hand and not wasting time with unproductive cohorts, I therefore get more work done in a lot less time than most. I'll work evenings and weekends if I have to, but that hasn't been necessary in the past."

- **How long do you think it will take for you to make a meaningful contribution to our organization?** This is somewhat of a loaded question. If you "guess" for too long a period of time, you don't look confident, and if you "guess" a shorter period of time than is real, then you look foolish. So, the best answer should be something along the line of, "In my present job, I began to make a significant contribution almost immediately. The nature of the work was such that I could go right in and immediately have an impact. It was really fun. In the job before that, because of the nature of what the company did, it took me five or six months to have a significant impact. All the people whom I have ever worked with have always said that I'm a quick study and pick things up very quickly. It's hard to speculate about how fast I can meaningfully contribute until I get into a job and get to know. I can assure you, though, that I will run as fast as I can. I realize that I or anyone else is hired to contribute as fast as possible."

- **How many hours in your previous jobs did you have to work each week to get the job done?** Don't fall prey to this loaded question. Your answer has to be something like, "Gee whiz, I'm not on a clock. I really don't know." If you have a job where you were paid overtime, the hiring authority may be concerned about having to pay a lot of overtime. So, in a situation like this, you would answer by saying, "I was always very careful to be sure that I didn't work overtime unless I absolutely had to. I'm a very fast worker and usually got my work done in the allotted time. Of course, my references would substantiate this." If you get a sense that overtime is not an issue, then you would answer, "I work very efficiently. I do whatever it takes to get the job done on time, with high quality. Whenever time it takes is whatever time it takes."

• **You don't have as much experience in some of the aspects of this job. How do we know if you can do it?** The answer should be something like this, "Looking back on most every job that I have ever had, I really didn't have the amount of experience my previous employers really wanted. Fortunately, I had very good managers in the places that I've worked. I noticed in the interviewing process here that people were willing to be involved in helping so that I'm absolutely confident I will have no problem in performing all aspects of the job."

• **What are some of the things in your last job that you didn't like?** Answer this question with things that have nothing to do with your performance or your abilities. Something like, "Well, I was frustrated because most everybody was so negative about the poor situation of the company. The company was eventually sold; unfortunately, most everyone had a negative attitude." Or something along the lines of, "Well, when work slowed down to a crawl, our major distributor stopped buying. Instead of looking around for things to do and thinking about what we could do to make the business better, most everyone in the firm complained. Some of us got together and came up with alternatives." Whatever you "didn't like" make it a values thing or something you could do nothing about.

• **What reservations might you have about working here?** The answer quite simply is, "None that I know of. No job or company is perfect, and I'm sure that you all have your positives and negatives just like any other company."

• **How many levels of management have you had to communicate with?** Be truthful, being aware that the purpose of this question is to discern how many levels above you are comfortable dealing with. If you only communicated to one or two levels above, you need to make sure you communicate that it was more related to the function of your job then your inability to communicate with upper management.

• **What do you think makes the position you are interviewing for is different from the jobs you've had or the other positions you are interviewing for?** Just be ready for this question and be aware of the unique aspects of the particular job that you were interviewing for. Make sure that you communicate very positive reasons as to why the job you are interviewing for would be "a better fit" than the ones you have had in the past.

• **Are you a good employee/manager/engineer/accountant/sales person/administrative support person/etc.? How do you know?** This very simple question requires a very simple answer: "I really love what I do. I really am very good at it because I get a lot of very positive feedback for the job that I do. My performance reviews and salary reviews have always been excellent."

• **In what way has your present job prepared you to take on greater responsibilities?** You'd better have an answer to this before it ever gets asked. You want to emphasize that there are certain aspects of your job that you have outgrown personally and professionally. Remember to make sure that you say you "love " your job, but you are ready for a new challenge. Emphasize that you have grown as much as you can in your current position and maybe cite one or two stories about how you could have contributed more but it just wasn't necessary because there were plenty of people who were doing so. Throughout the interviewing process you need to be able to communicate that you have one or two or even three skills and abilities that are on tap in the position. That way you always communicate, "I can contribute more, and I am not limited." Relate to your personal "growth" rather than a personal "issue."

• **Can you relocate either now or in the future?** The answer to any relocation question either now or in the future always has to be, "I will certainly do anything that is good for my company and my career. Relocation would certainly be included."

• **In what areas could your boss do a better job?** There's really only one way to answer this question: "I have a respect for my present boss. She does her job extremely well. There might be some little things that she might be able to do little better, but they certainly must be minor."

• **How well did you feel your boss rated your performance?** "All of the supervisors or bosses that I've had have done a good job in a rating my performance."

• **How did your boss or previous bosses get the best out of you?** This is a little bit of a trick question. It is as much to see how you react as it is to find out the answer. Just be ready for a question like this and realize that the simple answer is, "By telling me exactly what the objectives are and then leaving me alone."

• **Do you have budgetary responsibility? How large was your budget? Did you have any problems staying within budget?** Just be ready for any questions about your budgetary responsibility.

• **Give me an example of your past job experience that highlights your ability to build action plans or create programs that support management's strategic goals and direction.** You need to have three or four stories that could be used interchangeably with questions like this. If, in a previous answer, you told a story that could be an answer to this question, you don't want to tell the same story. In fact, there is a tendency for candidates, if they haven't prepared well, to tell the same one or two stories more than they should. Most of the questions that telling a story would answer are similar. If you keep answering different questions with the same two stories, you will appear shallow. So, be prepared with a number of different stories that can address different situations.

• **Tell me about an experience that illustrates your preference to be proactive in speaking to and maintaining contact with others or to wait for others to speak first or contact you.** Again, like above, you'd better have a positive story to tell. If you have to think about it, or ponder the answer, you won't appear decisive.

• **Do you know when to lead and when to follow?** Examples of both need to be given. You need to be prepared for this kind of question. Again, if you have to think about it or you ponder it, you will look like you don't know what you're doing. Short story situations where you lead and where you followed are appropriate.

• **Can you identify the critical needs in a situation, deal with them, and put the others on the back burner?** The answer is, "of course." And a story or two where you had to identify critical situations will work.

• **If you were offered this job, how long will it take you to decide?** "If I were offered the job, I should be able let you know within a day, at the most two."

How Do You Handle Difficult Situations?

• **Describe a difficult business problem that you had to deal with and how you did it.** Describe, in very positive terms, one or two business difficulties that you had to deal with and make sure that you reinforce them with stories. It is very easy, if you have ever had to fire someone, to use those firings as an example of the most difficult business problems you had to deal with. Describe how you did the firing, why you did the firing, and how everyone was better off in the long run for it. Nobody likes firing people, and it is very uncomfortable for everyone, so if you use this kind of example, you will usually satisfy the interviewing authority.

• **Describe a situation in your last one or two jobs where you made a mistake. What was the mistake and how did you rectify it?** Be ready for an "in hindsight" type of answer. Give the example, but highlight what you learned from it. Have one or two of these kinds of stories available for this question when you get it. Whatever you do, don't say that you haven't made any mistakes that you can recall. Talk about a challenge and what you learned from it.

• **Where have you made difficult decisions before and what were they about? What makes you think you can handle this position?** Again, any question like this should be answered with relying on how successful you have been in the past. Cite examples and stories about how you were successful in the past.

• **What are the things that you find most difficult to do? And how did you deal with them?** If you are an accountant, engineer, a technical person, or anybody who is analytical or kinesthetic, then the answer has to center around something along the lines of what your personality is not. For instance, if you are an accountant or an engineer in an organization, you would say that the most difficult thing you have to do is operate in a sales function. If you are a salesperson, then you would say that the most difficult thing you have to do is operate in an accounting or engineering function. This seems rather obvious, but the answer is very safe. Whatever you're not hired to do is probably the most difficult thing you could be doing, so use that as an example. You can always fall back on the proverbial issue of, "Well, I really get frustrated with people when they say they're going to do things by a certain time and don't do them. I'm somewhat impatient. I have a hard time appreciating slackers . . ."

• **What were the most important/difficult decisions that you made in your present, last job, or even your job before that?** This is not going to be a question you get asked very often, but you sure better have a good answer. If you have to think about the answer to this question for more than a few moments, you appear as somebody who doesn't know what he or she is doing. It is best to have at least two or three ideas about the most important or difficult decisions to make in all of the jobs, that you have had.

• **Has there ever been a situation where your work was criticized?** Be thoughtful about this answer, and if there was ever a time that your work was grossly criticized, you may answer something along the line of, "Well, there have been situations where I learned from the mistakes I made in some of the work that I did. I take criticism well and have learned from every time I've experienced it."

• **What are one or two things you wished you had accomplished in your present or last job and the job before that?** Again, not something that you're going to be asked very often, but you better have a real good idea about what those things are. You can even tie those issues to the reason you were looking to leave your present job or the reasons that you left previous positions.

• **The job you are interviewing for requires you to "wear a lot of different hats." You have never done some of these functions, so how do we know that you are going to be able to do them?** Something along the lines of "even though my primary functions were _____ and _____, in most of my positions I have worn a number of hats." Then provide examples of where you performed a number of diverse activities.

• **Describe a situation where you had to make a "seat of the pants" decision without a company policy as a model.** You may not get this question very often, but you need to have an answer. Think about two or three situations where you made off-the-cuff decisions and how they wound up being very good decisions. You can tie these decisions to a "working" philosophy of integrity, character, and "do the right thing" approach if you really want to look good.

• **Describe the situation where you had to work with a very difficult person. How did you handle it?** This is somewhat of a trick question because a hiring authority is trying to find out your definition of what a difficult person might be. Whatever you do, don't vilify, criticize, or present that person in a bad light. Describe the difficulties that the person caused you and everyone else in the organization in objective ways, then describe how you dealt with the situation. But present the person as a "positive" for you. "He or she was difficult to work with/for, but I found a way and learned so much from him or her. In the end, it turned out to be a great learning experience, even though painful at times."

• **Describe a situation where you had to make a quick decision in your last job. How do you make it?** Be prepared for this kind of question and have one or two stories about situations where you made quick decisions, and they turned out to be good ones.

• **Have you ever had to carry out unpopular policies or decisions?** Describe one or two situations where you were responsible for carrying out unpopular decisions that affected a lot of people. Be ready to describe the story of how you handled it and the outcome.

• **In your present or last jobs, were there any problems that you discovered that had been previously overlooked? How did you deal with them?** Be ready to communicate stories about problems that you initially discovered and what role you played in solving them.

• **How do you approach doing things that you really don't like to do?** A great answer is, "Well, attitude is everything. I have found that no matter how much I don't like any particular aspect of my job, if I take the right attitude toward it, I've been very successful. I try to break the particular job down into smaller steps and accomplish them a little at a time. I find that, along with my attitude, to be the major reason I'm successful in taking on parts of my job that I really don't like."

• **When faced with a very difficult business decision, what do you do?** Make sure that you communicate that you go through a number of processes that communicate wisdom. Do not say things like, "Well, I simply follow my gut instinct." You might want to say something like, "Experience has taught me to think long and hard about the decisions I make. I 'think' on paper by writing out all the issues, then see how they appear to me over a period of time. I seek the opinions of others who are both close to the situation as well as removed. I have two or three mentors that I have developed over the years whose opinions I respect, and I seek their counsel. Once I have exhausted all of the processes that I might go through, I then follow my gut instinct. Once

I have made the decision, I become committed to it 110% and throw myself behind it. Once I am sure of the best thing to do, unless there is a drastic change in the facts, I am unwavering about the decision."

• **What was the last thing you disagreed with your company about?** The best way to answer this question is, "Well, gosh. I really can't recall anything of any importance that I minded or disagreed with my company on. Whatever it might have been, I certainly don't remember." The only fundamental things one might disagree with are cheating employees or doing something immoral. But since employers indentify with employers and *not* candidates, unless the issues are public knowledge—i.e., bankruptcy, indictment by law officials—I wouldn't recommend saying anything.

• **Give me an example of when you were refused or told "no" by your company or supervisors.** Make sure you think of something that is a "safe" subject or topic. Do not mention something like, "When I went in and asked for 25% raise." If you can't think of anything even reasonably significant, simply state that you cannot remember any situation where you were told "no" or refused.

• **Give us an example of how you got your staff to support an unpopular decision.** Be ready for this kind of question and give an example of an unpopular decision that had to be made and the way that you presented it to your subordinates.

• **What special problems do you have with the day-to-day management of your staff?** This is the kind of question that nobody thinks about until it's asked. Be prepared with an answer. Maybe tell a story.

• **For what have you been most frequently criticized?** This is like the question about your biggest weakness. Think of something that could be positive or negative. Things like being a perfectionist or a driver or an extremely hard worker, and expecting the same of everyone are good answers.

• **Tell me about a time when you faced resistance or rejection to your ideas or actions. What did you do?** Think of a story where you faced some kind of resistance or rejection that you might experience. Even if you embellish on the story, make sure you communicated that, although you were disappointed in your ideas not being accepted, you were graceful about and accepted the results. If you complain, bitch, or moan about how other people treated you and your ideas, you won't make the cut. If you communicate that you lost your temper, got really upset, or alienated people, no matter how right you might have been, it will never be accepted by a interviewing or hiring authority. You have to come across as a "team" player no matter what the circumstance.

• **We sometimes run into a person who makes unreasonable demands of us. Tell me about a time when this happened to you.** Again, be ready with a story. Every businessperson runs into someone with "unreasonable" demands. Describe the situation and how you handled it gracefully and to everybody's benefit. You can talk about the solutions that you came up with. Make them logical, reasonable, and with common sense. If you've been in a position where the demands were made by a previous boss or other than customers, communicate that your "solution" was to explain that "we are all in this together" and that the unreasonable demand wasn't good for everyone. This may take a bit of thinking before the interviewing situation. But you must be ready for questions like this and have an appropriate story. Again, if you communicate anything less than, "I calmed the waters and (helped) save the day," you won't come across as positive as you want to.

• **Highlight your experience in dealing with interpersonal conflict disagreements by recalling a difficult situation that you were involved in.** As above, you need to have a story. You won't get ask this question very often, but you need to have a story prepared just in case. As with many of the questions in this section, even though you may not be asked very often, if you have to stop and think of an applicable story, you're definitely at a disadvantage. If you were unprepared for this kind of question and you have to recall an "interpersonal conflict," you're likely to relate the situation in an emotional way. When you answer questions in a less than a positive emotional state, you won't impress an interviewer. If you were caught off guard with this question and start "reliving" an emotional situation, it may not come across well. So, be prepared with an "interpersonal conflict" story. By the way, make it brief, factual, and unemotional.

• **How have you shown resilience in the face of**
  • **conflict?**
  • **frustrating circumstances?**

- **constraints?**
- **rapidly changing circumstances?**
- **shifting priorities?**
- **adversity?**
- **multiple demands upon time and other resources?**

Be prepared with stories that relate to each one of these factors. Rarely will you be asked about all of them, but you better be prepared for them. As with the questions above, if you have to ponder and think for too long a period of time, you don't appear decisive. Be sure to be detailed with things like constraints or rapidly changing circumstances. If you simply describe that "business was difficult" as a constraint, your answer will appear glib. You have to describe exactly how business was difficult—i.e., sales were down, overhead had to be cut, the company was up for sale, the CEO left, etc. Then describe, in detail, what all of the constraints were and how they made your job more challenging, i.e., "difficult."

Are You Management Material? What Kind of Manager Are You?

- **What is your management style?** Describe your management style. Something along the lines of, "I don't know if I can give my management style a particular title or description. I do know that in the past I've created an environment where people feel like we're all in this together. I've been very successful in getting people to do more than they normally would in many circumstances. People seem to be appreciative of that. I set examples for people and make them feel like that they are an equal part of the team. I have a number of examples of this kind of leadership." Then proceed to tell stories that all demonstrate your leadership capabilities. If you "label" yourself as one kind of management style as opposed to another, you might describe yourself differently then the hiring authority who is interviewing you. By not labeling yourself but providing examples of your management or leadership style as well as providing a story demonstrating your style, you play it very safe.

If you have paid attention to the metaphors and analogies that the hiring authority has been using, you will easily detect the management style of the hiring authority and maybe even the company itself. So, with that understanding, communicate a similar style of management. Tell stories about your management styles that are consistent with what you heard. Whatever you do, don't communicate a demanding, pushy, aggressive style of management because "that's just the way I am," when you detected that the hiring authority and/or the company have a kinesthetic, analytical, soft-spoken, amiable, or low-keyed management style. You were trying to get a job, not make a statement.

- **How would you define your job as a manager?** "My job as a manager is to reach the goals and objectives of the company by hiring and motivating the right kinds of people." Then maybe tell a story or two demonstrating the success you had as a manager.

- **What type of turnover have you had as a manager?** Be ready for this question and simply tell about the turnover that you have had. If the turnover has been high, then you might explain the nature of the jobs that you have hired people for and the reason that the turnover is high. Never blame your company or its management for the turnover that you've experienced.

- **How do you motivate your subordinates?** Be prepared to give examples of how you have motivated subordinates and staff. Tell stories about specific instances where the goal or task might have been difficult and you rallied your staff.

- **Explain your hiring procedure.** This is a simple question that you should be ready for. Since you know the hiring practices of the organization that you are interviewing with, try to describe your practices that are in line with these. Companies have had to be more careful about hiring in the last few years. So, make sure that the procedure that you describe is detailed and thorough. Communicate that you adopt the mantra of "hire slowly, fire quickly."

- **Describe the biggest mistake you made in hiring.** Be ready for this question. Whatever you'd do, don't say that you never made a mistake in hiring. Tell a story about the mistakes you might have made in hiring. Make sure that the story you tell isn't one that reveals that you made a bad hire based on bad judgment, like not checking references, or finding out long after you hired someone that he had an arrest record. Make sure it is the kind of a hiring mistake that most managers make, the credentials of the person were excellent, the references were solid, and that you "hired slowly," etc.; however, it just didn't work out. But make sure that you communicate that you rectified the mistake when you first detected it. Again, demonstrate that you employed the mantra of, "hire slowly, fire quickly."

• **How you handle dishonesty?** The answer is real simple: You simply don't! Don't try to equivocate the definition of dishonesty. You simply don't tolerate dishonesty.

• **Tell me about a situation where you were disappointed in your own performance.** Be ready for this question with the story about how you're disappointed in yourself and the way you or your team performed. Don't go on and on about how obsessed and disappointed you were. State the situation, and you might add that it was offset by a positive situation later on down the line and that you learned a lot from the experience.

• **Give me an example of a new or innovative idea that you came up with or implemented.** This is another chance to tell a story. Just be ready for this question. The last thing you want to do is to hesitate and have to think about the answer.

• **Do you communicate best with written or oral communications?** "I seem to do well with either one."

• **What are people's greatest misperceptions about you?** Think for a moment and pause. Come up with something that is relatively safe, something along the line of, "Well, sometimes it may appear that I take things seriously and come across as not having a sense of humor." Or something like, "I sometimes might appear to be a workaholic and have high expectations of others."

• **Tell me about a time when you had to "get your hands dirty" by doing a job that was one or two steps below you.** Just be aware that this kind of question is going to come, so have a story ready. Play up that, as a manager, you're there to lead the team and so nothing is really "below" you because you're there to make sure the job gets done.

• **As a manager, how have you promoted diversity?** You need to have a story or two about how you promoted diversity.

• **How much do you know about the duties or responsibilities of the managers or superiors two levels below you?** You'd better have an answer that communicates that you know very well what the managers two levels below you do. If you've been in one of those positions before and got promoted out of it, you'll want to communicate that. Just be sure you are not caught off guard and act like you have no idea what goes on in those levels.

• **You have moved up in the management ladder rapidly, but it seems like you've leveled off. Why?** Simple answer: "There are a lot of very good people and managers in the company that I am presently with. They've been there for quite some time. Their seniority and quality are hard to beat. That is one of the major reasons that I am looking to change. On top of that, my personal growth and expansion is limited in my current position. So, when I add these two factors up, it is best for both me and the company I am presently with that I find a new job. If I'm not growing and reaching my potential, I'm not going to contribute well. It's mutually best for both of us that I leave."

• **How long would you expect to be at this position if you got it?** This can be a really tricky question. If you are leaving your present position because there is a "ceiling," you are communicating that you would do the same thing if you were to work at the place you are interviewing with. If you have changed jobs every year for the past two or three years, you are communicating even more "risk." So, you have to change the focus to talking about personal growth, both intellectual and professional.

Something like this would work: "Every time I have left any situation, it has been primarily because I was really limited. I am very patient and have explored every opportunity to the maximum. There was no personal growth in the situations, even after I gave it time. As long as I am growing personally, intellectually, and professionally, I am committed to staying as long as I can. I hate changing jobs and companies."

This is the case of a staged, contrived event. Both you and the interviewing authority know that the odds of your being at this job or this company three years from now is not very great. But, as I've mentioned elsewhere, people interview as though the job and the company were a "forever" relationship.

• **How you deal with disgruntled employees/subordinates?** Don't say that you've never had any disgruntled employees or subordinates. Every manager has, to a certain extent. Telling a story here would reinforce whatever you say. Stating something like, "Well, I've been fortunate enough to establish personal policies and procedures so that most all of my subordinates in the past know where I stand on certain issues. I have found that being consistent, even about things that everyone may not agree with, has been the first and best 'line of defense' that I have needed. Second, I have found that 90% of the time, simply listening to people, especially when they vent, dissipates most issues. In checking my references, you will find that I have always managed people that way. I have found that even the most disgruntled subordinate respects fairness."

• **How often have you had to fire someone?** The longer you have been in management, the more you've had to do this. So, tell the truth. If you've been in management a very short period of time and have never had to fire someone, you can communicate, "Fortunately, I've never had to fire anyone. I've been fortunate enough to create an atmosphere and environment where people who aren't going to make it or don't fit in leave before I have to fire them."

If you've been in management for any length of time and have had to fire people, you want to communicate something like, "It is one of the most difficult aspects of my job. But it has to be done from time to time. I've always been sure that the reasons that I have released people are well documented and objective, and that firing is never capricious or reactionary. I've always tried to communicate that letting them go is best for them and the environment of the company. Fortunately, although an unpleasant task, I've never had any significant repercussions in letting people go."

• **Have you ever doubted your decision about firing someone?** Don't appear wishy-washy in describing this kind of situation. Something along the line of, "Well, if there are doubts to begin with, I have tried to work the situation out with the person before I have had to fire him or her. But once I have let the person go, I can't afford to look back and doubt the decision. If it comes to the point where I have to let someone go, I'm sure of myself."

How This Affects You

A positive answer to the question of "Can you do the job?" in my opinion, accounts for only about 20% of the hiring decision. Most hiring authorities are going to tell you that it accounts for 60 or 70% of the hiring decision, and they will never admit to the fact that it is really only 20% of the decision.

However, having said that, it is the *first 20%* of the hiring decision. If you can't get over this threshold and convince hiring authorities that you are capable of doing the job, you will never get to the other basic questions.

The answers to "Can you do the job?" questions need to communicate confidence. You need to be ready for questions that you don't think about every day. Your management style, for instance, isn't something that you articulate on a daily basis. But in the interviewing situation, it needs to roll off your tongue as though you recite it daily.

The "Can you do the job?" questions are probably the most taken for granted by candidates. Most candidates, since they don't look for a job very often, think that they will have a very easy time answering these questions. Don't take for granted confident, competent answers. Practice, practice, practice!

Chapter

8 Do I/We Like You?

··

Based on my experience, determining whether you are liked accounts for 40% of the hiring decision. Of all of the four basic questions that need to be answered affirmatively, this carries the greatest weight. No matter how good your skills might be, no matter how much of a risk you may or may not be, and even if working the money out is a foregone conclusion, you will never get hired unless you are liked.

Of the more than 100,000 face-to-face interviews that I have personally arranged over the past three decades or so, I've never had a candidate hired who wasn't, at first, liked by the people doing the interviewing and hiring. This fact defies logic and common sense. With all of the business acumen and wisdom that companies and the people in them are purported to have, you'd think that the emotional aspects of liking someone would have a minimal impact.

But the truth is that hiring people is like "buying" anything else. People do it for emotional reasons and justify the rest. I can't tell you the number of people I've placed over the years who were hired simply because they were liked by the hiring organization. The number of extremely qualified, excellent candidates that weren't hired because they weren't initially liked by the interviewing or hiring authority defies logic and common sense.

Companies and interviewing authorities often try to find out if they like you in very odd ways. These questions can have a tendency to get under your skin. Oftentimes you could be insulted by them if you let yourself. You can never let these or any other kinds of questions throw you off emotionally. You can't interview well when you are emotionally flustered. So the way to prepare for them is to either use the answers that I've given or come up with your own; but practice them with your coach.

Will You Be a Fit with Us?

• **Are you a leader or follower?** Simple answer: "Well, in certain situations I am a leader and in certain situations I am a follower. I can be both." Then reinforce this answer with stories, if necessary.

• **What do people like most about you? What do they like least?** Things like being a team player, getting along well with others, dealing well in tense situations, volunteering when you don't have to, perseverance, communication skills, etc., always work well. Reinforce the attributes that you spoke about in your presentation that make you a good employee. Regarding what people like least about you, laugh and say something like, "I'm a lousy golfer," or a poor tennis player or not good at telling jokes. Make it light.

• **What are your three greatest strengths? Three greatest weaknesses?** Strengths should be easy for you to come up with. Weaknesses are always difficult. What works well is saying things like, "Well, I'm very impatient with myself. I oftentimes expect the same passion and commitment from the others that I tend to have. I'm working on becoming a better listener." I have known people to say just plain stupid things like, "Well, to be honest, I talk too much." "I'm late a lot." "I seem to have bad luck in jobs and get fired." "I have bad luck with women and jobs." "I get bored easily." Don't do that. Make sure your "weaknesses" can also be "strengths." Ask your coach to help you with these because you are going to get this question.

• **What are your hobbies? Outside interests? Books you've read recently?** Don't hesitate to talk about some of your outside interests and hobbies, as long as they are reasonable and "business-wise." I would not recommend talking about your particular involvement with anything controversial. Church groups, political parties, or any organization that might be controversial, unless you were absolutely sure of the religious or political persuasion of the interviewing authority, should not be mentioned. Talk about hobbies like golf, tennis, running, cycling, gourmet cooking, etc.—anything— just be sure it is safe and not controversial. Make sure you are reading some kind of business-oriented book and briefly mention it if you have to. This kind of question is easy to prepare for, and you will give the same answer to everyone.

• **What do you like and dislike about your present boss?** This question has nothing to do with your boss; it has to do with how you express what you think of him or her. Badmouthing your present or previous bosses or company is the kiss of death. Something like, "I really like him as a person and have really learned a lot from him," is all that needs to be said. Employers identify with employers and whatever you say about your present or previous boss, you will say about the new people somewhere down the line.

• **How do you handle criticism?** How you react to this question is as important as your answer. If you look like a startled deer in headlights, you will be communicating the wrong idea. Just expect to get this question and immediately respond by saying, "I really do appreciate constructive criticism. Feedback is the breakfast of champions. I am my own worst critic, but I really like hearing what other people think."

• **Rate yourself on the scale of one to ten.** This is a stupid question, but you better be ready for it. "Well, my spouse thinks I'm a ten—sometimes! However, when I rate myself, I am an eight or nine in some things and a six or seven in others. But you will find I do my dead level best to do well and everything that I do." Then shut up!

• **How would others at your present or previous jobs rate you on a scale of one to ten?** "Again, I think some of them would rate me as an eight or nine in some of the things that I do and six or seven in other things that I do. But they do know that I try to do my best in everything I do."

• **Do you ever lie?** This is another Catch-22 question. Best thing to do is admit that you do lie in some rare instances when telling the truth has no consequences other than to hurt someone's feelings. For instance, you might say, "If I'm invited to a social occasion that I really don't want to go to, I will say that I have other plans. I guess, technically, that is a lie, but I see no sense in hurting other people's feelings by telling them that I don't wish to socialize with them." Then shut up. If the interviewer probes this question, simply say, "It is important to be truthful in every business dealing. I think lying is basically wrong and should only be used in situations as the last graceful alternative where the results are inconsequential."

• **What are one or two things your present or previous co-workers dislike about you?** Be prepared for this question, because you will get it more than you think. Answer it with something like, "Well, nobody has ever told me outright anything about myself that they said they disliked. I sometimes get the feeling that my work ethic and the striving for perfection irritate some people. But I'm not aware of anything that people have actually said they disliked." This, again, is one of those questions where how you respond is much more important than what you say.

• **What makes you mad?** "Well, there are very many things that make me mad, and I do get frustrated, especially with some of the things that my 16-year-old does (ha! ha!). But seriously, I have found that getting mad or angry doesn't help solve the immediate problem. I don't think any of us perform well under the emotional stress of anger."

• **How do you make your opinions known when you disagree with management or your boss?** "If my opinions are sought out, I respectfully offer them. If they're not sought out, and it is not within my responsibility, I probably wouldn't offer the opinion. If I felt strongly enough about the issue and thought it was important to voice my opinion, I would make a private appointment with the appropriate person to discuss my feelings and thoughts." The purpose of this question is more to find out how you go about voicing your opinions rather than what your opinions might be.

• **If you knew then what you know now, how would you change your life or your career?** This is a really good question, and you need to have a really good answer for it. You should mention things that might be obvious. For instance, if you have not completed your degree, you might say that, looking back on it, you would have finished your degree. If you have had several very short jobs on your resume, you might say that if you knew then what you know now, you wouldn't have taken those jobs. You should discuss any obvious mistake or misstep in your career, admit to it, and add the fact that you have learned a lot from the mistake and then move on. You might also add in summation that, "The important thing, for me, is that I've learned from every mistake I've ever made and, fortunately, I haven't made the same mistake more than once. I know I will make others, but I'm going to make the best of what I learn from them. It would be nice if the lessons hadn't been so painful." Do not say that you wouldn't change a thing because, even if it were true, not many people would believe you.

• **What is your definition of success? Of failure? And how do you rate yourself in these two categories?** This is a loaded question that has no absolutely correct answer. But something along the lines of, "Well, success for me is the constant pursuit of a worthy goal where I am personally growing and economically providing for myself and my family. The only definition of failure, for me, would be to quit trying and give up. Failure is not an option for me, nor should it be for anyone else."

• **What makes you better than any other candidate I can hire?** "Well, I don't know that I necessarily am better than anyone else you could interview, at least on paper. But I am a very hard worker and am determined to be successful. In the final analysis, I have more passion and commitment to the job than most people do. So, with me, you get passion, commitment, and determination far above what you'd probably get in most anybody else." You can then demonstrate those features by telling stories that speak of how you have provided benefit to your previous employers.

• **I'm sure that there were some policies in your previous companies that you didn't agree with. . . . How did you handle those?** This is one of those questions where the interviewing or hiring authority is trying to find out how you respect your previous employers. Obviously, if you think your previous employers and their policies weren't good, a hiring authority will assume you will feel the same about his or hers if you were hired. So the answer is, "I guess there might have been some minor policies and procedures that may not have been clearly understood, but, for the most part, it was apparent that most all of the policies and procedures were for the good of the company and everybody in it." Don't ever badmouth a previous employer!

• **What kind of people do you hang out with?** Be a little careful with this question. Some interviewing authorities may be trying to ask you about church groups, ethnic groups, or things like that. The best answer is something along the line of, "I have a diverse group of friends that are all very interesting." If you were asked about hobbies and you mentioned golf or tennis, you might mention that you hang out with people like that.

• **Tell me a joke.** This is a stupid question. Be careful here. Whatever you do, don't tell anything off-color or inappropriate. If you have little kids, tell a joke your 5-year-old told you.

• **How would you describe your personality?** Consider the kind of opportunity you are interviewing for when you go and answer this question. If you were interviewing for a sales position, you certainly wouldn't want to say, "I'm an introverted quiet person who doesn't like people." If you are interviewing for an accounting position, it would not be intelligent to say, "Well, I'm a wild and crazy guy, and people never know what to expect of me in the way of my moods." Think, be honest, but don't go overboard.

• **We're a very aggressive organization here. You seem to be a fairly laid-back, rather quiet person. How do you get along with very aggressive folks?** A simple answer like, "When people get to know me, they don't think that I am really 'quiet.' I am intensely interested in the opportunity with your company, so I'm trying to listen very well. I've always been able to get along with just about every kind of person and personality."

• **On a personal level, what would your previous boss or present boss say about you?** "I've always got along very well with my bosses. Even though I think that everyone that I've ever worked for both directly and indirectly thought highly of me, beyond social engagements like dinners or golf games, I've always tried to keep our relationships business."

• **What was it like for you growing up?** This could border on an illegal question, if the interviewing or hiring authority seems to be asking about your religion, ethnic background, etc. Most hiring authorities, when they ask this question, simply want to get a sense of your character or values. A person who might describe his or her growing up as a tumultuous experience or, as some people would say, "I was a mess," might communicate that he or she is presently "a mess." As in any other question, answering it with "true confessions" that communicate personal instability doesn't bode well. The best answer is to describe your growing up as a "great" experience. If, in growing up you had overcome personal or family challenges and they communicate a positive attitude or strong work ethic, then certainly describe the experience.

• **Have you ever had to overcome any personal hardships?** Whatever you'd do, do not describe your terrible, acrimonious divorce; your run-ins with the law, your DWIs, your being thrown out of your house by your spouse, your three bankruptcies, or anything that communicates poor judgment. Even things like overcoming cancer will frighten an employer. Describing "character-building" challenges, like growing up without a lot of money, having to work from a very young age, being forced to put yourself through college, overcoming the death of a parent at a very young age, etc., will answer the question to your benefit.

• **If you were to invite three famous people to dinner, whom would you invite?** This is a dumb question, but if you are asked it, you pretty much have to answer it. Be careful of answering this question politically or religiously. If you say something like, "Jesus Christ, Buddha, and the Pope," you open yourself up to judgment that has nothing to do with getting the job. I would recommend to sticking to business-oriented individuals. Saying something like, "Warren Buffett, Bill Gates, and Donald Trump," whether they're presently alive or not, is safe.

• **If you were me, what question should I ask that you really don't want to answer?** This is also a dumb question, but it gets asked more than most people might think. The idea is to take you off your guard. Be ready! Keep it something very light and almost funny. Say something like, "Looking back, who did you first have a romantic crush on and what do you think of him or her now? Answer: "My fifth grade teacher. I think she died last year." Do not take this question real seriously, ponder it, and come up with some answer that puts you in a positive light. (I had a candidate one time who was asked this question by a very attractive female hiring authority. He was so thrown off by the question that he answered with his instincts. It cost him the job!)

• **Do you like me as a person?** Simply responded by saying, "Well, I don't know you very well at all, but I think we have good chemistry. You are a very good interviewer."

• **Describe a situation where you personally or professionally failed.** Watch out for this trap. Be ready for this question and answer it with a "safe" story. Something like not making a high school or college basketball team, getting a B in a very difficult class when you felt like you performed on an

A level, not getting a promotion that you felt you deserved will all be good answers only if you explain how you learned from the experience. Again, stay away from divorces, personal bankruptcies, etc. Although you might think that these kinds of personal "failures" were the best lessons that you experienced, you never know how an interviewing or hiring authority is going to respond.

If you describe a professional failure, make sure you don't blame other people. Take responsibility in the right way. "We misjudged the market" or "We didn't see the recession coming" will work. Never blame others for your mistakes, even if they were part of it. You don't want to be perceived as a blamer.

• **How do you rank yourself personally and professionally among your peers?** You neither want to be too boastful nor to humble in answering this question. If you have concrete examples, like superior sales performance or accolades that been bestowed upon you by your company or your supervisors, you would mention them. If nothing concrete is available like this, then an answer something like, "I've been fortunate to work with a very successful, hard-driving organization where the performance 'bar' is set pretty high. It is a great challenge to work with such a high-caliber group. Sometimes I outperform most everyone, and sometimes I am outperformed. The neat thing is that regardless of my 'rank,' I am impressed to perform my best every time. Whether I come in first, second, or third isn't as important as the fact that I grow personally every day."

• **Do you have personal and professional goals?** Answer: "I have spiritual, personal, and professional goals. I write them at the beginning of every year, review them daily, and assess them quarterly. I believe everyone has to have goals."

• **Who is your greatest personal mentor?** One has to be careful here. You need to be careful. Saying something like, "Jesus Christ, my Lord and savior," might be the truth, but it is really risky to say. Many employers get concerned that an answer like this would only come from someone that is going to try to "sell" religious values to other people. You might be better off to answer this with a very "safe" answer like, "My mother, my father, my older brother or sister," and then give a short story about how this person has been your mentor.

• **What is the biggest personal mistake you have ever made?** This is a loaded question. If you say something like, "I married the wrong person, and it turned out to be a disaster," you run a real risk. It is simply too emotionally charged, and you never know how the hiring or interviewing authority is going to interpret the answer. So, it is best to play it safe and come up with maybe a personal investment that went badly, maybe not finishing a degree, or taking a job that turned out to be a poor decision by not doing enough due diligence. Make sure that no matter what you say, you make it clear that you learned a lot from the mistake. Tell a story with a beneficial lesson.

• **How did you get your last job?** The answer to this should be fairly simple. If it appears on your resume, though, that you have always worked for family or followed the same supervisor from place to place, you might want to make it clear that you competed for your last job, there were a number of people running for the position, and you got it. Tell a story of how you got it.

• **What do you do in your spare time?** The answer to this minor question could wind up being a major mistake. If you say something like, "I work on my golf handicap every chance I get," the hiring authority may fear that you were going to be playing golf when you are supposed to be making sales calls. Reading, gardening, fishing, woodworking, spectator sports, tennis or golf, etc., should be all right to speak of as long as you don't come across as a fanatic. (I once had a candidate who is such an avid Dallas Cowboys fan that she bragged that she had never missed a Cowboys game in twelve years—including the away games as well as attending the preseason football camp in August. The hiring authority refused to hire her because he thought that all the time she wanted to devote to the Dallas Cowboys would possibly detract from her work.)

• **What do you think about yourself is most important to us?** If this question comes in the beginning of the interviewing process, then you want to "sell" the simple but important aspects why a company would want you as its employee. Saying things like hard worker, determined, committed, going the extra mile, good listener, excellent with people, dependable, etc., are all good to start with. Just be certain that you mention a couple of stories that demonstrate as many of these basic attributes as you can. Remember: Stories sell!

If you were deeper into the interviewing process and you have really done your homework, you should be aware of the most important attributes that the organization is looking for in any candidate. Be sure to emphasize your particular attributes that relate to that issue. Again, a story is great.

• **Tell me about a business experience where you had to decide to either lead or to follow. What choice did you make and how did it turn out?** The most important aspect of this question is to find out not so much whether you chose to lead or follow as to why you chose to lead or follow. Never claim to be the leader "because everybody else was a schmuck." Whenever you cast dispersions about anybody that you've worked with or for in the past, you put yourself in that a poor light. So, whatever the reason for leading or following, make a positive reflection on the people that you have worked with or for.

• **Tell me about the last time one of your subordinates made a big mistake. What did you do?** Make sure that the story you tell or what you talk about demonstrates how you tried to improve this situation by helping others learn from their mistakes. Now, if the mistake was grievous enough, you might explain what the reprimand might have been. Just be sure to keep it positive.

• **What have you done to implement improvements in your work group organization?** You'd better have a real good answer for this one. If you have to ponder this question, it will be obvious that you haven't done anything to improve working conditions. The answer must be decisive.

• **Describe how you make decisions.** If this question catches you off guard, you will be dead in the water. You better have a memorized methodology that you can explain to a prospective employer. Saying things like, "Well, I just follow my gut" won't be a good answer. You'll only get asked this by relatively analytical hiring authorities. But you need have a step-by-step approach to the way you would do it.

• **We all have times when we are very proud of what we've accomplished but sometimes we don't receive the recognition we think we should. Tell me about a time that this has happened to you and how you dealt with it.** If you say something like, "I made it real clear to my superiors that they should recognize what I've done," you have just ended your prospects of getting hired. The proper answer is, "Getting external recognition isn't as important to me as *me* knowing that I have done at a good job." Describe a situation where this kind of thing might have happened. Just be sure to communicate that external recognition isn't that important to you.

• **Describe a situation where you demonstrated a high level of commitment to an organization where you worked.** Be ready for a question like this. You'd better have a very good story to tell. If you say something like, "Well, I stayed late when I needed to, worked overtime when necessary, and came in on the weekends when I had to," or something weak like that, you will lose points for a poor answer. A "high level of commitment" means something that is well beyond the call of duty. Have a good story ready and make sure that it communicates how you really went the extra mile.

• **What have you done in the past that has demonstrated a high level of personal integrity?** You won't be asked this very often, if at all. But if you are, you'd better have a good, solid story that relates to your integrity. You have to be a little careful about a question like this, because if you say something like, "Well, I never cheat on my expense account, when everybody else does," you won't come across as a person with high integrity. It isn't an issue of integrity not to cheat. So, make sure that you have a story that demonstrates your integrity. Something along the lines of, "I encouraged us to be honest with a major client about the mistake that we made, even though it might have cost us the contract and our relationship."

• **What was the last creative idea that you came up with that affected the group or company that you now work for? How did you come up with the idea?** You'd better have a good answer for this question. If you have to think about the answer for more than just a moment, you won't appear like you're telling the truth. This kind of story can relate to any other story that you might have told in the interviewing process. Just be ready for it by having at least one or two applications of your own personal "creative idea."

Do You Work Well with Others?

• **How do you deal with people whom you don't like and who don't like you in the workplace?** This is a really good question. The hiring authority is more interested in the way you react to this question than in the answer itself. An answer along this line will suffice: "Because I give all lot of respect to all of the people that I encounter, and even the people I don't particularly like, I seemed to gain their respect. I deal with everybody on a professional level and try to keep personal relationships at work to a minimum. I have to appreciate everyone but I don't necessarily have to like them."

• **Describe a very difficult person that you had to work with and how you handled it.** You can begin to answer this question in a light-hearted way by smiling and saying, "Well, my spouse at times . . . or my 16-year-old at times . . ." Then add, "Seriously, I've never really had a problem with difficult people, even if they did not respect me personally. I found a way to deal with difficult people as with all other people in the workplace and that's to perform so well that my work would 'speak' so highly of me that what people thought of me personally didn't really matter."

• **Have you ever gotten personally involved or socially close to anyone at your work?** This is a question that comes up more than most people would think. You might be amazed at the number of people who willingly admit that they have dated or got personally involved with some of the people that they have worked with before. Don't go there! The answer has to be, "I keep my personal and business life separate. I have seen situations where people have become personally involved when they work together and it usually leads to nothing but a disaster. It just plain isn't smart."

• **We play a lot of poker (golf, tennis, bowling, etc.) are around here. Are you any good at it?** Even if you are a scratch golfer, never admit to being really good at any "social" game or endeavor. You set yourself up as "someone to beat." A number of years ago, I had a hiring authority who, I could swear, didn't hire my candidate because my candidate was an excellent golfer and this guy won the company golf tournament every year and didn't want the competition. So, you might want to admit to enjoy watching a particular social endeavor, but never claim to be really good at it.

• **Tell me about a time when you practiced diplomacy when communicating with another person or group.** Simply be ready for this question with a reasonable story. It is important here to be ready with a business-oriented story. Do not get trapped into talking about a social situation.

People are trying to evaluate your personal business skills not your social skills. Besides, if the first thing that comes to mind is a social situation, you won't appear businesslike.

• **Sometimes we have to bring conflict out into the open and other times we avoid it or sacrifice our own needs in order to placate others. Tell me about when you've had to make a choice like this.** This is a pretty sophisticated question and not many people are going to ask it of you. But you need to be prepared with a story about how you confronted conflict and/or how you avoided it. Again, if you hesitate or stammer without being able to answer quickly with an example, you will appear indecisive.

• **We all have to deal with "power struggles" or resolve win/lose situations. Tell me about the last time you were involved in such a situation.** Depending on how the interview is going, you might laugh and say, "Well, the last time was when my spouse and night were deciding where to go to dinner. . . . I let him/her win." Then follow up with a more serious work environment situation and how you resolved it. Be ready with a short and to the point story. The answer to question like this can be a recipe for disaster if you go on and on and make the story too long without getting to the point.

• **Describe a time when an external customer tried your patience or tried to get something from you or your company that he or she didn't deserve—maybe not outright cheat, but close to it. How did you handle it and what did you do?** Even if you are not directly involved with an external "customer," you better have some kind of answer or story for this. You need to communicate calmness and clear thinking. If your answer is, "We sued the bastards," you won't come across in a positive way. As with other answers, have a short, to-the-point story.

• **Describe a time when an internal customer tried your patience.** If you were in a support or service role to other departments in your company, it won't be hard to come up with an example of this. If you were in the estimating department, for instance, you can relate that the sales department is always pressing you to provide estimates faster, no matter how accurate they might be. You need to communicate courage and responsibility over and above relinquishing to pressure.

• **Priorities constantly change in our firm. Recurring challenges and limitations to resources push us really hard. Often it is hard to maintain a positive attitude, and the department gets emotionally down. Has this ever happened to you and how would you deal with it?** If you claim to have never had an emotionally "down" time, no one will believe you. Most of the world is negative about most things. Something along the line of, "All emotions are infectious. I really try to look for the 'positive' in every situation. That doesn't mean that I ignore reality." Then tell a story about a situation in your present or previous job where you were "pressed for resources" and how you handled it. If you badmouth your present or past company by saying something like, "Well, the finance and accounting departments could never keep the cash flow positive. It really screwed up our department and I was yelling at them all the time," you won't get hired.

How This Affects You

Most people think that it is terribly unfair that being liked has as much to do with getting hired as it does. Hardly any hiring authority is ever going to admit that it is as much as 40% of the hiring decision. It is true that the first 20% of the hiring decision is based on the candidate's ability to do the job. But being liked or "fitting in" with the rest of the company and the individuals in it is a bigger question.

"Cultural fit" is the term that many hiring authorities will apply to the kind of people that fit into their organization. In the vast majority of these hiring situations, "like attracts like." These are companies that, as a whole, look for people that are just like, or at least mostly like, everyone else in the company. Instead of an individual hiring authority passing his or her own personal judgement, the company does as a whole.

Even when a candidate is not being judged by the people in the company, there's still going to be a personal compatibility assessment on the part of a hiring authority. People will not hire someone they don't like. It's just that simple! (And you probably won't go to work for someone you don't like. It works both ways.)

I've experienced more qualified candidates not being hired because they weren't liked either by the individual hiring authority or by the company as a whole *more* than any other issue in the hiring process. We've all experienced the same kind of thing in our workplace. How many times have we all experienced an individual being promoted who may not be very qualified but is "liked" by management so he or she is promoted? It is unfair. But let's face it, life isn't fair either.

Now there will always be people who may not like you as much as they may like others or vice versa. That's fair. And it would be foolish to tell people who simply dislike each other to stop it. But, as a candidate, you need be prepared to be evaluated personally. You need to be ready to be judged by your social skills as well as your professional skills.

Based on my experience, 35 to 40% of the hiring processes include some kind of social "interview" interaction. These can be anywhere from a lunch interview, a golf or tennis match hiring authority, an invitation to a Christmas party, or a trip to a company function before the candidate is hired. The social events during the interviewing process don't have anything to do with the candidate's ability to do the job. Companies and hiring authorities are simply trying to find out how well the person might fit in from a personal point of view.

I've also seen candidates blow their chances of getting hired by screwing up these social interviews. I've had candidates who have stuffed themselves at lunch or dinner interviews. I had a candidate one time who played golf with the CEO and didn't get hired because the CEO thought that he had lied about his score on a couple of holes. I've known candidates to get into political and moral arguments with potential peers at social interviewing events. I've had candidates drink too much at Christmas parties, and spouses of candidates who embarrassed themselves and their spouses at such social events. I'm not a fan of social interviewing situations for the very reason that too much can go wrong.

I know, it's hard to "practice" being liked. What is important is to be aware that being liked is part of getting hired. Once a candidate realizes that, he or she is better prepared for success in the process.

Chapter

9 Are You a Risk?

....

These are going to be the most difficult questions you will be asked. They're going to encroach on your character, your judgment, and the quality of your decisions, both personally and professionally. Of course, the truth is that everyone is a risk. Everyone who has ever been hired is a risk. The real question imbedded in this subject is, "What kind of risk are you?" And along with that, "Am I, as a hiring authority, willing to run the risk and put my reputation on the line with this person?"

A hiring authority is trying to minimize risk and maximize a return on investment. It's a tradeoff. A hiring authority wants to minimize his or her risk but get as many benefits as possible from hiring someone. The greater the risks you might present, the more they have to be offset by a greater reward. With every risk you present, and you know exactly what they are, you have to offset those risks with the benefits you can provide. The greater the benefits you can demonstrate and the more risks you can mitigate in your being hired, the better chance you have.

Candidates don't recognize the risks that they present to a prospective employer. In fact, many things that you think are a positive might very well be a big liability. Get your coach to help you recognize what the risks are with hiring you. Then, be ready for the questions.

Are You Going to Be a Long-Term Employee or Will You Leave Quickly?

• **Why do you want to leave where you are? Or, why did you leave your last position?** This is one of the biggest "what kind of a risk are we taking" questions you will be asked. The answer to this question is one that will either immediately end the interviewing process for you or enhance the rest of it. This is one of the most crucial questions that you will be asked in every interview. You better have a consistent reason as to why you are looking to leave or why you left your last position; and, as with many other answers, you will need to stick with it. The key to this answer is to be as non–"self-oriented" as you can make it. The major reason that this is an important answer is that the interviewing or hiring authority will assume, just by the nature of his or her relationship with the employee, that you will leave them somewhere down the line for exactly the same reasons that you are leaving where you are now or for the same reason you left your last position. Employers identify with employers.

Being presently employed and looking to leave when you have been employed by that firm for a relatively long period of time, say five years or more, because you are not growing personally or do not have the opportunity to grow beyond your job is a better reason to be leaving than because, for example, new management was coming in and they didn't really like you. You absolutely have to be truthful in this answer, but you also have to "spin" it so that you communicate a really good business reason for yourself and for a future organization. Now, if you have been caught in a layoff because you were one of the last to be hired, and therefore one of the first to go, there's not much you can do about putting a "spin" on the isolated reason. Even though you were laid off, you can add comments and statements about the job that would make a prospective employer feel really good about you. To ease any concerns, say something like, "I really liked the job and the people. I appreciated their company and the opportunity. Unfortunately, I was simply part of a layoff. They were great people." Again, saying anything negative or disparaging about the company that you are presently with, or are leaving, is not going to do you well. Saying anything negative about the people you were working for or have worked for won't reflect well on you.

If the hiring authority and hiring company have a tremendous amount of "pain" (that is, they really need to hire somebody or are desperate to fill a position), the less likely they are to care about why you are looking to leave or why you left your last employer. So, if you sense that the need to fill a position is great on the part of the hiring company, you don't have to be quite as concerned about how analytical interviewers will be at the answer you give to this question. If an organization is desperate to fill a job, as long as your reasons for leaving your present one are anything short of "Sometimes, I'd just like to strangle my boss," the answer to this question won't matter too much.

However, most organizations that are looking to fill a position are not so desperate that they are not going to very carefully analyze the answer to this question. If you're presently employed, answer along the lines of, "Well, I really love my job, I really like the people who I work with, and I appreciate everything the organization has done for me. However, the organization is in the process of being sold (or under new management or has been contracting for the past few years, etc.) and I am personally stymied in my professional challenge and personal growth. I can stay in the position that I am in, and I am not threatened; but for the next number of years I'm not going to be able to 'grow' beyond the job I'm in now. Since my growth is limited, both personally and professionally, everything else, including my earnings, will stagnate. I owe it to myself and my family to seek a new opportunity where I can grow and be challenged beyond the opportunity that I have now."

Whatever you do, you have to communicate that you like your present job, the present organization that you work with, etc., and that you are leaving simply because you are capable of doing more for an organization and therefore growing both personally and professionally. If you communicate self-oriented answers like, "I need more money," "I want a better title," or "I'm going nowhere in my present firm," you'll be dead in the water.

Another way to approach this is to center your answer around the position for which you are interviewing. Something like, "I really love the company that I work for, and I have done well by them. They have been very good to me and I really appreciate that. But in the position I am in now, I am not as challenged, nor can I contribute as much as I could in the position we're discussing here at your firm. This particular position that I'm interviewing for will give me the opportunity to _____, as well as really contribute to the growth of your organization. I'm just not able to do that where I am now. It isn't anybody's fault. It's the nature of what we do and the size of our organization."

• **Gee whiz, you have sure stayed short periods of time in your last three jobs. What's wrong?** The obvious fear behind this question is that, if you are hired, you will only stay at that job for a short period of time. In fact, we will discuss this topic in a little more detail toward the end of this chapter. But your answer has to be one where you do what we call in sales "changing the base." The answer goes something like this: "While you are correct that I've had three very short stints in my employment, there are two things that are very important. First of all, I realize that someone like you is going to look at this as a liability. I don't like it any better than anyone else; in fact, it has really concerned me. I made a couple of mistakes in taking several of those positions, and if knew then what I know now, I would never have done that. The truth is, however, that I really learned from the mistake. The fact that I've had three relatively short positions is one of the very reasons I can guarantee stability. I cannot very well afford another short stint at a job, so I am being very careful about the job I take. Whoever hires me is going to get a passionate and committed employee for at least seven years. The second thing is that even though the opportunities did not last very long, I worked very hard while I was there, and the references that I have from those organizations will substantiate how hard I worked and how much I contributed."

It does not do any good at all to try to justify two or three short jobs that appear on your resume. That is a road to disaster. I've had candidates who casually dismissed the fact that they had two or three short stints on their resume and justified it by saying that it was just a condition of the economy. I have also had candidates who spend so much time trying to explain why they made such poor business decisions, and going overboard to explain it, that neither they nor the interviewing authority ever got beyond this one question. The point is to address it, make it to be as much of a positive as you possibly can, ask for understanding and empathy, then shut up. If you have this problem in your background, this will be one of the answers that you have down pat. Practice it.

• **You've been the president of a firm (or the owner of your own firm). How do we know that you know how to work for someone else and that**

you will take direction? This is the underlying fear and concern that all employers have when it comes to hiring someone who has either been the president of an organization, run an organization, or owned his or her own firm. The idea that the highest manager of an organization would actually work for someone else scares companies. What scares them is that if they hire you, and you have been in those kinds of positions, you won't take direction, and you will never really work for someone else. They are concerned that you really won't be happy unless you are "running the show." They believe that after a taste of working for someone else, you will leave after a relatively short period of time.

It is difficult for most presidents or owners of organizations to work for someone else. It is an emotional adjustment that is very hard to make. But it is done, and it does work. So, the answer to this question is really simple: "Well, you know as president of an organization (or owner of a firm), I 'worked' for a lot of different people and I answered to the entire company. I answered to customers, employees, the government, the IRS, my attorneys, my CPAs, insurance companies, vendors, and, very often, my spouse. We all answer to someone. Even the president of your organization or owner of your organization answers to someone, and usually many people. I have never met a good leader who couldn't work within any organization and be part of a team, as well as be a good follower. The truth is that we are all really self-employed. In reality, we all work for ourselves within an organization. The organization is simply a group of people working with and for themselves. Someone in the organization signs the paycheck, but the truth is that it's earned by the diligence of each individual. That's the way I approached business when someone else signed a paycheck or when I was responsible for signing the paycheck. In this opportunity, I may not lead the organization, but I still work for myself. My future earnings will depend on how I perform. In this case, the only difference is that someone else will sign the paycheck. One greater advantage in hiring me, over others, is that because I have been self-employed (or president of my own firm or owned my own company), I really understand how difficult it is to run a business. I, more than anyone else you will interview, will treat your money like my money because I really understand how that works. Most people see themselves strictly as employees. They act as though there is an adversarial relationship between themselves and their management. Little do they realize, as I do, that we're all in this together and whatever I do for management I do for myself, and whatever I do to management I do to myself. I am as careful with the company mission and money as I am my own, because I see them as the same. So, what this all means is that I'm going to work for someone just as hard as I work for myself. It is one and the same. I take direction just as well as I give it, I follow just as well as I lead, and I do what needs to be done. My ego is in check. I'm interested in the opportunity because I could do a good job for a very good company."

• **This position with our company requires a college degree and I noticed on your resume you only state that you attended college but it didn't say you graduated? Why did you quit?** This question goes to tenacity or staying power, and so is another way of determining whether you'll stick around. The way to answer is by saying, "I realize that most companies look for a degree in this position. I didn't get a chance to complete my degree because _____." Explain why you didn't finish college—and it better be a good reason, like a death in the family, I was married with a kid and I had to go to work, or I was putting myself through college and the money ran out and I had to go to work. Don't list anything like: I was bored, college and I didn't get along, I was so busy partying, I flunked out, or I just didn't value the chance I had enough and I regret it. Even things like, "Well, I just wasn't mature enough for college and didn't appreciate it" don't work. It has to be a good, palatable reason that doesn't signal a lack of steadfastness.

Then the candidate has to say: "I do wish I'd finished. But, every job I've ever had has required a degree on paper, and I have performed well at every job. In fact, when you analyze my background and check my references, you will find that not having a degree has never negatively affected my performance."

Say no more; don't make it a bigger deal than it is. If there is a corporate policy about not being hired without a degree, you may not get hired, and there is not one thing you can do about it. So, putting up a big stink like, "Well, it is ridiculous for company's to require a degree. A degree doesn't mean people will perform. It's stupid" and on and on will just make your perceived "deficiency" more pronounced. Even if it is stupid (and I believe it is—no one ever asked me about my Ph.D. before they hired one of my candidates), your protest will not change things, and you will embarrass yourself.

So, just stick to the "I don't have a degree. It might be better if I did, but it hasn't kept me from being a performer" type of answer. Answer calmly, somewhat briefly, and then smile and shut up! If companies really want to hire you, i.e., if you establish enough of a value for yourself, they will overlook this kind of thing no matter what the policy is.

• **This position is one or two levels below the ones you have had in the past. How do we know we won't hire you and then in six or seven months someone calls you with a position like that and you leave?** This is one of the biggest fears that any hiring manager or hiring authority has. To hire somebody and then have him or her leave, for whatever reason, is a big risk. Other candidates may stay a short period of time and then leave for all kinds of reasons, but the issue of having held higher positions is so glaring, at the onset of the relationship, that the hiring authority is very afraid.

This is esoteric and "graduate level" stuff, but I will tell you the reality of this fear. It is groundless! Here is the truth. If people are reasonably happy in the job that they're doing, they're not going to think about leaving the job, even to interview for a better one on a whim. I personally call to recruit people who are supposedly happy in their jobs on a daily basis. When people are genuinely happy, even reasonably content in their jobs, they really don't want to interview, and they really don't want to leave, even if the job that I describe or might have for them is better than the job they've got. The reason is simple. People really don't like looking for a job. If you have been paying attention, you probably know by now that looking for a job is a pain in the butt, and nobody really likes doing it. So, the idea that a reasonably content employee will get a call six or seven months, or even nine months, into a new job to interview for the level of job that he or she used to have and run off and leave isn't realistic. Most people just are not in a situation where they have nothing better to do on a Tuesday morning than think about changing jobs and interviewing. It's just too emotionally stressful, and rarely does anybody do it unless there is just cause.

Reasonably happy employees usually don't have to leave to look for another job. It's just too stressful to do that, so as long as they are reasonably content with the positions they are in, they have a tendency to stay where they are. Of course, to complicate matters, the only way that a hiring authority can prove or disprove the theory is to take a chance on hiring someone in this situation. I have placed enough people over the years at levels far below the positions that they held before, ones who went on to be very happy and content over many years, that I have proven the stereotypes to be unfounded.

Now to make matters more interesting, you as a candidate can't explain this to a prospective employer. The problem with this truth is that it is predicting the future, and the hiring authority simply isn't going to try what he or she believes to be a great risk just to prove a theory. And the problem with this theory is that you can argue both sides of the myth and be right.

So, here is your answer: "Mr. or Ms. _____, in every company in which I've ever worked, I've always started out at a position one or two levels below what I eventually attained. I realize exactly what I'm getting into with this job and the opportunity that you have outlined for me. I have no intention of wasting anyone's time, money, or effort—mine or yours. I wouldn't be trying to get this position if I didn't think that it would be challenging, gratifying work, and I wouldn't have a really good future with this organization. In the past, when I have been in the lower level positions with the companies in which I worked, I would get calls from time to time about interviewing at other organizations or other companies for higher level positions. But I was very happy where I was. I enjoyed the work, I was challenged and, frankly, the compensation followed my being happy, content, and challenged in the job. If we can make this opportunity happen, I can assure you that I know exactly what I'm getting into and the idea of leaving, or being recruited away for a position one or two levels above it, just isn't realistic for me. I've been in the 'shoes' of this kind of position before, and I know exactly what I'm getting into. I like the job, the people, the company, and if we can work out the compensation, I am more than confident that I will make you an excellent employee for a long, long time."

• **Why did you leave your last job so abruptly? Or why do you want to leave your current job? How do I know you won't do the same here?** For more than thirty-one years that I've been in this profession, this is one of the most difficult and treacherous questions you're going to be asked. Underlying this question is a concern on the part of the hiring authority that whatever reason you used to leave your last job or are using to leave your present one, you're going to use when you leave them. Depending on the state of the economy, a hiring authority is going to be more sensitive to the answer you give to this question. When the employment economy is robust, hiring authorities are more concerned about what you can do for them immediately than they are concerned about why you left your last position or why you want to leave your present one. This was true in the early 1980s and the late 1990s. When the employment economy is more difficult and there are many candidates to choose from, most hiring authorities are more concerned about the reasons you might have left your last employer or why you're looking to leave your present one. No matter what the economy, all hiring authorities are very concerned about the answer to this question. But, the answer is more important in a difficult economy than in an expanding one.

The biggest mistake candidates make when it comes to this question is that they, first, don't mention how much they appreciate the job they had or presently have and then, second, talk about selfish, or self-centered, "me" reasons for either leaving or changing jobs. Anything related to what you wanted when you left or want to leave will not fly. Answers like, "Well, I wanted more money (or a bigger company or more prestige)," anything related to your needs, before the needs of the company you were with, will destroy you. Remember, whatever you say, the hiring authority you are talking to will take it personally and envision a time when you will say the same thing about him and his company.

So, you have to find a relatively "antiseptic" answer to this question that neutralizes any kind of negativity. Something along the lines of, "You know, I really loved that job for _____ and really appreciated all of the people who I was working with. Unfortunately, the company had to downsize because of the economy and since I was one of the last hired, I was one of the first to go." Or, "I really love my job and I love the people with whom I work. Unfortunately, I have reached a point with my position that the opportunity for me to grow both personally and professionally just isn't there. They are good people and have been good to me. I will certainly miss them, and I'm sure that they will miss me, but I am capable of greater responsibility and authority and the odds of me getting that where I am just aren't very great." You absolutely have to spin the answer to this question into a positive.

Never criticize, denigrate, badmouth, or in any way speak poorly of your present or past employer. If you can't say something good, at least make it neutral. If you try to make your present or last employer out to be a "bad guy," no matter how justified you are, a hiring or interviewing authority will never, ever buy into your excuse or reason.

The answer to this question kills more opportunities for candidates than probably any question that can be asked. You need to really think about whatever answers you are going to come up with and put yourself in the shoes of the interviewing or hiring authority and ask yourself, "If I didn't know me as I do and I was being compared to a number of other equally qualified candidates, how does the answer to this question make me look?" If the answer to this question makes you look like a dedicated, committed, reasonably well-performing employee, who for very good business reasons is looking for a job, you'll be fine. If your answer does anything less than that, you're dead in the water.

• **Where do you see yourself five years from now? Or how does this job fit into your career goals?** The purpose of this question is not so much to get a "right" answer as it is to see what you will say. If you answer the real truth, which is, "How the hell do I know?" you'll shoot yourself in the foot. If you answer anything along the lines of, "I have no idea," you're dead in the water, too. If you are too audacious and say something like, "I want be the president of this company," you'll appear foolish.

In the vast majority of cases, it's going to be very difficult for any candidate to be able to predict where he or she will be or what he or she will be doing five years from now. The expansion and contraction of business in the United States doesn't bode well for accurate predictions five years into the future. Unless you were in a very narrow kind of profession where it's fairly easy to predict what you might be doing five years from now, it is safest to say something along the lines of, "Well, I'm not really sure of exactly what kind of position I will have in five years, but my goal is to be performing in a challenging position where my company feels like I'm contributing to its success, taking advantage of every attribute that I have. If I am doing my best and contributing to the best of my ability to the growth of the organization I'm with, my personal growth and advancement will take care of itself. I'm a firm believer in what Lincoln said: 'the harder I work, the luckier I get.' So, I have come to the conclusion that if I do the very best I can every day, push myself to the limit, grow personally and professionally, tomorrow, as well as five years from now, will take care of itself."

• **If you inherited a lot of money, say $2 or $3 million, what would you do?** This is somewhat of a silly question, but what the interviewer is trying to find out is if you would quit work if you could afford it economically. The answer to any question like this absolutely has to be, "Well, I worked all my life and no matter how much money I might have in the bank, I would foresee continuing to work." No one really knows what he or she would do if inheriting a lot of money, so I admit that this is a silly question. However, the hiring authority is deathly afraid of hiring someone and then having him or her soon quit.

• **You are awfully young for this position, aren't you? I'm afraid that, in building your career, you would only stay with us for a short period of time.** This is not an illegal question regarding age, unless the candidate is 40 years of age or older. Companies can legally put a minimum age requirement on just about any job except for the age of 40 or older. So, it would be legal for an organization to discriminate and not hire anyone less than, say, 38 years old, but it could not legally discriminate by stipulating that somebody needed to be 42 or older. That would be discriminating against anyone 40 to 42 years of age.

This question has to do with how long a company thinks it might keep you as an employee. It may have to do with your being younger than most of the people in that kind of position, but the major concerns are that you would only be there a short period of time and then leave. The answer to this question is quite simple as long as you remember that the issue is a fear of turnover and your leaving just when you might be contributing your best. So, you say, "I know that I'm a bit young to have accomplished what I have accomplished, but I find that 'maturity' is more an issue of experience and being able to perform then it is one of age. As long as I am contributing to the business endeavor of the organization and personally growing, there is no reason for me to leave."

• **You are awfully young for this position, aren't you?** See the answer above. This question without the following statement may more relate to your "fitting in" than your age. So, it might be a good idea to clarify the question in your answer. Something along the line of, "I have found that maturity is more an issue of contributing to an organization than one of age. I have been fortunate enough to be in situations where I was able to contribute and grow. Are you asking this because there are few people in the organization my age?"

Once you get the answer to your question, you can assure the interviewing or hiring authority that you have been in this situation before. Saying something like, "I have always been in departments where I have been younger than most anybody the group. In checking my references you'll find that this has never been an issue for them or for me" will get the job done.

• **You will be older than anyone else here. How does that make you feel?** This is a dumb question, but you may hear it. The answer is simple: "I have worked in organizations where I was older than the majority of the employees, and it wasn't a problem. In fact, I've provided a great balance of 'experience' that others didn't have. It was great."

• **You will be younger than anyone else here. How does that make you feel?** Another dumb question. Refer to the above answer.

• **You live a long way from here. It will take you 45 (or 1 hour or 1.5 hours) minutes to get to work one way. With the price of gas, as well as your time, after a while you might lose enthusiam for the job.** Companies certainly worry about this because they have employees who complain about the commute to and from work. The answer is, "I have had to commute before and I am not bothered by it. In fact, it gives me a great opportunity to listen to motivational tapes and CDs. I use the time to learn and get better. If you check my references, you will find that I was rarely late for work."

• **Were you ever denied a pay raise, got a poor performance review, or were passed up for a promotion? What did you do?** This is a very loaded question. The biggest concern that an employer or hiring authority is expressing in this question is, if you don't get a raise, or if you get a poor review or are passed over for a promotion, you will leave. An answer along the line of, "Well, I've never had a poor performance review (be sure it's true), and the one or two times in my career that I might have been passed over for promotion, it worked out best for the organization, and therefore it worked out well for me. My experiences have shown me that if I perform well, pay raises, promotions, etc., always take care of themselves."

• **This job and this company are real big risks. We don't know how long we're going to be able to make it. What do you think?** Well, this is a question that comes up from time to time. Sometimes it is a question to "test" you to see if you are a risk taker. Sometimes it's simply to tell you the truth about how the company is doing. Sometimes the interviewer wants to see if you'll make a mad dash for the door at the first sign of trouble. If you're not sure of the reason for asking the question, then keep in mind that you have nothing until you have an offer. I've known people that have taken tremendous risks with companies that were on the brink of failure and wound up being phenomenally rewarded when they turned around and were successful. So, the answer to this question is something like, "I am by nature a risk taker. I don't have a problem with a risky company or a risky opportunity as long as the rewards are there."

• **Your resume shows that you been with one company a long time without any appreciable increase in rank or salary. Tell me about this.** You absolutely have to say something along the line of, "I really love my job and the company that I work for. We aren't the kind of company that has a lot of turnover, so opportunities to get promoted have been very rare. My company has given salary increases when it can, but it has been strapped for the last few years. One of the reasons that I am looking to leave is to experience personal and therefore economic growth. Frankly, that's why an interviewing with your firm."

If you badmouth your present employer and bitch, moan, or complain about not getting promoted or not receiving salary increases, you will shoot yourself in the foot. You communicate that you are a poor employee and that's why you haven't received promotions or salary increases.

• **When do you expect a promotion?** This can be a trick question. If you say you hadn't thought about that, you won't appear ambitious. If you say something that communicates that you expect a promotion quickly, you won't appear patient enough and you will appear to be the kind of person who is more interested in a promotion than doing the work—and that you might leave if you don't get a promotion you think you deserve. So, an answer something along the line of, "I have found in the past that promotions have come after I have performed successfully. In the past I really haven't worried about promotions, because I know that if I do my job and I do a better than others, the opportunity to go beyond my position will present itself."

• **When do you plan on retiring?** This is especially difficult if you are over 55 or 60 years old. The answer, simply, is, "My goodness, I love working so much, I don't know that I would ever retire."

• **How long will you stay with us if you are hired? Or, how do I know that you will stay with us for a reasonable period of time to be effective?** I know that this sounds like a really stupid question, but people get asked this quite often. Now, there is no way of being able to tell anybody how long you will stay on a job. If you stayed on your last few positions for a long period of time, then you might answer, "Well, as you can see, I've been very stable in the positions I've had before, and I would expect that as long as the opportunity is fulfilling and the company is pleased with my work, I will stay equally as long here. As you can see, I have never really left my jobs so much as the jobs have left me for one reason or another." Or, something along the lines of, "My experience has been that as long as I'm challenged and the company I work for is pleased with my work, we both grow. As long as both of us are growing, there's no real need for either one of us to make a change."

How Much of a Liability Might You Be?

• **Were you fired? And, why were you fired?** Hopefully, if you were in a position to be fired, you got your most recent organization to lay you off rather than fire you. If there is one small saving grace in an employment recession, it's that layoffs are rampant. When the employment economy is expanding, people don't talk about layoffs quite as much. But when the economy is contracting, layoffs are fairly common and it is much less a stigma to be "laid off." Unless you were fired for a very serious cause, like embezzlement, threatening a co-worker, or sexual harassment, most organizations will be amenable to stating to people that you were laid off. Different companies have different policies regarding what they will tell a prospective employer about why a person was terminated or laid off. The terminology may not be very important to your employer, but it is very important to you.

The difference between being fired and being laid off connotes an adversarial discharge for cause in the former and an involuntary, at least on your part, separation for, usually, economic reasons on the part of the company that let you go. So, you are much better off if you can communicate the idea that you were laid off rather than fired. The truth is that the result is the same. Most companies, rather than create a picture of an adversarial "bad guy," would rather lay you off than fire you.

I do not recommend that you answer this question with something like, "Well, it's the best thing that ever happened to me" or "it was a blessing in disguise" or "the job wasn't working out, anyhow" or "the job just wasn't for me," etc. These kinds of answers have a tendency to come across as flippant and arrogant. The employer thinks, "Well, if getting fired was such a blessing, or the job wasn't working out anyway, or the job wasn't right, why did you keep the job?" This would especially be true if you were at the last job for three years or more. What your comments would communicate is, "This was a really great job until I got fired, then it was a bad job." This is an incongruent idea that most employers will not feel comfortable with.

If the last organization you were with formally states that you were "laid off," rather than terminated, you can honestly look at the interviewing or hiring authority in the eye and say that you were "laid off." It is really important to say something along the lines of, "I really loved that job and the opportunity it afforded me. I really learned a lot from those people and the time I spent there was gratifying. Unfortunately, because of management changes and economic issues, we had to go through a layoff and I happened to be one of the ones who was affected."

If you have been at an organization for three or more years, it is not likely that a prospective employer is going to question your performance or the fact that you might have been fired for cause. It is very rare for an employee to do well in the company for two or three years and then all of a sudden become a "bad" employee. So, the longer you have been on the job that you were ultimately terminated or fired from, the easier it is to say, "I really love that company and I was there for a reasonably long time. I performed well, but there came a time for us (the company and me) to make a change." And then smile in a very friendly way and shut up! Just stop talking and keep looking the interviewer in the eye. You can then quickly follow up with, "And before that, I was at _____ company, where I performed very well."

If you follow the script that I have recommended about the presentation of yourself and the job you had (how you performed and why you left) this question may never come up. But, if it does, you must not communicate any kind of emotion or anger. And whatever you do, don't get into a story of "true confessions." You will absolutely annihilate any chance you have at getting the job if you go on and on and on trying to justify being fired. If there's no way of avoiding having to say that you were fired, simply acknowledge that you were: that you really enjoyed the time you were at that particular organization; that you learned from that organization and appreciated all that they did for you; and that it was simply time to make a change.

Answering this question, when you have no other choice but to admit you were fired, even for cause, takes more practice than probably any answer you will ever give in an interviewing situation. Practice! Practice! Practice!

Where being fired really causes a problem for the organization that let you go is in a reference check. The laws about what can and can't be said in a reference check are so subject to individual interpretation that most companies have resorted to simply confirming the dates of a person's employment, confirming or denying earnings, and confirming or denying whether a person is a "rehirable." Any other comments made in a reference check have the potential of creating a litigious situation between the ex-employee and the employer. Regardless of whether anyone agrees with the state of the situation regarding references, most employers with any brains are only going to confirm or deny these three things: dates of employment, earnings, and eligibility to be rehired.

If you were fired for cause and you're pretty sure that a prospective employer is going to find out that you were fired rather than laid off, the best thing to do is to explain exactly what happened in your opinion. You shouldn't criticize or denigrate your previous employer. Communicate the idea that although you don't agree with the decision, you do respect it. In order to overcome the situation where you were fired with cause (and there is no way around having to talk about it in the interview), you are going to have to "counter" being fired with excellent references. So, you say, "Well, Tony, how can I get good references from a company or individuals that fired me?" Well, you do two things.

First of all, you find some individual at the company that you were fired from who will, on a personal basis, speak to a prospective employer about what you did, how well you did it, and, at least, provide a personal reference that might offset the formal "negative" reference, if that is the case. In other words, you are going to counterbalance and neutralize the negative reference with a positive personal reference.

The second thing that you absolutely have to do is have a plethora of positive, glowing references from previous employers that you worked with before your last job. Being fired, or let go, just doesn't have the same negative impact if it stands alone. But you're going to have to get at least three or four glowing, positive, enthusiastic references from previous employers to offset one negative reference—even if this is an implied negative reference from your most recent employer.

• **How much time did you take off last year?** This seems like a relatively simple question, nonthreatening at all. The "risk" issue here is really the question of, "How many times are you going to be out of here and other people will have to do your job (which they will resent)?"

Be truthful about this answer. After all, if a company checks your previous employment reference, one question it might ask will be about inordinate absences. If you are one of those people who are rarely absent, you realize how frustrating it is for everyone in an organization to take up the slack for those people who are out a lot. Being absent an inordinate amount of time irritates management and frustrates the dickens out of other employees. So, if you were absent from work an inordinate amount of time in the past year, be sure to communicate that the circumstances were out of the ordinary and that being absent from work is not something that you make a habit of.

• **Have you ever had personal financial difficulties?** This question tries to get at how responsible you are. If you were in the banking, accounting, finance, or credit profession, you know how treacherous the answer to this question can be. Many companies run a credit report after getting your permission to do so. If you have had personal credit challenges caused by a bankruptcy, divorce, being out of work for so long, or any other less than positive circumstance, the best thing to do it is to admit that your credit has been "bruised" and enumerate the circumstance that caused the issue. If you note that a rough credit history may be an issue for a prospective employer, don't let him or her find out about it when he or she does a credit check. You are much better off to be proactive and explain the situation before it is discovered.

• **If a personal commitment conflicts with a business emergency, what do you do?** This is a somewhat loaded question. If you communicate that you drop all personal commitments for business reasons, it will be construed that your values are out of place, and if you communicate that you always put personal commitments ahead of business, you will be questioned on your commitment to your job. The answer is, "Fortunately, I've never been caught in that bind. I've always been able to be sure that unexpected personal commitments have been cared for by someone else. Because of my personal situation, I doubt that I would have to make that choice."

• **If you could start your career over again, what would you do differently?** This is kind of a trick question. Whatever you do, don't go overboard about all the mistakes you made and what you would've done much differently. Something along the lines of, "You know, I've been fortunate, I haven't made too many mistakes in my career and I sure learned a lot from the ones that I made. There aren't very many career choices or decisions that I would change."

• **Have you ever been asked in any of your jobs to do something unethical? How did you handle it?** Tell the truth. In rare instances candidates leave companies because they're asked to do unethical things. If you did leave because you were asked to do something unethical, don't make a big, long emotional harangue about how somebody asked you to "cheat" and you wouldn't do it. Simply state that you were asked to do something unethical (and it is best to say exactly what it was that you were asked to do, especially if you are asked), and you elected to leave the organization because it put you in an awkward position. You don't want to come across as a "holier than thou" and have contempt for people who might ask you to do something out of line. Likewise, you need to make it clear that you didn't agree with what you were asked to do so you refused to do it.

Also, if you were asked to do something highly unethical or illegal, it wouldn't be wise to open up this kind of discussion. So unless you were asked to do something grossly unethical, simply state that you never have been asked to do anything of the kind.

• **Do you object to honesty or psychological testing?** This is only going to be asked by an organization that does this kind of testing. As I mentioned before, if you object, you were probably going to be eliminated.

• **What do you think about _____ (any controversial issue, i.e., politics, religion, anything in news that might be controversial)?** If it is that controversial, no matter what your opinion, don't give it. Say something like, "You know, I am trying to learn more about _____. I'd be interested to know what your opinion is." I wouldn't necessarily agree or disagree. Simply state, "That's very interesting, I'm going to do more research on it myself."

• **How would you describe your personal character?** This is another dumb question, but you may very well hear it. The answer has to be along the lines of, "honest, a high degree of integrity, cooperative . . . ," and anything else that might fit. Don't go on too long. Two or three descriptive words would do.

• **How would you describe your own personality?** Simply describe your personality in positive terms. Three or four descriptive terms will do.

• **Have you ever been involved in a lawsuit? Business or personal?** You have to answer this question very carefully. Lawsuits are usually public records, even if they are settled. So, if you have been involved in a lawsuit, state that you have and give a very brief description, one or two sentences about it, and then be quiet. Whatever you do, do not go on about how gruesome it was, who was right and who was wrong, what a mess it was, etc. Most businesspeople, if they've been around for any length of time have been involved in lawsuits. It would only become a big deal in an interviewing situation if you make get a stumbling block.

• **What will your boss say when you resign? Will he or she be upset?** This is a bit of a loaded question. It might be asked so that the interviewer can find out if you confided in your present boss, if your present organization knows that you were probably going to leave, or the interviewer just might throw the question out there to see how you will react. The best answer will be along the line of, "I'm sure my boss will be somewhat disappointed, but he or she has always been the kind who wants what's best for everyone in the organization. If finding a new job is best for my family and me, well, my boss might be unhappy about the situation for his and our company, but he will be pleased for me."

• **Can we contact your references, present/former employers?** The only alarming thing about this question is that you might not want anyone checking your present employer as a reference until after you have left your job. The only reason someone might ask you this question is to see how you react to it. So, you want to say, "I have no problem with your checking my previous employment references when we get to the proper offer stage. But I certainly would not want anyone checking with my present employer as I have not left, and they have no idea that I'm looking for a job."

• **Knowing what you know about the job you are interviewing for, what are the things that you're going to dislike the most?** Simple answer: "Well, from what I know so far about it there might be some things that I may not like as well as others, but I haven't found anything that I would dislike."

• **What is the least relevant job that you had?** Be pensive and think about this for a few moments. Then say something like, "Well, in just about every job that I've ever had, I learned something. There were jobs during college and right out of college that were not as relevant to my career growth as they could have been, but I sure learned a lot by working at them. I've always felt that, no matter how menial the task, I really need to do my best."

• **Sometimes people stretch the truth or don't tell the truth in order to protect themselves or their organization. Have you ever found it necessary to do this?** This is a really tough question. It ranks up there with the question of, "Do you ever lie?" Something along this line would work, with somewhat of a smile on your face, you say, "Well, I have been known to embellish a bit, but I've never been comfortable with covering up or stretching the truth. In situations where I've seen people fib, it inevitably comes back to haunt them. My experience is that one lie leads to another, then to another, and it's never really in anyone's best interest. Part of being successful in business is being able to present things just as they are, for better or for worse. I've always found that honesty is appreciated by most people."

What Kind of Worker Will You Be?

• **What are the reasons for your success in this profession?** This should be an answer that should roll off your tongue quickly and decisively. Something along the line of hard work, determination, passion, and willingness to go the extra mile will do.

• **What is your energy level like? Describe one of your typical days.** I have discussed it in other parts of this book, but you must always communicate a high energy level. As you know, interviewing is a staged, contrived event.

People confuse your ability to perform with your ability to interview. A low-energy, slow, apathetic interviewing style will communicate low-energy, slow, apathetic work habits. So, you always want to communicate a high energy level. You do that by sitting up and leaning forward with relaxed intensity. When you walk during the interviewing process, make sure you walk at a rapid pace. When asked about your energy level, you must say that your energy level is high in a fairly animated way.

Describe your day by making sure you are up and at your job very early, getting a lot of work done, i.e., undertaking lots of activity, and going home later than most people. You have to communicate doing a lot of work and doing it quickly.

• **Why do you want to work here?** If you were early in the interviewing process, you would want to say something like, "Based on what I know, there seems to be a very good opportunity here for both this company and myself" and then elaborate a little bit on it and the opportunity as it might appear. Be sure to have a better answer than, "Well, I need a job and you've got one here." That won't get you hired.

If you were a little further along in the interviewing process, say your third or fourth interview, then you should have a very good idea about why you would want to work for the firm. Make sure your answer focuses more on what you can do for them rather than what they can do for you. If you say something like, "Well, there seems to be lots of room for advancement (or lots of money, great titles, etc.)," you won't win the job. You need to have three or four very well-thought-out reasons as to why you want the job, focusing on what you can do for the company and therefore what it might be able to do for you.

• **What kind of personal experience, outside of work, do you have for this job?** If you have some experience outside of work that helps in the job, then relate it. But do be careful here, and don't simply come up with something that is an embellishment or contrived. Also be sure to stay away from anything that might have to do with politics or religion. Being an elder in your church or being the Republican precinct chairman might show leadership, but these kinds of organizations may not be good to mention in the interviewing process for obvious reasons.

• **Have you done the best work you are capable of doing?** This can be a trick question. If you say that you have done the very best work you're capable of doing, it may come across as a bit egotistical. If you say that you haven't done the best work that you were capable of doing, you may come across as an underachiever. So, the best answer has to be along the line of, "Based on the experience that I have had, I was doing the best work that I was capable of doing. The more experience that I have, the better my work gets."

• **Tell me how you moved up through the organization.** If you were promoted a number of times, you should relate instances in which you were promoted. Don't laugh, but I have known candidates to say things like, "Well, I simply sat around long enough and eventually someone promoted me." That will not get you the job. If you were promoted, you should have real good reasons as to why.

• **Can you work under pressure? Tell me about the most pressure situation you were in.** You should be able to relate a good story here. One or two situations where you performed well under extreme pressure will do. If you have to think about this or you are hesitant in your answer, you won't appear decisive.

• **Describe the most difficult problem you had to deal with.** Watch out for this kind of question. It is better to describe a difficult business problem rather than a personal one. If you say something like, "Well, I'm going through a very ugly divorce," you may be describing a difficult problem, but it won't help your candidacy. You should have a rehearsed answer for a question like this. Describe the problem and describe how you solved the problem directly and specifically.

• **What have you done that shows initiative?** Again, you should have the answer to this question down pat. It should roll off your tongue as though you've answered this question many times. The answer to this can be either a personal story or a business situation. It might be good to have both, and having two or three or even four instances where you showed initiative would be good.

• **How do you manage to interview while still employed?** This is a question that's going to put you on a spot a bit regarding your integrity or character. If you communicate that you simply took all lot of time off to interview, you will appear to be a person who takes advantage of your employer. Sell, and answer something like, "I have accrued quite a bit of vacation, and I've been taking it to interview" will suffice. Just don't be flippant or casual about the answer.

• **What kinds of decisions are most difficult for you?** An answer that communicates compassion and empathy for other people is usually a good answer for this kind of question. Something like, "It is difficult when I have to fire someone or lay him or her off, and I know it affects not only that person but other people. I have done it, and know I'm going to have to continue to do it, but it still isn't easy."

• **What area of your skills/professional development you want to improve at this time?** Most people never think of this question until they get asked it in an interview. And that's the worst time to start thinking about the answer. Most every professional needs to be working on his or her "game" all of the time. If you are a professional in, say, the technology area, you need to communicate that you are taking courses or improving your skills in some aspect of technology. If you are not in a profession where this kind of thing is that clear-cut, you need to communicate that you are constantly taking personal development and personal growth types of training or seminars, such as motivational and inspirational books and CDs centered on simply growing, as a person will do. So, mentioning any kind of course, book, or program that you are involved with will make you stand out.

• **Why should I hire an outsider when I could fill the job with someone inside the company?** This is a great question, and I'm always surprised that it doesn't get asked more often. In fact, it's one of the questions that you as a candidate will need to know somewhere down the line before you accept a job with the company that might ask. However, if you are asked the question, you need to answer it in a careful manner. If you say something like, "Well, obviously you don't have anybody in your company as qualified as I am or you wouldn't be interviewing me," you'll kill the interview with your ego. If you say something like, "Well, you wouldn't," then you are coming across as weak.

It is true that most of the time if a company was going to move or promote someone from within to fill a job, it would have done so already and it wouldn't be interviewing you. Once in a rare while, the company will interview externally to simply compare with the people that it has internally who might be qualified. So, the odds are in your favor to start with. An answer like "My experience has been that if companies can find equal candidates internally and externally, they should be hiring internally. But I have also found that hiring externally brings new blood, new ideas, and energy to the organization, and it usually works out very well," will work.

• **Do you set goals for yourself?** If you haven't set goals for yourself, start before this question gets asked. And for goodness sake don't say something like, "Well, I have goals, but I don't write them down." That's a sure way to get eliminated as a candidate.

You absolutely should have specific, written goals when it comes to a job search (and in life, if you want do it right). They don't have to be sophisticated, mesmerizing, or miraculous. Simple, specific, timed, measurable, and attainable goals are a necessity for a superior life as well as a superior job search.

• **How do you organize yourself for day-to-day activities?** An answer of, "Well, I just show up and react to what happens," won't get it. It certainly doesn't hurt to have a copy of your day-to-day activity/goal sheets. You have to communicate the idea that you plan every day and you work your plan.

• **What interests you most about this job?** This is a "trick" question. If you say something like, "Well, I hear it pays really well," you're dead. You've got to say something that is complimentary to the organization, as well as to yourself. Something along the line of, "As I see it, there's a great opportunity for me to really contribute to the growth of what appears to be a very strong organization. I would be able to push my limits and skills beyond what I have experienced in a job before. I'm excited about it," would be great. Communicate being able to provide your skills to what appears to be a great organization. Anything that appears to be a "what this job can do for me" answer will not be good.

• **What can you do for us that someone else cannot do?** Any question like this has to center around the idea that what the company gets when it hires you is that it gets YOU in the deal. The way you communicate that will make all the difference in the world. Saying something like, "I have been very fortunate to be blessed with skills that fit my personality very well. I not only bring my personality to the party, but also a unique way of communicating and being motivated. I also bring success" is appropriate. It certainly doesn't hurt to have a story of how your unique approach to things solved a problem in a previous position.

• **How long have you been looking for another position?** If you have been looking for a job for, what might appear to be an inordinate amount of time, like six months or so, you have to answer this question with the outright statement that you are looking for the "right" opportunity. So, if you've been out of work or been looking for a job for six months or so, it is appropriate to say, "I've been actively looking for a position for the past few months, and although I've had a number of opportunities to accept a job, I haven't found the right match for both me and a prospective employer."

Hiring or interviewing authorities will be concerned if you have been on the job market too long. They will wonder, "What is wrong with this person?" So, be sure to give a logical and reasonable explanation of why you might still be looking. If you just started looking for a position or in the early stages of your job search, you may simply state that you've just started your job search.

• **What do you think of your current/last boss?** This is a great chance for you to destroy your candidacy. The metaphors and analogies that you give here are extremely important. No matter what, even if you were fired by the biggest jerk in the world, you absolutely have to present your current or last boss in positive terms.

The reason for this is very simple. Employers and hiring authorities identify with employers and hiring authorities. Whatever you say about your present or last boss, they will assume that you will say it about them. This is one of the few ironclad rules about interviewing. Never forget that in interviewing, a hiring authority is not going to identify with you more than they're going to identify with your previous or present boss. If you badmouth your present or last boss, you are presenting yourself as a phenomenal risk. You cannot afford to do that. So, if you get along very well with your present or last boss, state that. If things were a little rocky, even if you were fired, say something like "We didn't see eye-to-eye and our chemistry was never great. I do respect him (her) and appreciated the success he (she) has had. I'm sure he respected me too in spite of our differences." Even if you disagreed with your previous boss or he or she fired you, this is a neutral answer. If your previous boss tries to destroy you in a reference after you have said something like this, he or she will marginalize him- or herself. The interviewing or hiring authority will have a tendency to think, "Well, after the relatively respectful things that this candidate said about his previous boss, I can't believe that he badmouthed this person that way. This previous boss must be a real jerk."

This kind of strategy doesn't work 100% of the time, but at least you neutralized whatever your previous boss might say. Just remember to take the high road. Because if you take the low road and present your previous boss in any negative terms, you probably won't get hired.

• **What would you do when you have a great deal of work to accomplish in a short time span? How have you reacted?** You'd better have a couple of stories to reinforce your theory for this answer. Your answer should be something along the line of, "I am constantly setting goals and planning. So, I set priorities for myself and for others. If I have a great deal of work to accomplish in a short time span, I have to analyze my priorities and pick the ones that are most important. Years ago I reacted too emotionally and tried to get all of it done. I have found that, in cases like this, unless someone can put 26 hours in a day, I have to decide what the priorities are and act on them."

• **Tell me about a time when your team fell apart. Why did it happen? What did you do?** Again, to reinforce your ability to deal with stress and strain you need a story or two. Know why the minor crisis happened and explain in detail what you did.

• **How did you feel about your workload at that company? And how did you divide your time on your major areas of responsibility?** Never, ever complain about your workload. Explain that you appreciated the amount of work you were assigned and that all of the best managers seem to be somewhat overloaded. Explain how you divide your time to deal with your areas of responsibility. Again, you need to reinforce how you "make your plan and work your plan" in a calm deliberate manner. Communicate that you always found that good planning always works.

• **What have you learned from the jobs that you held?** Whenever you get the opportunity to talk about what you have learned, always have that center around how you have grown as a person. You can relate different kinds of "character building" traits in certain jobs. Things like, "In my present position,

I've really learned to be patient with impatient people. Although I report to a particular individual, I wound up really working for three very demanding people. It has been a real challenge, but I've grown as a person."

Or, you can say something along the line of, "I have become more focused (detailed, understanding, assertive, positive, a better leader, etc.) because I have been fortunate to have a good mentor in my last (or previous) job." You can never answer this question wrong if you stick to something that you learned from a mentor where you grew personally. You can even reinforce whatever you say with stories.

• **What do you know about the position for which you are applying?** Don't feel like that you have to relate more than you know. You can even add that, "From what I've learned so far, it seems very exciting and would be a great opportunity for my skills and for your company. I'm sure that as I get into the interviewing process more deeply, I will gain a better idea of the opportunity for both of us."

• **In your current/last position, state your five most significant accomplishments.** You better have these ready in case this question comes up. It is always good to give some kind of "figures" when you talk about significant accomplishments. Talking about increasing percentage of sales, increasing productivity in percentage figures, lowering costs of sales and expenditures in a department with an increase in productivity, etc., always make you stand out.

"Soft" types of accomplishments, like instilling a positive attitude in the team or turning moral around in the organization are OK to mention once, maybe twice. But don't do any more than that, and if you do, you need to be sure that you associate measurable productivity and/or savings with them. At least three or four of these most significant accomplishments need to be able to be measured with objective numbers.

• **After I get to know you, what will annoy me about you?** Don't take this bait. Say something like, "Well, although I try to work at it, I'm not a very good golfer (tennis player, bowler, poker player, etc.)." Then smile. Don't get into anything more personal than this. It simply can't help you.

• **I see you are working on your MBA/graduate degree. What are you going to do when you get it?** Some companies really like people getting graduate degrees and some don't care. It is helpful if you know how many of the managers or people in the organization have MBAs or graduate degrees.

There might be a fear that, if you get the MBAs or graduate degree, you will leave. This is especially true for companies, industries, or professions that don't necessarily appreciate or need for a graduate degree. Finance and banking, for instance, appreciate graduate degrees more than manufacturing or sales organizations.

If you suspect that the organization is ambivalent about an MBA or graduate degree or it is fearful that you may leave once you get it, you may say something like "I decided to pursue an MBA or graduate degree as much for personal growth as anything else. In my experience, I have seen that having an MBA or graduate degree doesn't necessarily make you a better professional. But, I am a constant learner and if it helps along the way, it will be of value."

• **WOW . . . your grades are really low. What happened?** Take this question very seriously. Respond by saying something like, "It did take me a couple of years to really get focused on college (or graduate school). I was very active in college in organizations and held leadership positions. I also had to work to earn money for college and its expenses. If I had to do it again, I would probably work a little harder." If your college or graduate school was more than a couple of years ago, mention that your working performance has been excellent.

How This Affects You

After the question of being liked or disliked, the issue of being a risk destroys more job possibilities than any other question. Although it still only amounts to 20% of the hiring decision, it is a very crucial 20%.

When hiring authorities hire an employee who doesn't work out, they look bad. Next to one's own poor personal performance, hiring people who don't work out leads to a very poor reputation. Hiring poor performers can lead to being fired. No matter how many people are involved in the hiring decision, the immediate hiring authority is held responsible for the decision. If it turns out to be a bad decision, the hiring authority is perceived to be a poor businessperson.

The *fear* of making a poor hiring decision is a much greater motivator than the *vision* of a good hiring decision. A good hiring decision is expected, but a poor hiring decision is remembered and ruminated over much longer than a good one.

A hiring authority with any reasonable experience can recount every detail of every poor hiring decision he or she ever made. The outstanding hires may be remembered also, but hiring authorities will never forget every aspect of the poor ones.

This fear is a great motivator. If a hiring authority has an equal number of good reasons to hire a candidate and good reasons not to hire a candidate, the candidate will never get hired. Because of the risk, a hiring authority is going to err on the side of safety and may pass up an excellent candidate for a lesser person who has fewer risks.

The vast majority of candidates don't recognize the risk they pose to the hiring authority. The very things that some candidates think make them excellent to hiring authorities are their biggest liabilities. Here's a list of the major "risk factors" that candidates present to hiring authorities. If you fit in these categories or situations, reread this chapter and mitigate your own risk.

- Being the president of a company
- Being fired
- Owning your own company
- Being out of work for an extended period of time—no matter what the reasons
- Too many jobs in the short period of time—i.e., three jobs in two years
- For women, coming back into the workforce after raising a family
- Being at one company *too long*
- Changing careers
- Working in a small company and interviewing at a very large company
- Having worked in nothing but large companies and interviewing at a small company
- Poor performance as a salesperson or poor performance reviews
- Going through a divorce
- Being in one company for a very long time and never getting a promotion
- Leaving a job for "personal" reasons that you can't explain

- Being unhappy in just about every (or any) job you've ever had
- Being motivated by your spouse or family members to change jobs
- "Philosophical" differences with your present employer (that don't make sense)
- Reasons for changing like, "it's just time for a change"
- "I'm not really looking to change, but if the right deal came along . . ."
- Poor previous employment references
- Too many traffic violations, misdemeanors, or brushes with the law
- Casual reasons for leaving your present or past jobs
- Poor credit

There are others. You just need to be sure that you think critically about what your risk factors might be. Ask your spouse or a close friend about your risk factors. Even better, a good recruiter who is been in the business for a long period of time might help you strategize about your risks.

10 Can We Work the Money Out?

∙∙

Most people think that these are some of the most difficult questions to deal with in the interviewing process. Frankly, though, if all of the other questions about being able to do the job, being liked, and being a risk are answered, even reasonably well, these questions are very easy to deal with. In fact, the answers to these questions are merely an outgrowth of all of the previous ones. The more an organization would like to hire you and the more you would like to go to work for them, the easier it is to work out the money. So, the better you sell yourself and the more desirable you are to an organization, the more likely it is to compensate you fairly. We will get into the final economic negotiations at the end of this chapter, but here are some of the questions that you're going to get asked that relate to money and compensation.

∙ **What are you currently earning? Or, what have you been earning most recently?** This is a pretty simple question and requires a really simple answer. Simply share with the hiring or interviewing authority exactly what you have been earning or presently are earning. Whatever you do, don't inflate the numbers. Over the years, I have had a number of employers ask this question during the interviewing process, and then after a person is hired, call the previous employer to verify earnings—only to find out that the candidate lied and is therefore terminated. If you were in sales, do not extrapolate the best month that you ever had and annualize it. If you are asked for a salary history, give it accurately. Some interviewing processes require the candidate to provide previous W2s.

• What kind of money would you like to earn? Hopefully, you will have some idea about the salary range for the position that you are interviewing for. However, your stock answer in a situation like this is, "Well, I'd like earn as much as I can commensurate with the service that I give. I am just as interested in a fulfilling and challenging position as I am in the money I want to earn. I have found that if the position is right for me, and I am right for the company that I'm going to go work for, the money is usually going to take care of itself. What kind of money for this position did your organization have in mind?"

Always, always, always discuss money along with the relationship it has to your contribution to the job. What this communicates is that you were just as interested in doing a good job as you are interested in the money you will receive. People who focus on money too much in the interviewing situation without bridging its relationship with the job, the quality of work, and the challenge don't do themselves any favors. Just remember: Always discuss money in relationship to the job that needs to be done.

• You have been making $XXX,XXX, and the money that is associated with this position is significantly less. How do we know that you will be happy? In this situation, you have to find out exactly how much of a difference there is between what you have been making and what this particular position pays. If you've been out of work for any amount of time, the truth is at this point you are making absolutely nothing.

No matter what the difference between what you have earned in the past and what the company is paying, your answer to this question needs to be something like, "Well, I realize there is a difference between what I have made (or what I am making now) and this position. However, I have found that if the opportunity is right and I am able to perform at my best, the difference in the money isn't as important as the quality of the job and the opportunity."

The idea behind this whole interviewing process is to get a job offer. Just because you get a job offer doesn't mean you have to accept it. But your goal is to get an organization to make you an offer. If you communicate the idea that there is going to be a problem with the money it can pay you and what you will accept, you run the risk of eliminating yourself before you ever get to the offer stage.

Any questions you get asked about money during the interviewing process before you get to the final offer stages need to be handled gracefully, but gracefully postponed until the final offer stages. Once you get to that stage, you have established yourself and the value you can bring to the organization. The greater the value you establish for yourself, the more money you will be able to negotiate.

• **What is the most money that you have ever made?** Answer this question judiciously. If you have been in sales, for instance, and your earnings have been really high in some years and lower in others, give an average of the last few years. Bragging about making a lot of money will never help in negotiations. If you made an inordinate amount of money several years ago, I would recommend not even mentioning it. Again, the answer to a question like this needs to center around not just what you've earned, but the challenge of the job opportunity itself. Something along the lines of, "There have been a few years in which I've been fortunate enough to be with organizations where bonus earnings were sizable. But I realize that those are very uncommon. I am more interested in the opportunity, the challenge of the job, and the potential. If those things are taken care of, my earnings will reflect my performance."

• **What do you consider most valuable: a high salary, job recognition, or advancement?** Again, combining earnings with job performance is the most important thing you can do. Something along the lines of, "Well, I have found that the better job I do, the harder I work, recognition, advancement, and, especially, money usually take care of themselves."

• **What kind of benefits are you expecting?** In the past few years, benefit plans, especially in the insurance arena, have skyrocketed in cost—especially for companies with a hundred people or less. So, there is no such thing as "standard" benefits. It is not uncommon for organizations to have drastically reduced their benefit plans for their employees. The purpose of this question is to find out if there is going to be a great deal of difference between the kind of benefits that you have had before and the kind of benefits that might be offered with this company. Again, you really don't want concerns about benefits to interrupt the interviewing process until you have fully sold yourself. So, an answer something like, "Benefits, like money, to me are as important as the company, the job, and the professional challenge. I will certainly take the benefits package into consideration if an offer is made, but right now those kinds of things shouldn't be an issue."

All You Need to Know About Money Negotiations

Most people make a much bigger deal about salary and compensation negotiations in the final step of getting a job offer. I have always contended, and my candidates over the years agree wholeheartedly, that if you keep a few principles in mind, successful negotiations, when it comes to money, just aren't that hard. Here is what you need to know.

People have all kinds of funny, usually wrong, ideas about compensation. It becomes real important because money is a common denominator, and it is easily equated with success in a job (which really isn't true). Many people say they are primarily motivated by money. If that were true, more people would rob banks or something illegal to get money quickly. The truth is that just about every psychological study about the motivation of money rank it as the fourth or fifth reason people work. It always falls behind job satisfaction, contribution, security, personal growth, and so on.

If you have "managed" the interviewing process correctly, you already have a good idea of what the salary and compensation for the position are. You know how close your idea is to and the hiring authority's idea of what is fair. Money is simply part of the job offer negotiation. There are lots of things that might be negotiated in a job offer. So, before we get to the exact way to address money, let me share them with you:

401K investment and retirement plans

Car, car allowances, insurance, parking fees, other car expenses

Business expenses

Title

Salary review dates

Insurance—health, life, vision, dental—for you and family

Disability insurance, both short-term and long-term

Overtime pay

Vacation time

Sick leave

Educational reimbursement

Flextime

Pay for extra personal time off

Health club/country club membership and expenses

Real-estate assistance

"Custom designed" bonus plans

Stock options, stock used as a sign-on bonus

Sabbaticals

Stock purchase plans

College tuition reimbursement plans

Daycare programs

Ability to work from home a designated percentage of time

Membership to buying clubs

Separation packages

Sales territory realignment

There can be all kinds of other benefits that a company might be able to provide. I have seen such things as time off to train for the Olympics, time off to attend executive MBA programs at far away schools, bike race team sponsorship, and hunting lodges.

Make sure you know all of the aspects of a job offer before you start negotiating. The larger the company, most likely the less flexible it can be. But you won't know until you try. Here are some things to remember:

- The better you sell yourself in the interviewing process, the more a company likes you and wants to hire you, the more leverage you have in negotiation. If you are a "nice to have" instead of a "can't live without" candidate, you may not do as well in negotiating. Make yourself indispensable!

- When it comes to money, always try to negotiate with the hiring authority—the one with "pain" to hire someone. You don't have as much leverage with a removed third party, like H.R. An H.R. department isn't as interested in alleviating the "pain" of a hiring authority as it is in keeping with the salary guidelines that make the department look good. So, if the H.R. department starts talking to you about money, insist on talking to the hiring authority.

- Don't assume that you are going to have a hassle over the negotiations. If you approach the negotiation as though it is just part of the other conversations, you are much more likely to do well.

- Remember, the first rule of negotiation is to never be afraid to walk away! Now this might be harder to do if this is the only offer you have received in six months. And don't lead with an aggressive attitude. Simply know that you can walk away any time.

- Make sure you know everything about the job before you negotiate. It is not uncommon for a candidate to be so intent on getting an offer that he or she misses a number of important parts about the job. So, when you go in to negotiate, if you don't already have a crystal clear understanding of the job, get one!

- Approach the negotiation with a "we are all in this together" attitude. You have to say, in the beginning of the conversation, "Mr. or Ms. Hiring Authority, I really want this job and I want to work for you. I would like to see if we can work the money out together." This removes the employer's fear that you will *reject* him or her. Studies have shown that this kind of "Let's all win together" attitude is the best negotiating statement a person can make.

- Contrary to what most people think, most employers are not interested in "paying as little as possible." Most know that we all get what we pay for. The employer needs a good employee more than he or she needs the money.

- Make sure you hear all aspects of the offer before you start negotiating. Write this down so you can see them in front of you.

- Don't negotiate over the phone or by e-mail unless you absolutely have to. Face to face is always best.

Once you have done all of these things, repeat back to the hiring authority what you understand. Then take each item you think you would like to discuss and talk about it with him or her. As you go through each item, it doesn't hurt to ask, "Is that the best you can do?" Now, some things like life insurance or health insurance benefits are cast in stone. They can't be changed for each individual in the company. However, things like base salary, salary reviews, etc., may be greatly variable. I recently instructed a young candidate who was changing jobs for the first time to automatically ask this question when he got a verbal offer. He was making $65,000 and was offered $68,000. The young fellow simply asked, "Is that the best you can do?" The hiring authority told him that he would call him back in an hour. The hiring authority called back and offered $71,000 with a $2,000 signing bonus. The candidate was elated. He got a $5,000 raise before he even started simply because he asked.

Even if you ask this question and discuss each money item in an offer, you may not get any more money. The offer might be the same when you sat down to discuss it. Don't worry about that. It still may be a good offer. But, at least you will be respected for trying.

Remember that in the coming economy your job with any one firm is likely to last only 2.5 to 3 years. You may, for a number of reasons, be willing to take a little less than what you think you or the job might be worth in order to gain experience that you can leverage in the next job.

How This Affects You

Be aware of every aspect of an offer, especially the monetary part. Give good answers and ask good questions. Treat "money" with grace and ease, like any other part of the interviewing process.

Practice, practice, practice. Go through a number of role-playing sessions and mock negotiation situations with your spouse, friend, or coach. This kind of thing does not come naturally to most people. Get use to having to do it: Every three years or so is more often than you expected!

Chapter

11 Illegal Questions

I take a bit of a different approach toward illegal or inappropriate questions than a lot of authors or experts. For the past thirty-plus years, I've experienced thousands of companies and individuals in those companies who ask illegal questions. Most of the companies in this country have fewer than 100 people, and it may not come as a surprise that many hiring or interviewing authorities just don't have any idea what is legal and what isn't.

Some of them do it unknowingly and ignorantly, although that's really hard to believe. But it is true. Some of them do it because they're simply going to intentionally discriminate based on what they consider to be their prerogative. Some people ask illegal questions just to show interviewees that they're going to get away with it. It's all rather insane and stupid.

Many experts will tell you to flat out tell a prospective employer or hiring authority that a particular question is illegal. They will normally recommend that you tell the hiring authority that you don't have to answer that question, because it is illegal. I'm not going to tell you to do that. I'm going to tell you to do what you think is best about answering the question.

You may have a chance to be righteous and right and proceed to put some hiring or interviewing authority in his place by letting him know that he's breaking the law, or you can try to get a job. I assure you that if you make an interviewing or hiring authority uncomfortable by informing her that you know that the question she asked was illegal by saying something like, "That is an illegal question; I don't have to answer it," you won't get hired. Now, you may not really want to go to work for an organization or individual stupid enough ask obviously illegal questions. But if you need a job, and he or she has one, I certainly wouldn't recommend losing the opportunity by getting your nose out of joint over an illegal question.

Use your own judgment. You may want to consider answering the question, depending on the context in which it is asked. If you feel like someone is asking your age or your marital status because the person will probably use that information to eliminate you from consideration, you might say something in a startled, surprised, but very kind manner like, "Oh, goodness! I didn't know you could ask that question, but . . ." then answer the question in a way you think is appropriate.

You might also answer the question with a question, such as, "How does the answer to that question have an impact on my performance of the job or my ability to getting it?" This is a very nice way of saying, "That's an illegal question. It has nothing to do with my ability to do the job and I'm not going to answer it." If you feel that the question is being asked out of genuine interest and sincere empathy, like in a casual conversation after a formal interview, feel free to answer it in any manner that you wish.

Again, follow your instincts and the answer these questions in whatever way you are comfortable doing. I don't recommend "winning a battle" but "losing the war" over illegal questions. If you think it's appropriate to set someone straight about the illegal questions, feel free to do so. If the questions offend you, just don't go to work there.

Here's a list of the most common illegal or inappropriate questions:

- Anything about the candidate's parents, spouses, nationality, ancestry or lineage
- The name of next of kin
- Birthplace
- How a person might have acquired a second language
- Any religious questions, political questions, religious holiday observances
- Asking about a change of name or name of origin
- Asking about marital status
- Asking about the number, names, ages of children or dependents

- Asking if a person has childcare for children
- Asking if a person is planning on having a family
- Age
- The branch of the military that a candidate has served in and the type of discharge
- Asking about a candidate's preference to work with any identifiable "group," such as men, women, religious or ethnic group
- Any questions about a person's native language or accent
- Questions about organizations that the candidate might belong to
- Asking candidates if they have ever filed a Worker's Compensation claim
- Asking if a candidate has ever been arrested
- Asking if the candidate has ever filed a claim against your company's insurance company

PART

III

Asking Your Own Questions of Yourself, Your Recruiter, and Your Potential Employer

Chapter

12 Questions to Ask Yourself Even Before the Interviewing Process

∙∙

If I've learned one thing since I got into this business, it is that the candidates who get the best jobs and make the best opportunities for themselves are the candidates who ask the best questions. They ask questions of the right people and ask them in the right way. It often has been said that the difference between average people and the most successful people is in the questions that the most successful people ask.

Most every book or program about finding a job will address the kinds of questions you should ask during the interviewing process. The list of questions can be endless. Teaching you the questions to ask isn't difficult. However, the difference between candidates who get the best job offers and negotiate the best opportunities for themselves and those who don't isn't the questions they ask. The difference is knowing whom to ask the questions of, when to ask the questions, and how to ask them.

The timing of asking the right questions during the interviewing process can make a difference of everywhere from either getting the job or not to a $15,000 to $20,000 increase in salary over what a prospective employer wants to pay. The key isn't just asking questions, it is the timing of those questions and asking them in a manner that catapults you ahead of your competition.

Asking even the right question of the wrong person can destroy your chances of successful interviews. For instance, if you ask a Human Resources representative or a third party interviewing authority a question like, "What is the most prominent deficiency in the department I will be interviewing with?" and they don't know (which they probably won't), or something like, "What are the personality strengths and weaknesses of the hiring authority's supervisor?" and they don't know (which they probably won't), you will embarrass them and they won't "look good." And, since you have made them look incompetent, you most likely won't move up the interviewing chain. After all, who wants to "promote" someone who makes them look bad? The last thing an H.R. or interviewing authority wants is for you to tell a hiring authority that the person that initially interviewed you just didn't know a lot about the job.

I'm going to teach you when to ask the right questions, whom to ask them of, as well as how to ask them so that you give yourself every advantage to get the best offer. I have personally been involved in more than 100,000 interviewing cycles since 1973, one candidate at a time, referred to individual hiring authorities for anywhere from one to multiple interviews for each hiring situation. Sometimes my candidates got hired, sometimes they did not. But I have experienced candidates asking every kind of question you can imagine, including the ridiculous and the absurd. I know which ones work and which ones don't.

My experience has taught me well. Asking the right, intelligent question in the right way, of the right people can make you. This is an obvious example, but take the question of salaries and compensation. If you ask, "What does this job pay?" (wrong way to ask the question) in your initial interview (wrong time to ask the question), you will probably eliminate yourself from being considered. If you ask about the work environment, like "What's it like to work here?" (wrong way to ask) before you get a job offer, you have probably just lost the race.

So, I have broken down the questions you should ask in the interviewing process into sections based on events before, during, and after the interviewing process. I will not only explain how to ask most of the questions, but I'll share with you what you need to look for in the answers you get, depending on the person answering them.

Keep in mind that, whether you like it or not, you are not likely to be at this same company four or five years from now. You have to interview as though you were going to be there forever, but reality is that you are going to use this job as a stepping stone to the next one. So, the answers you get to certain questions regarding your future may mean something different than they did a few years ago.

In this chapter, we'll look at questions to ask yourself—even before the interviewing process begins. In the chapters to follow, we'll look at questions to ask throughout the rest of the process, from before your initial interview to questions to ask yourself after each interview, and finally questions to ask when you get an offer.

Questions to Ask Yourself Before You Begin to Look for a Job if You Are Employed

The purpose of all of these questions, if you are presently employed, is to make sure that you are committed to the emotional and psychological difficulties you will encounter in changing jobs. Next to death of a spouse, death of a parent, death of a child, coupled with divorce, looking for a job is the next most emotional thing that we do.

Many, many times people forget how difficult it is to look for a job, and this is especially true when they have one. They often decide on a whim or in a fit of emotional anger that they're going to leave the job they have and find a new one. They find out after months of looking for new job that it is a difficult thing to do. Changing jobs is a lot more difficult than they thought it was going to be.

This is especially true with individuals who all of a sudden want to leave their present job for a single reason. Maybe they are passed up for a raise or promotion or they don't get the amount of the raise they think they deserved. So, in a fit of emotional unease, they've decided to just change jobs. Three or four months later, they find out that it was a lot harder to do than they thought it would be, so they quit looking.

The point is to ask yourself these questions in order to be sure you are going to have the mental and emotional stamina it is going to take to change jobs. It is going to take a lot longer than you think. It is going to be harder to do. There's going to be a whole lot more rejection and refusal then you expect.

Sometimes, you have no choice but to have to change jobs. Just be sure that you are emotionally and mentally committed to the challenge it is going to be.

If you are being forced to look for a job while you have to keep the one you have, you will want to consider the following list of questions. They will help you deal with the emotional strain of having to change jobs. Here is a list of the key questions you should ask yourself before embarking on a job search:

- What is the major reason that I need to change jobs?
- How long ago could I have seen this coming?
- How can I affect the issues that might force me to look for a job?
- Is my need to look for a job caused by others or me?
- If it is my choice, do I have a realistic idea about what the job market might bear?
- Can the issues that are causing me to look for a job be resolved? How long would it take?
- Realistically, how long will it take me to find a new job? (90 to 180 days if you are employed)
- Am I willing to make and keep the intense effort it is going to take to find a new job?
- How will I work interviewing around the job I have now?

Looking for a job is hard work. It always takes longer than most people expect, and it is normally a lot harder than they imagine. So, if after you look at these questions very hard, ask yourself if you really need to look for a job or if you should give the present situation a chance to resolve itself. You may not have a choice, but you need to be sure that your decision to change jobs is a knee-jerk reaction to some short-term situation that might get resloved.

Questions You Should Ask Yourself Before You Look for a Job if You Are Looking Full Time

These questions have to do with two things. The first is to help you check your emotional state so that your disappointment and frustration in losing a job don't interfere with your interviewing. Many people spend a lot of emotional effort in expressing the damage they experience in losing their job. The sooner you neutralize those feelings, the sooner you can move forward with a positive attitude.

The second thing that these questions will do is to get you in to the mode of looking full-time for a job. Looking for a job is a job in itself. If you approach looking for a job in a systematic, planned manner, the process will be easier.

Don't ignore your feelings or try to deny them. The purpose here is to delve into these issues so deeply that you understand your feelings and therefore become able to release them from being distracting to you and your emotions and your mind.

Questions Regarding Your Feelings

The questions below are designed to help uncover the feelings that might well prevent you from successfully interviewing. Take your time with these and answer each one fully. No one else is going to see your answers, so be as truthful as you can. Key questions to ask yourself about your feelings:

- How were you frustrated in the last or present employment?

- What were the disappointments you had with the job or company you left or are now experiencing in your present employment?

- Did you lose or are you losing self-esteem? How?

- Were you shocked at being laid off, fired, or forced to look for a new job?

- Who is to blame for your having to look for new job? Describe the situation in detail.

- Describe your disillusionment with the whole situation. How did it come about?

- Describe the shame you have in needing to look for a new job. Describe what other people will think and say about you, about your having to find a new job, about your being fired or laid off, etc.

- Do you feel isolated by having to look for a new job? Can others really understand?

- Are you denying any of the things or situations that happened? Can you describe them clearly, even if emotionally?

- Toward whom do you feel hostile, if anyone? Why do they deserve your hostility?

- Complete this sentence: I am angry because. . . . Really go into a very in-depth explanation as to why you're angry. Be as angry as you want to be; write as long as you would like.

- Do you feel guilty about what happened in losing your job or the reason that you have to look for a new one? Is there anything you could have done to prevent the situation?

- Describe the depressed feelings you might have about the whole situation. Do you feel sad, empty, fatigued about it? How does "poor you" feel about this whole thing? How do you describe "poor you"? Describe in detail.

- Describe, if it applies, how unfair the whole situation is. Describe it in detail. Write down all of the things that make you fearful about this whole situation. Be as detailed as you need to describe exactly what you are afraid of, even ridiculous fears.

After you have written down your answers to these questions in detail, read them at least three times, preferably out loud. As you read each one, ask yourself out loud, "Can I let this feeling go?" Then ask yourself out loud, "Do I want to let this feeling go?" You cannot be surprised if the answer to each one of these questions is no.

It is not uncommon to want to hold onto these feelings during the grieving period. You realize that you may never let all the emotions go or completely eliminate them from your emotional memory. The objective is not to eliminate them altogether but minimize their impact on you, so you can move forward toward a positive emotional state to interview well and attain a new job.

Questions to Ask Yourself About Your Strengths and Weaknesses

The most important aspect of these questions is to make sure that you see yourself realistically for the eyes of a hiring authority. Most people have inflated opinions of their strengths and minimized opinions of their weaknesses. Most of the candidates I've interviewed think they can do most any job they interview for.

But there is a big difference between being able to get the job and actually performing on the job. In my opinion, I might make the best President of the United States that this country has ever seen. But I'm not going to get the job because I'm not going to survive the "interviewing" process. Don't laugh. I can't tell you the number of candidates I've encountered over the years who just knew they could be the best anything they wanted to. But they neglected to take into account first, their ability to really do the job, and second, and most important, their ability to get the job in comparison to all the other candidates who were interviewing for the position.

Most people judge their talent and ability to do a job based on their own personal experience. Most candidates rarely see themselves and their talents relative to the other candidates they're competing with. This happens to the best of us. For example, Michael Jordan was one of the best athletes in the world, but when he went to play baseball, his athleticism wasn't as important as his baseball skills, which weren't as developed as his basketball skills. No matter how much Michael Jordan might have said, "But I'm the best athlete in the world," his baseball skills still couldn't compare with the people he was competing against. Just because he thought he might make a good baseball player didn't mean that he was going to get the job or do well at it. His skills were measured relative to the skills of other baseball players, and, in the end, baseball wasn't his strong suit.

So it is with you. You need to be realistic about not only what you are capable of doing, but also realistic about your ability to qualify for and get the job.

In this same vein, you need to ask yourself questions about your strengths and weaknesses as though you were in the shoes of the hiring authority. Assessing your abilities with only your opinion as a reference will do you no good at all. You have to evaluate yourself based on how a hiring authority, who is interviewing ten people just like you, would evaluate you.

You also have to be aware of your liabilities in the eyes of a hiring authority. As I've emphasized throughout this book, most people do not see anything in themselves or their background that is a risk or liability. But every hiring authority is asking every candidate either bluntly or implied, "What are the risks and liabilities in hiring this person?"

Every one of us has some liabilities in the eyes of a hiring authority. Every hiring authority is evaluating the risk he or she runs of any candidate not working out as a good employee if hired. So, you have to be aware of what your liabilities—either real or perceived—are in the eyes of the hiring authority.

As I established in the previous chapter, if you have been out of work for a long period of time, if you've had too many jobs in the last few years, or if you've been fired or laid off, you may appear as a great liability to a hiring authority. It's then your job in the interviewing process to offset or mitigate those perceived liabilities. But if you don't know what your liabilities are, you will never be able to address and overcome them.

So, with that, here is a list of questions you should ask yourself to assess your strengths, weaknesses, and liabilities:

- What are my professional and personal strengths?
- Can and do I explain my experience, background, and previous positions clearly and concisely?
- How can I demonstrate that my strengths have been benefits to the people I've worked for in the past?
- What are two or three of the most important features of my background that will be benefits to a company that I might be interviewing with?
- How will I clearly communicate myself and my benefits to a prospective employer?
- What are the facts or issues in my background or experience that might be perceived as liabilities to a perspective employer?
- How am I going to offset, minimize, or mitigate these perceived liabilities?
- Can I turn these perceived liabilities into advantages to a prospective employer? (For instance, if you have had three jobs in three years, you might turn those "lemons" into "lemonade" by stating something like, "You can rest assured in hiring me that I can't afford another one-year stint with any company. Because I have had three jobs in three years, I absolutely plan to stay on this next job at least five to seven years.")
- How can I avoid being defensive about the mistakes that I've made in the past? How can I make them positives?

- Are the things that I think are important in my background the ones that a prospective employer will think are important?
- What makes me unique? What are the three or four of my most important features and benefits that make me a better candidate than my competitors? Is this just my opinion or have others confirmed them?

Remember to look at these answers the way an employer would. An employer needs to minimize risk. If you have made mistakes, admit them. Present them as lessons. Think about how what you say will be compared to other equally qualified candidates.

13 Questions to Ask Before the Initial Interview

....

Most candidates looking for a job don't prepare well for an initial interview. Even though they may practice interviewing techniques, they often overlook preparation for interviews with specific companies or individuals. So, ask yourself these questions:

• **What do I know about the company I'm speaking with?** I can't tell you the number of candidates I have worked with over the years who knew nothing about the company they were interviewing with. Or, what is worse, they researched the wrong company and showed up being totally uninformed or misinformed. The more you know, the better you will interview. This is especially important the longer you interview. People often start out doing this right, but after they have been looking for a while, they get lazy and a bit depressed and stop doing it.

• **Have I done my research on the company?** Not just by using the Internet. Talk to clients/customers of the company, its suppliers, its competitors, and some of its present or previous employees. Get a leg up on your competition and think of innovative ways of doing your research.

• **Do I know anyone in the company?** People often move around in the same business from company to company. If you are interviewing with a competitor, supplier, or any organization that might employ someone you know,

193

or even know of from a second-hand source, you might want to call that person and ask about the company. Don't do this, though, if you are presently employed and don't want to run the risk of your looking for a job being discovered. Unfortunately, people love to gossip. I can't tell you the number of times where one of my employed candidates did this only to find out that it got back to his or her company. Think before you do this!

• **Have I taken good notes about the company to refer to during the interview?** You look like you know what you are doing when you have made notes about your research.

• **What do I know about the person I am interviewing with? Is he or she the hiring authority or an intermediary? Did I "Google" all the individuals? What do I know about them personally?** The more you know about the people you will talk to, the better. It may never come up, but it sure is a great "talking point" if you find that the hiring authority went to one of the universities in the South East Conference as you did, and you can break the ice by talking about the school's rivalries. Or, if your MBA is from Columbia and so is his or hers, you automatically have something in common.

• **Did I get a copy of the job description before the interview?** Job descriptions are often on the company websites. Or, can the specific one be e-mailed to me before I show up? These, more often than not, are ridiculously generic, but it can't hurt to know it. By the way, don't be too taken with the requirements that are posted with the job. These descriptions are usually written by people who have nothing to do with the job function.

• **What makes this company good—or not so good?** You may not be able to form an answer to this question yet, but it certainly can't hurt to ask yourself as you do your research.

• **Does this company have any glaring problems that I should know about?** You do need to know about any issues. But, if you find out that it does have problems, that doesn't automatically mean that it isn't a good job or company for you. Besides, if the problems are even remotely known to the public, you won't look good in the interviewing process if you aren't aware of them.

• **Can I articulate my unique features, advantages, and benefits for this position or the company based on what I know about it?** You better have some idea of what you can do for them that no one else can. "I'm just a great person to be around" doesn't do the trick.

• **Do I have a list of good questions to ask the interviewer based on the research I have done?** You may not need them all, but you will look intelligent when you do have them.

There are some things you should not ask on an initial interview, especially with the research capabilities offered by the Internet. If you have to ask these questions in the interview, the interviewing authority will know you aren't the sharpest pencil in the box. So, before you go on an interview you should already know:

- How large is the company? How large is the department?
- What are its major markets?
- What is its position in the marketplace or ranking in the industry?
- What is its market share?
- What are its products or services?
- Is it growing? Contracting?
- How fast has it been growing (or contracting)?

Questions to Ask When Working with an External Recruiter

An external recruiter can make a tremendous difference in the effectiveness of your interview. Some of us have worked with the same hiring authorities for years. If we have been at our profession for a number of years, we even may have placed the hiring authority we are referring you to. Many times we have a strong personal relationship with them. But even if we don't, it certainly doesn't hurt to ask your recruiter about the interviewing or hiring authority because a recruiter can be an excellent source of information as you research the company.

Here is a list of questions you should ask your recruiter:

- How long have you worked with this interviewing or hiring authority? The company?
- What does this company want to find in a candidate?
- Tell me everything you know about the job: major duties and responsibilities, money, travel, territory, quota . . . everything!

- How long has the company been looking? When does it need to fill the job? What is the interviewing process?
- Why is it looking? Is the job a replacement or a promotion? What happened to the last person?
- How many other candidates is it looking at? What has it not seen in other candidates that it would like to find?
- Does it have any internal candidates? Are you representing any of them? If so, what is my competition like? How do I stack up with them, in your opinion?
- What are my strengths relative to the job and the person doing the interviewing?
- What are my weaknesses relative to the job and the person doing the interviewing?
- What in my background should I emphasize in the interview?
- What is the personal background of the hiring authority? How long has he or she been there? What are his or her personal likes or dislikes? Has he or she hired for this position before?
- What issues am I going to have to overcome in the interview?
- What do I need to do or show interviewers to get beyond the initial interview?
- What do I need to do to get the job offer?

An external recruiter may not have all these answers, but you need to ask. You might find out crucial information that could help give you an edge over the competition. The more you know about the job, the interviewer, etc., the better you will do.

Chapter

14 Questions to Ask in the Initial Interview

··

I n this chapter, we'll address the questions you might ask in an initial interview. Depending on who is doing the interviewing, you can learn a lot about the job, and, more importantly, sell yourself to the next level of interviews. The level of responsibility and authority of the people who conduct initial interviews can vary dramatically. As you will see, you will want to vary your level of questions to the kind of person you are interviewing with.

Questions to Ask an Internal Recruiter, Human Resources Representative, or Third-Party Internal "Screener"

Your plight in being interviewed by any one of these "interviewing" authorities could range anywhere from excellent to disastrous. I have experienced "screeners" who have run the professional gamut from the daughter of the president of a firm, who, home from college, was tasked with doing the initial screening for a controller, to experienced H.R. leaders who knew more about hiring than the hiring authority did (and should have been listened to more often).

Most of the time, if you are being interviewed by a person who does not have direct, personal responsibility for the job—i.e., the hiring authority— you are being interviewed by someone who is more concerned with how he or she appears as a screener than finding the best candidate. The tendency is to screen you out rather than screen you in.

These people have the responsibility to help identify the best candidate, but they rarely have enough intimate knowledge about the job and the hiring authority's real "pain" (i.e., need) to understand or know the gives and takes of the kind of person who could be hired. They have no real authority, just the responsibility. They screen candidates from a wish list that may be realistic or not, given to them by a hiring authority, or even worse, a hiring committee.

These people don't want to personally look bad to the people they are screening for, so they will try to screen for the "safest" candidate. They don't want to run the risk of looking inept. If a hiring authority, for instance, decides that he or she would like to have a candidate who has a degree, even though a degree may not be necessary, a screener without a lot of experience will eliminate an excellent candidate who can do the job but doesn't have a degree. Or when a hiring authority arbitrarily decides that he or she would like to get someone with five to ten years of experience, most screeners will eliminate a perfectly good candidate who only has three years of experience or one with fifteen years of experience because he or she doesn't "fit" what the hiring authority asked for.

Your mission is to get beyond the screener to the people who are they real decision makers. You need to sell yourself well enough as a quality candidate to get passed up the interviewing chain.

So, you really want to be careful if you are initially interviewed by a third-party screener.

You should ask many of the same questions that you would ask an external recruiter.

• **How long have you been here at the company**? If you get an answer like "fifteen years . . ." then you might be in really good hands. If you hear "fifteen days (or months)," unless you are a perfect candidate (and who is perfect?), you really have your work cut out for you. Good luck!

• **Why did you come to work here?** People love to talk about themselves. It is a great way to break the ice and get them to talk.

• **Why do you like working here?** Notice the metaphors. This question gets people to talk again and tells you about them. It gets the spotlight off of you.

Now ask all of the questions (from Chapter 13) that you would ask an external recruiter that make sense. Stay away from asking any questions that might put these people on the spot. Your goal is to get beyond these screeners and get interviewed by the hiring authority—the person with "pain." If you get the sense that the screener really doesn't know much about the job or the hiring authority or his or her job is to simply "check the boxes" on someone else's criteria page, don't embarrass the person by asking, "How many people on my level have you hired here?"

Likewise, if you are an accountant with twenty-five years of experience, and you are being interviewed by someone young enough to be your daughter who talks to you about getting her braces off, don't act paternalistic, egotistical, or superior. You have to get this person's support to get to the next level of interviews. In fact, you want to get the support of this screener, to not only promote you up the interviewing ladder, but to actually tell the hiring authority that you are the best candidate.

There is a real strong tendency to want to dismiss these screeners, especially if you have been looking for a job for a while, have been to umpteen interviews, have a ton of experience, and feel like you are being interviewed by a very inexperienced know-nothing intern. I have had some of my own candidates get up and walk out of the interview when they found out that they were going to be initially screened by an H.R. person. Bad move!

Don't let your frustration show. Interview well, just like your job depended on it. Gear your questions to ones that will sell you but also make the screener feel comfortable. If you ask, "What are my strengths relative to the job and the person doing the hiring?" and you get a blank stare, you know that questions like that aren't going to get you promoted to the next round.

Questions to Ask in a Telephone "Screening" Interview

No one, especially candidates, likes telephone screening interviews. They are one dimensional, and even the people who conduct them aren't thrilled. But they are very popular and lots of companies do them.

If you have to conduct a telephone interview, make sure you establish a few things. Conduct the interview on a land telephone line. Do it at a private place with no distractions. Never do it on a cell phone while you are driving. Be focused and be ready. In the next few pages, we'll discuss the questions you can ask to give you a better chance of getting a face-to-face interview.

Remember, you can't get enough information over the phone, especially in an initial telephone screen, to make a decision about the job. So, unless there is a total mismatch (i.e., there is 75% travel in the job and you can't do that), don't eliminate yourself from the interviewing process at this time. Get the face-to-face interview.

If the interviewer is a screener, reread the above section about questions to ask an internal recruiter, human resources representative, or third-party internal screener. He or she will usually have a list of standard questions to begin asking you. If you can, try to interject a question near the beginning of being questioned. Why? Because then you start asking questions, and when you ask the questions, you will begin to control the interview!

So, if the person interviewing you asks, "How many years of experience in our business do you have?" You ask, "Well, how many would be ideal for the job?" If the person answers you, then you ask, "Tell me, what kind of experience and background would be perfect for the job?" Once the person starts answering that kind of question, you keep asking questions and getting answers. The more information you get, the better you will be able to "customize" your experience when you restate to that person the information he or she wants in the light of your own background. Ask factual questions and be ready to sell the face-to-face interview. In fact, the overall question you want to ask in a telephone screen situation, is: When can we get together face to face?

Open-ended, factual questions that give you information by which you can sell the face-to-face interview is what you want to ask. Many of the questions to ask over a telephone interview are similar to those you'd ask of a screener. But, remember that a telephone interview is two-dimensional, so listen closely to how the interviewer responds.

• **What is your role in the interviewing process**? The answer tells you how much authority this person has.

• **Can you describe the ideal candidate?** If the screener reads it off to you, you know he or she doesn't know much about what he or she is doing. It might be difficult to tell over a phone interview whether the screener is reading, but you can usually tell by a change in his or her voice pattern.

• **Is this an addition or a replacement? Why?** If the person doesn't know, don't embarrass them. Just move on.

• **When would you like to fill the position**? Nonthreatening question and should be easy for the screener to answer.

• **Who will be doing the initial interviewing**? Again, you need to know, and it tells you who the next step is with.

Remember, after about 20 minutes, any telephone screening/interview begins to get old. So, about the time you sense it, say something like, "Based on what we have discussed, my experience and background fit well. When can we get together?"

If the interviewer/screener says, "Well, we will get back to you if we are interested." You now have the hiring authority's name, so call that person and state that you had a telephone conversation with _____. Tell that person that you fit what the company is looking for and you'd like to meet with him or her face to face.

If the telephone screener is the hiring authority, which happens 50% of the time, your questions can be a lot more professional and direct. You don't have to worry as much about embarrassing him or her with what he or she doesn't know.

Your goal is to still sell the face-to-face interview—the next step. But you can still have a good conversation on the telephone if you ask questions. Again, don't eliminate yourself over the phone. And again, when you ask questions, you control the interview.

In the next section, we will discuss initial interview questions you can ask that make you look good when the interviewer is the hiring authority. You can ask some of the same questions when you are on the phone with the hiring authority. The difference is that when you are on the phone, you will want to close for the face-to-face interview faster: "It sounds like we need to get together, face to face. Would tomorrow afternoon work for you?"

Questions to Ask When the Interviewer Is the Hiring Authority

Now we are getting somewhere. You are in front of someone with authority. Now the rubber really meets the road, and your ability to ask the right questions at the right time will make all the difference in the world.

Most interviewers start by asking the (dumb) question: "Tell me about yourself." If you do it right, you will come to the right time in the interview for you to start asking questions. See Chapter 5 for more details.

Remember to take notes during the interview. You are going to want to use the answers you get to sell yourself to the immediate hiring authority as well as to the people in the second and third round of interviews.

Begin by asking easy, nonthreatening questions:

• **How long have you been here?** This is a good question because people like to talk about themselves. It opens rapport. If the answer is something like, "a long time (i.e., five years or more), you are dealing with someone who ought to know the ropes. He has probably done lots of hiring for the company and has everyone's, including his higher up's, confidence and support. So, this person probably has a lot to say about the hiring decision. (Just because a person is a hiring authority, doesn't mean he or she has authority. Lots of hiring managers "screen" possible candidates, and their superiors really make the decisions. You can't assume anything.)

If the person says, "Well, I'm new here, been here six months." That is going to tell you something different than the above situation. Let's face it—a person who has been in the job for six months is just getting her feet on the ground. There is nothing inherently wrong with that. You just need to be aware that she may not know as much about the company as others, and some of your questions may not be able to be answered by this person.

• **What makes this a good company to work for?** This is another way of complimenting this hiring authority. Most aren't going to say, "Well, it isn't." You will probably get some insights that you will be able to feed back to not only this person, but to others you are interviewing with down the line. If you sense enthusiasm and excitement, you can do the same as you go through the interviewing cycle.

• **What was your background before you got here?** Again, this leads a person to talk about him- or herself. It also tells you about the person. If the answer is, "Look, sonny, I have no college education. I started out in the warehouse twenty-six years ago and came up the hard way. I know this company inside and out, and these people that want to come in and just change things because they read it in a book or got it in a class drive me crazy," you might want to underplay your brand new MBA from Columbia University. Simply take note of the story. Everyone has a story. The more analogies you can make with your story, the better you will be able to sell yourself.

• **How long have you been looking for a person?** There is a big difference between just starting to look for someone and "We have been looking for six months." You need to know the situation. It will lead to better questions. A company that has been interviewing for six months either doesn't have any "pain," they are looking for Superwoman (or man), or there are some problems . . . maybe big ones. Pay attention.

• **Are there any internal candidates?** You need to know this. There are usually internal candidates. So, why wasn't one hired? I have experienced many hiring situations over the years where external candidates were interviewed to simply satisfy the "Well, we looked outside the company and couldn't find anyone as qualified as the internal candidate we promoted" syndrome. After all your trouble to interview, you just might be the bridesmaid and were from the beginning.

• **How many candidates have you interviewed**? There is a big difference between "four or five" and "fifteen or sixteen." It isn't uncommon to hear companies say they have interviewed fifteen or sixteen. Some readily admit it and don't care. Some are embarrassed. The answer will lead to some of the next questions. A company that has interviewed fifteen or sixteen people either doesn't know what it wants, doesn't have much "pain," or is incredibly picky or stupid or both. It doesn't mean that you may not be "the one," but don't spend your first paycheck because you probably won't get hired.

• **What are you looking for that you haven't found in the candidates you have interviewed**? You might get a real sane answer like, "We did make an offer to one candidate, but he took another job." You might also get a less-than-sane answer like, "Well, we just haven't found the right chemistry," or "Well, there are five people who make the decision, and we can't agree on anyone" or "Well, I found three I liked but the boss nixed all of them."

Listen carefully to this answer. You may be treated the same way. I have seen situations, though, where, as in the last answer, the boss just got tired of saying "no" and approved the next candidate that made it to her or him. Also, what someone might say of other candidates, he will say of you. If every other candidate was a "jerk," "incompetent," "a fool," "not good enough," etc., you will likely be in the same category.

The answer to this question also may be the "magic bullet" that if you can prove you possess the right attributes, will win you the job.

• **Is this an addition or a replacement? What are the circumstances**? You already may have asked this question of a screener or during a telephone interview, but it's an important question. Really listen carefully to the answer here. If you hear, "Well, we gave the guy six months to get it right and he couldn't do it—and he was the third one in a year. We'll keep churning them until we get it right," you have a challenge ahead of you. If you hear, "We promoted the last two people out of the job," you will feel differently. If you hear, "Well, the job doesn't pay that well, so people leave it after two years or so," it may still be a good job for you, but likely you'll be there two years or so.

This is one of the best questions you can ask. It could give you real ammunition to help you sell yourself. For instance, if you hear "We wanted the person in the job to take more graduate courses so we could promote him, but he just wasn't motivated," you can sell your desire to further your education. Just listen and take notes. You may want to feed this information back to the hiring authorities.

• **What is the most difficult part of the job**? This might be a question you save for subsequent interviews, but if things are going well in the initial interview, it can be a great question.

The answer can "load your shotgun" so you can sell yourself better. It also can tell you the greatest challenge you may have with the job. An answer like, "It's working for me, and I have a real reputation to live up to . . . ha!" (don't laugh, I've heard it often) might give you the opportunity to mention that you have worked for some of the most demanding bosses. It might also tell you about the ego you are interviewing with. Or it might tell you to run away. If you hear, "It's keeping up with the accounting for nine different subsidiaries and getting the reports out on time," you will want to mention where you have done that kind of thing before.

Initial Interview Question Mistakes

One of the biggest initial interview mistakes people make is to ask questions that either put the hiring authority too much on the spot or ask questions that expose sensitive issues. A question like, "In doing my research, I noticed that you had to restate your company earnings the last year. Can you tell me what the circumstances were for that?" might be a good question and one you would want to know before you might take the job, but you don't want to ask a question like that in an initial interview. Or, something like, "I see the company has lost money and contracted the last two years. What happened?"

Stay away from uncomfortable questions like that, at least in the initial interview. It may show your business acumen but now is not the time. As you become a finalist for the position, or are offered the job, there will be plenty of time to ask these qualifying questions. In fact, most astute employers will expect you to ask them. But do it at the right time. And ask the right person. Asking a screening H.R. assistant about the company's involvement in a lawsuit isn't smart. Now, asking the V.P. of finance about that kind of thing as you are being offered the job might be a good idea. You need to know what you are getting into and how it will affect you.

Remember that your purpose for asking questions in an initial interview is to sell yourself to the next stage of the interviewing process. Don't qualify yourself out of what might be a good opportunity by asking too many of the wrong kind of questions in the initial interview.

You will notice that I don't recommend asking any "what's in it for me" questions in the initial interview. Questions like, "What kind of money is associated with this position?" are not good questions for an initial interview. Now, if money or benefits come up in the interview, go ahead and address them, but don't delve into them much at all. There will be plenty of time for that in subsequent interviews. You want to sell yourself to the top of the candidate stack. Once you are there, most everything else takes care of itself. If the money isn't right, you don't have to take the job.

Take notes, and as you go through the interviewing process you can get clarifications on things you don't understand. You don't have to know everything right now.

Final Question in the Initial Interview

The average initial interview lasts about one hour. I've been involved with employers who spent as little as five minutes and hired the person on the spot, and others who spent four hours in an initial interview, told the candidate she was perfect for the job, then neither of us ever heard from them. Your goal is not to eat the elephant all in one bite. You do it one bite at a time.

You want to sell yourself to the next interview. You are asking questions so that you can make yourself look better to the hiring authority. Any question that puts you in a position to sell yourself helps.

The final question you need to ask in an initial interview is: "What do I need to do to get the job?"

Yes, blunt and to the point. You can preface it with something like, "This is a great opportunity for both of us. I'm a great fit for your job. What do I need to do to get it?"

Forget the namby-pamby, weak questions like, "Well, what is the next step?" "Where do we go from here?" "When can I expect to hear from you?" Yuk! Terribly weak! You are supposed to be a decisive businessperson who can ask the cold, hard business questions. So, act like one! Ask the ultimate initial interviewing question.

Questions to Ask Related to Subsequent Interviews

The average interviewing cycle involves three to four interviews with decision makers (five, if you count screeners, H.R., etc.). The cycle usually includes an initial interview with the hiring authority, an interview with his or her superior, and, once in a while, depending on the level of position, that person's superior. (I have been involved with cycles that had as many as ten interviews and took six months.) Often there are committee interviews with three or more people at a time.

If you are promoted up the interview chain by the hiring authority, you now have the opportunity to ask tougher, more qualifying questions, while you sell yourself at the same time. There is still a delicate balance of selling yourself and getting information you may need to make a decision about the job, should you be offered it.

The first thing you need to do, once you get the word that you are moving up the chain is to ask the initial interviewer, probably the hiring authority these questions:

• What is the next person (or groups of persons) I will be interviewing with like? How old is he or she (i.e., what generation in the workforce?) Get the person to describe the role and personality of the next interviewer or group. Try to get him or her to tell you everything he or she knows. If you hear something like, "Well, my boss has been my boss for ten years and he and I think alike," you know the hiring authority will have most of the decision power. If you hear, "My boss is new to the company. This is the first position we have worked on together," you aren't sure if the hiring authority will have a lot of input or not.

• What is his or her role in the company? What is his or her role in the interviewing process? It is the second part of this question you want to really listen to. The hiring authority might say something like, "I send people to him with no comments. He interviews them, then we get together and talk about it." Or she might say, "My boss simply 'kicks the tires' just so we have two people talk to you. I'm really the decision maker."

Don't trust this last comment. If the superior couldn't say "no" to any candidate, he or she wouldn't be interviewing you. I can't tell you the number of candidates over the years who believed this, and thought since they had such a good interview with the hiring authority, they were a cinch for the job. Wrong! So, be careful of the "tire kicking" line. No superior simply "kicks tires." There is a reason he or she is in the interviewing cycle.

So you have to sell yourself just as hard as you have done before. Take nothing for granted. Keep asking the questions below.

• How involved is this person (or group) in the day-to-day function of the job? Whether the person is fairly removed from the day-to-day function of the job you are interviewing for or very present in your possible day-to-day functions will make a difference in his or her interviewing you.

• How has he or she felt about other candidates that you have sent? You'll find out if you are the first or one of many.

• **Does he or she usually agree with your opinions?** Rarely are you ever going to hear a hiring authority claim that his or her superiors never agree with him or her. Don't ever believe a hiring authority if he tells you that his superiors always agree with them. It is more reasonable to hear the hiring authority say something like, "Most of the time, they do."

You might want to get into a conversation about what the hiring authority and his superiors may or may not agree about. This will give you insights into the relationship between the hiring authority and his or her superiors.

• **What is this person going to like or dislike about my experience or background?** Try to make the hiring authority tell you where your strengths or weaknesses might be in the eyes of the next interviewing authority. You will be surprised what you might learn.

• **What have you told him or her about me?** Sometimes a hiring authority will only send one or two people to a superior. Sometimes she will tell the superior who she thinks will do the best job, sometimes she doesn't. You need to know what she has told the superior so you know how you stand.

• **How many people is this person going to interview**? Are you one of three or ten? It makes a big difference. It doesn't hurt to ask what succession you are in the interview lineup. If you are the first of three, there is a tendency for you to be the one to "set the bar." If you are the third of ten, you may not be remembered. You are going to have to do a lot of active follow-up to be remembered.

• **When will this person get back to you with feedback**? Most people assume that the person or persons who do the second interviews will get "right back" to the hiring authority. Wrong! Don't be surprised if you hear, "Well, she is going on vacation next week for a week and will get back to me when she gets back." Not good news. You will have a tendency to think the feedback will be immediate.

• **How do you stack/rank the candidates? Am I your strongest one? Are you going to recommend me as the best candidate to your superior?** This is a great question and really tests how you are doing. Most hiring authorities will be taken aback a bit at your boldness. But this is a great test of where you stand. And, after all, you need to know. Listen carefully to what the hiring authority says. If he or she says that you are one of many that is talking to the superior and that he or she does not really have a favorite, then you need to be on your guard. It is likely that you are simply one of a number of people that the hiring authority is sending up a ladder. It is not likely that you are considered by him or her to be the strongest candidate.

If the hiring authority says something like, "Well, I have two candidates that I think can do the job, and you are one of them," then you know where you stand.

Sometimes, hiring authorities will simply try to find two or three candidates that can do the job, send them to their superior get this superior's blessing, then choose one. Most of the time, however, the hiring authority has one or two favorites in the group. If he has a long-standing relationship with the superior, he will probably tell his superior whom he likes best. But you will never know this. So, it is best not to take any chances. Ask the hard question of, "Where do I stand with you and are you going to tell your superior that I'm the best candidate?"

Unless the hiring authority says that you are his strongest candidate, then you need to ask a question along the lines of, "What do I need to do to become the strongest candidate?" and then shut up. A confident hiring authority will be very impressed with your courage to ask these difficult but telling questions.

How This Affects You

Remember that your purpose and goal of an initial interview is to get to the second and subsequent interviews. You want to be sure that the questions you ask "position" you at the top of the list. Every question you ask should not only give you information you can use later to decide if you will take the job, but also demonstrate your intelligence. If you ask intelligent questions, you will know how to sell yourself "up" the interviewing ladder.

Chapter

15 Questions to Ask Yourself After Each Interview

....

You need to ask yourself questions about how each interview went right after each interview. Take notes every time. You will need to refer to these notes before each follow-up interview with the company. Please don't try to rely on your memory. Hopefully, you will have so many opportunities you are pursuing that you will get confused about which one is which if you don't take good notes.

So, right when you get to your car, after the interview, jot down your immediate impressions of the interview and how you did. When you get to your desk, ask yourself these questions:

- Who did I interview with? Is she a real decision maker or an intermediary?

- What was her position?

- Did I make a "connection" with her?

- What are the most important things the interviewer was interested in finding out?

- Did I communicate those well enough?

- Who is the real decision maker?

- What are the names and titles of all of the people I talked to today?

- How much input does each person I talked to have in the decision?

- What was the job I was interviewing for?
- What seemed to be the two or three most important requirements of the job?
- Can I do the job?
- In light of the job requirements, what are my most unique attributes?
- Was I clear about my unique features, advantages, and benefits?
- Was my presentation clear, concise, and smooth?
- What questions could I have answered better?
- Could I have asked better questions?
- Do I have a clear understanding of the job?
- Did I ask for the job like I should have?
- Did the interviewer(s) like me personally?
- If I am in the shoes of the interviewing authority(ies), how did I do?
- From their point of view, what are my greatest strengths?
- If I interviewed with more than one person, with whom did I "connect" the best and who is most likely to support me beyond this interview?
- From this person's point of view, what are my most prominent weaknesses (objections to hiring me)?
- How would I overcome them in subsequent interviews?
- Who else did I meet, office administrators, potential peers, etc?
- Based on this interview, what are the risks in hiring me?
- Am I clear about the next steps in the process?
- What can I do now to further my candidacy?
- What aspects of my experience or background should I emphasize in a follow-up email to the interviewing authority?
- Based on what I know and feel, will I be invited back for subsequent interviews?
- Do I know the interviewing and hiring process?
- What are the next steps and what can I do to move them along sooner rather than later?

- Do I know who else I will interview with next, if I am called back?
- The grade I would give myself on the interview based on a scale of 100% _____.
- If put in percentages, my odds of moving to the next step in the interviewing process are _____%.
- Put in percentages, my odds of getting this job offer is _____%.

Summary: _____

_____

_____

_____

_____

Answering all of these questions at the time right after the interview will give you a great idea of exactly how you stand and what you need to do next to get the job.

Chapter

16 Questions to Ask in Interviews Beyond the Initial Interview

•••

I have often referred to these interviews as the "second season." They are like the playoffs in sports. It is really time to bring your A+ game. Win or go home! It's that simple.

These kinds of interviews can be anywhere from a short, casual interview with the hiring authority's boss, to an elaborate, all-day meeting with "corporate" people (my candidates have experienced as many as nine individual interviews in one day). If you asked the right questions of the hiring authority, you will know what to expect. But never take for granted any information you may get.

I have seen many hiring authorities totally underestimate the process beyond them. Keep in mind you are dealing with people and things change. When you are ready for one thing, you will get something else. Just be prepared.

Normally, interviews beyond the initial interview with the hiring authority at the most will be two. Most of the time it will be with the hiring authority's superior. Sometimes, you may go beyond that to the superior's boss.

The kind of questions you will ask each of these people will be similar. Just remember that the further removed the person is from the day-to-day function of the job, the less he or she may know about it. This is especially true if the superior or his or her superior is in a distant office or new to the company, etc.

Again, if you asked the right questions, you will have an idea of the situation. Keep in mind that you are still selling yourself up the interviewing ladder.

We will cover one-on-one interviews first, because they are the most predominant in the interviewing process. I will address peer and group interviews at the end of this chapter. They can be very treacherous if you aren't ready for them. Fortunately, they don't happen as much.

Once you have completed most of the interview with the superior, you will want to ask many of the same questions you asked the hiring authority.

Questions to Ask in One-on-One Interviews

• **What do you think are the most difficult aspects of the job I'm interviewing for?** Be ready to hear something that you did not hear from the hiring authority. If you do, you may have to alter the way you sell yourself to this person. If you hear relatively the same thing you heard from the hiring authority, then you can present your features, advantages, and benefits to this person, assuring him that you can deal with the job.

• **What has been the most difficult challenge in finding the right candidate?** See if this is consistent with the hiring authority's answer. Listen well. Again, you may need to alter your presentation of yourself.

• **How many candidates have you interviewed?** Good to know the number. See if it jives with what the hiring authority told you. If the hiring authority told you there were three candidates and this person tells you there are five or six, you will want to follow up by asking, "Well, (hiring authority) stated there were only three. How has it changed?" Then shut up and listen. You have asked a rather uncomfortable question for this person. You're saying, "Wait a minute. Was I not told the truth?" You demonstrate courage.

• **Is there anything in my background or experience that needs to be clarified?** As in previous interviews, people will act like they know what you are talking about, then, later on, not be sure. This gives the person the opportunity to ask for clarification if it is needed.

• **I understand that the company is considering a merger (acquisition, buyout, etc.). How do you think it will affect the company?** If there is a glaring "elephant in the room" type of issue that is going on with the company, like a merger, buyout, downsizing, etc., that you feel it is appropriate to ask about, now is the time to do it. This is a real balancing act. You have to decide what is best to do. On the one hand, you don't want to bring up difficult issues for the company you are interviewing with. But on the other hand, you don't want to appear stupid by not acknowledging an issue like this and asking about it.

So, my suggestion is that if the issue is common knowledge in the company and has been brought up in the interviewing cycle as something that might impact the company and therefore your job, you might ask. If it is a sensitive issue like a class action lawsuit, or bad publicity, though, don't touch it.

Don't ask, "How will the merger (or buyout or downsizing, etc.) affect this job?" It is too obvious that you are more concerned about yourself. Whatever the event is, if it is going to impact you and the opportunity, you will hear it then. Keep in mind that if there are any serious problems like this that you will really need to know about before you take the job, if offered, you can ask them at the time of the offer. In fact, as you will see, that is when you are going to really qualify the opportunity and ask every question you ever needed to know.

Too often, candidates ask hard qualifying questions too early in the interview process and make bad judgments about an opportunity because they don't wait until they are "at the altar" ready to get hired. I have seen numerous impending events that would appear to be "bad" actually work well for a candidate. I recently placed a regional manager who was concerned about my client company's pending merger. Whereas all of the other candidates were scared off by it, he took the job with a written agreement that, if the merger took place, his 50,000 shares of stock that came with the offer (to be given him over four years) would be immediately vested. So, he got a good job, and if the company merged, he'd get a very good "bonus."

• **Based on our interview, do you have any concerns about my ability to do the job?** This will be a personal view of your experience and background. If you hear "Yes," then you need to ask, "What are the concerns?" Find out what the concerns are and be prepared to sell yourself. Write them down in a businesslike manner, then counter them.

If you hear "No" then you need to ask, "Are you going to recommend to (hiring authority) that he or she should hire me?" This is the kind of bold question most candidates don't have the guts to ask. You are going to know exactly where you stand when you ask this question.

If you get confirmation that you'll be recommended to the hiring authority, then you need to say, "Great, I will call him or her today to arrange a time we can get together and hammer out the details." This doesn't mean you are going to get the job by any means. What it usually means is that this interviewing authority can live with your getting the job. It is one more small step to getting an offer. Exactly what you want!

If, though, you hear, "Well, it isn't really my decision. I just give a 'go or no go' opinion. It is (hiring authority's) decision," then it is absolutely a must that you say, "Look, Mr. or Ms. _____, I wouldn't be talking to you if your opinion wasn't really important. Mr. or Ms. (hiring authority) thinks very highly of you. Are you going to support my candidacy and tell (hiring authority) to hire me?" This is bold and takes courage, but you might as well know now what this person thinks of you. Best case, she tells you she will tell the hiring authority to hire you. If she hesitates and goes back to her first statement, you should probably assume that you aren't the number one candidate in the eyes of this person. It doesn't mean that you won't get the job. It does mean that you don't have a strong endorsement from this person. You may not be totally out, but you aren't a sure bet either.

• What is the next step in this process? This question is useless unless you have asked the two or three questions above. Many candidates ask this as though it were a "closing" question. As far as closing goes, though, it is very, very weak. But if you have asked the other hard questions, this becomes an informational one.

You might become surprised at the answer to this. Don't be surprised if you hear that there are two or three more steps in the process that you weren't expecting. Surprises like, "Well, we are in our 'quiet period' before going public," or, "I'm getting a new boss, and we don't want to hire anyone until he gets into the job," might come out, but at least you'll have a better picture of where things stand.

There may be other pertinent questions specific to the company or the job that you may want to ask this interviewing authority. Just remember to keep them in the realm of "selling yourself" questions, rather than "qualifying questions."

You can take all the information you get in all of these kinds of interviews and ask everything you need to in the final interviews. Remember, get to the altar first, then you can qualify as much as you want before you say, "I do."

Questions to Ask in Interviews with Potential Peers

Many companies, as part of the interviewing process beyond the initial interview, will have you in for interviews with the "team." The idea here is to get the group you might be working with to talk to you. Hiring authorities will tell you that it is a chance to get to know everyone for your sake. Don't buy this at all. This is an interviewing situation and these potential peers can nix you big time.

I can't tell you the number of times I have seen candidates who think that these are nice social events so that they can get to know everyone they might be working with find out that, after the event, a "vote" is taken on their candidacy and they lost. Every meeting with anyone at any company that you might be interviewing with is a "formal" interview, no matter what anyone says.

These peers are going to give an opinion about you to the hiring authority. Their opinion counts, no matter what you are told. They can't hire you, but they can sure tell the hiring authority not to hire you. They won't say totally negative things like, "Don't hire that person. He or she isn't qualified." It will be comments like, "Well, I'm not sure this person would fit in the group," or "I didn't really get a good feeling about that candidate. I don't know why, but I just didn't."

Very few hiring authorities are going to hire you if most of the people on the team don't want you on board. The last thing a hiring authority wants is someone who might change the chemistry of the group she already has. So, be ready, this series of interviews is like all the rest: serious.

In fact, if you do this right, you may find out some things about the job or the hiring authority that no one wants to tell you. Once in a while, these peers will give you the "real deal" information about the job or the hiring authority. Just pay attention.

If these peer interviews are in a group, like a lunch or semisocial event, keep your questions light. Let the group or the individual you are with take the lead. They may begin by asking you about yourself. If they do, remember you are still interviewing and you need to be selling yourself. Remember that you need to ask good questions, too. You need to let the individual or the group feel important.

A recent Department of Labor study, reported by *Trends* (June 2007), found that one out of every four workers today is working for a company for whom they have been employed less than one year. More than one out of two is working for a company for whom they have worked less than five years. So you have to be aware that many of the people who are "interviewing" you haven't been with the company that long.

• **How long have you (or you all) been with the company? What was your background before you got here?** The major reason this is a good question in the potential peer interview is that it gets people to talking about themselves, and they love to do that. There is going to be, whether you like it or not, an implied "we are judging you" on the part of these peers. The best way to not make a mistake is to say as little as you can without being stupid. Simple, one-word answers, like "yes," "no," or "maybe" don't work well in an interviewing situation. Getting people to talk about themselves keeps the spotlight off of you.

If you find similar backgrounds, values, or experiences that you can identify with, make a note and bring them up in future interviews. Companies often hire people with the same cultural values almost subconsciously. People like people like themselves. So, if you discover issues like this and they are compatible with yours, you can use it to your advantage.

• **What is it like to work here?** Watch for metaphors and analogies. See if all team members are consistent with what they tell you. But don't be alarmed by the answers. It is going to be different for most folks. However, if everyone says it's like a gulag and the boss reminds them of Hitler, take note.

• **What are the most difficult aspects of working here or the job itself?** Again, this question gets others to talk. You may be amused at the answers. Take what they say into account, but don't judge the job based on what they say. I have been involved in hiring situations where the peers really didn't want anyone else on the team or in the group. The hiring authority did, but they didn't. There may be all kinds of reasons for this, but it can happen. For example, the group of salespeople may have to each sacrifice some clients or territory to help get a new person started, and they may not want to make that sacrifice, because it may cost them sales or commissions. Just be perceptive. Pay attention and listen carefully.

• **How many people have you interviewed for this job?** This is a great question for potential peers. Most hiring authorities aren't going to waste a lot of their subordinates' time having them interview people they probably won't hire. Sometimes, though, companies set up a procedure involving peers as part of their interviewing process. Nonetheless, the answer to this question will tell you volumes about the situation. Potential peers will be a lot more honest with you than a hiring authority or his or her superiors.

• **Why haven't they hired anyone yet?** Only ask this if you get the sense from the hiring authority or his or her superior that they have been interviewing for a while. Potential peers will be more open about answering this question honestly than the interviewing authorities. Don't be surprised if you hear, "Well, they offered the job to two people who turned it down. Then they rethought the criteria, and you are the third one I (we) have talked to." And, the hiring authority told you that you were the only one they were interviewing! Liars!

• **Why did you get hired here? What did you do to get the job?** You only want to ask these questions if you really start "bonding" with your potential peers. You want to get them to help you get the job. You will be amazed at how much they can help you and coach you through the process.

Questions to Ask in a Group Interview Beyond the Initial Interview

This is a situation when you are paraded into a room with four or five people in a conference room. The idea here is to save time and have a bunch of people interview at once. This situation can be treacherous. Suffice it to say that this situation may be more than an interview. It can be a political game and you might be the pawn in a one-upsmanship game.

There is not much you can do about this scenario except to do your best. You will normally give a presentation about yourself, be asked a few questions, and then, maybe, be given the opportunity to ask questions yourself.

This is a bit tricky, but experience has taught me that you don't have to be compelled to ask questions here. If you don't ask questions in the one-on-one interviews, you probably won't get hired. But the group interview setting is different. Asked if you have any questions, you might say, "Most of the questions I have had have been answered by (hiring authority). The others I have would be best in a one-on-one conversation."

If you think it is smart to ask questions in this situation, and it will make you look better as a candidate, ask nonthreatening questions that are not personal. Asking five people, "Why do you like working here?" won't be good. Generic questions that show you have done your homework are good. Some examples:

- I learned that your competitor is coming out with a new product to take away market share from you. Are there plans to counter that effort?
- You all have a high customer satisfaction rating. What has been the key to that?
- In talking (interviewing) with your competitors, they say (something really positive) about your company. How have you managed to get the competition to feel that way?
- I noticed in your annual report that profits were up 25% over last year. What is the major contributor to that?
- What are the major business issues that keep you awake at night?

This is one of the best "group" of interview questions you can ask. It makes people go inside themselves and think about the answer. I guarantee you, not one in a hundred candidates is going to be as perceptive and wise as to ask this question. The answers you get from the group will create an atmosphere of a conversation rather than an interview.

You can think of many more when the situation arises. Notice that all of these are positive questions that force fairly positive answers. I wouldn't recommend that you bring up anything negative in a group setting. It is too easy for people to get defensive, not only with you, but with each other. The last way to get hired is to start a small civil skirmish. So, something like, "I noticed that you have lost money the last three years and your debt to equity ratio is way out of kilter. What's up with that?" is not a smart question.

If the group you are interviewing with is only two or three people, you can be less careful about what you ask. Two or three people is more intimate and personal. When the group gets bigger than that, there is a totally different dynamic. Two or three people in a group is intimate enough for you to ask the same kind of questions that you might ask an individual.

If the group is larger than three people, a "political" dynamic takes over. Each interviewer is not only trying to interview you but also trying to show his or her peers how smart he or she is. You may be a person in a group ego game. If this happens, ask broad, general questions that are safe to answer. Asking why the sales department didn't perform well is not smart—it gives other departments room to criticize the sales department. Questions around such topics as "What does the future hold for the company?" "What kind of growth might be expected?" fit better.

Questions to Ask in a "Marathon" Interview Session

Marathon interview sessions are where you are shuffled from one interviewing authority to another. Most of the people you will talk to in a marathon interview setting won't have much to do with the job you are interviewing for. Sometimes they are in the loop of the interview process just so the company can look like it has a thorough interviewing process.

These people may not have a lot of responsibility in the job you are interviewing for, but their big impact on you is that they can say "no" to your being hired. So, you had better make a good impression on them. I have experienced numerous situations over the years where candidates took these interviews for granted because they were with people that had absolutely nothing to do with the job, only to find out that these people nixed their candidacy.

Sometimes the interviewing authorities in the marathon are simply asked to talk to you so it won't look like you were dragged to these "important" interviews to only talk to two people. I assure you that at least half of the people you will "interview" with could probably care less about you or the job you are interviewing for. They will never admit it, but that is the case. So, catch on! If they are going to interview you, they have to have an opinion. If they have an opinion, they will be asked about it. So, you had better make a good impression.

Be ready for some of the people you are supposed to talk with, to, all of a sudden, not be available. Be ready to wait longer than you should for some and end up only meeting a very short time with others. This type of marathons start, stop, get stalled, etc. The time you have with each interviewing authority will dictate how many questions you might be able to ask. As before, you will want to have more questions than you will probably need. The *most important* question that you have to ask *every* interviewing authority in the marathon is: Are you going to support my getting the job?

You absolutely have to ask this as a final question of every interviewing authority you talk to. No matter how insignificant you might think any person is in the decision-making process, you have to ask him or her this question.

You can ask other questions of these people, very much like the ones in the preceding scenarios. Questions about the person that get him talking about himself, his opinion about the biggest challenges in the job (providing he is close enough to the job to really know), challenges in the company, etc., are all appropriate.

The most important thing you can do in these interviews is to get your interviewers to commit that they will recommend you for the job. You haven't done your job in the interview unless you get this question answered affirmatively.

You may not get much time with some of these people. Don't be surprised if you are told you will meet with some of these people for an hour or so, and find out that they can only give you fifteen minutes. So, you sometimes need to sell yourself quickly.

• Mr. or Ms. (interviewing authority), you are obviously respected by your company. I wouldn't be here if they didn't value your opinion. Is there anything in my background or experience I may need to clarify? If you get hesitation when you ask the question "Are you going to support me," or the person says something like, "Well, I don't know . . . it really isn't up to me . . . it is up to (hiring authority)," or the person says, "Well, we will get together and discuss it." You need to state, in a question form, "You obviously have a hesitation, can you tell me what it is?" If the answer is "yes," then ask the obvious question, "What might I need to clarify?" If the answer is "no," then ask, "What concerns might you have in recommending me?" Most of the time, there won't be any. Some people don't want to commit to you. It isn't that they don't like you. It is that they just don't think they should without the rest of the committee. If they say there are not any concerns, then you can ask the same question another way: "Do you see any reason that you wouldn't recommend I be hired?"

Unless this person simply doesn't like you and totally won't support you, she will likely tell you that she will support you. This doesn't mean by any stretch of the imagination that you are going to get the offer, but this question to each interviewing authority will, at least, keep him or her from standing in your way 95% of the time.

Most good managers—and the higher up the ladder you go, the better—will really appreciate your courage to ask the tough questions. This question puts it all on the line. It doesn't force, but certainly nudges, these decision makers to lean toward recommending you to the hiring authority.

Ninety-nine percent of the candidates you might compete with won't have the courage to ask these questions of every interviewing authority. They will say stupid things like, "Where do we go from here?" "Who else do I need to talk to?" "What do you think?" etc. Soft and namby-pamby! Not a decisive businessperson's approach.

17 Questions You Can Ask at the Time of an Offer

· ·

There is no time in the interviewing process that you will ask more questions than now. Remember that we advised you to hold off on some of the tougher, qualifying questions until you get an offer, lest you be perceived as having a "what's-in-it-for-me" mentality. All those qualifying questions that you were tempted to ask during the interviewing process, all those "what can you do for me" questions that you were disciplined enough to avoid, are all going to get answered now.

If I haven't made it clear, let me state it one more time: Your purpose in the interviewing process is to sell yourself into getting a job offer. If you get a company and the individuals in it to want you badly enough, they will do everything they can to try to hire you. The more they are convinced that you can do a better job than anyone else, the more they will satisfy you with answers for every question you can ask.

When people want to hire you, they want you as comfortable as possible with the company, the people, and the position. Once you are at this point, you can start really deciding if the job is right for you.

The first group of questions you will want to ask are of the hiring authority. The second group will be of yourself. They are simple but very profound and will make a difference in your career.

Questions to Ask the Hiring Authority at the Time of an Offer

Most companies in the United States have the direct hiring authority, the person with the "pain," make the formal job offer. When you get that call from the hiring authority, you know you have done your job right so far.

Unless you are in a distant city or have absolutely no questions about the job opportunity, you can listen to the offer over the phone. But 98% of the time, you want to say, "I'm excited about this opportunity. When can we get together face to face to discuss the details?"

Up until now you have been outright selling yourself and telling this person and the company that you were right for the job. It is now your turn to find out if the job is right for you. And now is the time to do it.

You need to be sure that you have as clear an understanding about most of the aspects of the job before you decide about it. Just because you have been selling yourself into the job, to this point, doesn't mean you will take the job. Don't worry about that yet.

If you didn't have a reasonable interest in the job, you wouldn't have made it this far. So, now it is your turn. Set an appointment with the hiring authority. Write down every question you need answered. Don't all of a sudden be coy. Keep your enthusiasm up and be excited. Don't play silly games and say to yourself, "Well, if I say or do this, they will say or do that, so I'll do this and they'll do that," etc.

You have to approach the offer stage in a "we are all in this together" manner. This is not an adversarial situation. Your taking a job offer has to be a win-win for everyone. Too often candidates approach a job offer with the idea that "they are going to try to give me as little as they can, so I have to try to get as much as I can" attitude. Bad business! If a company has made you feel like it is you vs. them in the hiring process, you probably shouldn't go to work there.

Now that we have laid the groundwork, get a face-to-face appointment with the hiring authority. If, for some reason, and it does happen with some firms, the formal offer is made by the H.R. department, tell the person who calls you that you want to meet with the hiring authority before you make a commitment.

If the hiring authority calls and expects you to commit to the job over the phone, don't alarm him or her by saying, "Whoa! Wait a minute. I have a ton of questions and I don't even know if I will even consider taking your job." He or she may simply hang up on you and call the next candidate. Again, say that you are excited and you want to meet face to face. We all know that phone conversations and (especially) e-mail conversations are one-dimensional. It's impossible to read or appreciate body language over the phone, and e-mails are emotionless. Hiring is still a personal, emotional endeavor. Accepting a job is personal. You need to know as much as you can about the facts and feelings of a job offer. Do it face to face!

If you have sold yourself like you should have, the hiring authority wants to answer all of the questions you may have. He or she wants a win-win deal, too. You have no obligation to tell him or her that you aren't sure about taking the job anywhere along the line. You have nothing to decide about until you have an offer. Don't think that because you were selling yourself hard that you are implying that you are going to take the job. You never promised that you would accept their job any more than the company promised you it was going to hire you.

• **I understand we are here to discuss an offer, correct?** Make sure you have a clear understanding that you are meeting to discuss an offer. I have had a number of situations over the years where the candidate as well as I thought that the final offer was being made at this meeting and it wasn't. So, simply ask if you are unsure. Most of the time, you will be correct. But this will clear up any doubt. As the hiring authority begins the meeting to make an offer, he or she will probably say, "Before we get to the nitty-gritty, do you have any questions?" Your answer is, "Yes." And, during this meeting, just as with the others, take notes! You may have to review them before you make a decision about the job.

• **What are your professional and personal expectations of me?** If you don't already know, you certainly want to—and need to at this point. Don't be surprised if you hear some aspects of the job that you don't recall hearing before. Often, in the interviewing process, assumptions are made by both parties. Because you have been focused on selling yourself pretty hard, you now want to be sure you totally understand the expectations.

• **Please describe the working environment.** The interviewing process probably gave you a really good feel for this, but you want to hear it. Pay special attention to the metaphors and analogies you will hear.

• **What is your management style?** Listen to the metaphors again. Remember, on average, you have probably only spent one or two hours with this person in a rather contrived atmosphere. You want to listen to see that what you hear is consistent with what you saw or experienced.

I should mention here one of the hundreds of lessons I've learned about employment since I started in this business in 1973. I'd never recommend taking a job strictly because you like the boss and you want to work for him or her. Often, candidates are so impressed with the hiring authority that they confuse liking the person with liking the job and want to take a job because of whom they would be working for.

Now I'm not saying that you shouldn't consider whom you are going to work for in the process of evaluating a job. Whom you work for is crucial to your success. But, with the transient business environment today, your boss could be here today and gone tomorrow. (By the way, it's the same with you.) Just don't take a job exclusively because of the hiring authority.

Make your possible future boss a part of the decision. Go to work for someone you can hopefully learn from. But ask yourself, "Would this be a good job if this person weren't here?" It may change how you feel about the job, but in this day and age, you can't assume anyone is going to be anywhere for any length of time.

• **What is the management style of your boss and the company?** If you hear, "Well, my boss is totally different than me. He's a real piece of work," or, "This company is pretty tyrannical, but we operate differently in this group," you'll get one impression. If you hear, "It's pretty consistent with my style here," you will get another impression. You just need to know.

• **What are your personal plans with the company?** By throwing in some personal questions now and then, you create a conversational environment, rather than an interview environment. "We are all in this together" becomes more real when you ask about personal futures.

• **How would you describe the philosophy of the company as well as your personal philosophy?** You may have already gotten a picture of both of these in the interviewing process, but it doesn't hurt to ask again to see if you get consistency. Some people and companies say one thing and act differently (duh!). So, just listen. You don't have to agree with everyone's philosophy, but you do have to feel compatible with it. If the hiring authority says something like, "Well, the company is committed to the good of mankind, but I'm here for the money," it doesn't mean he or she is a bad person or it is a bad job. You just need to know.

• **How would you describe the culture and values of the company?** If you hear, "Well, we work hard and party hard," and you are the kind of person who doesn't, you may not "fit in." If you hear, "We are here for the money, and that is all we care about," and you have a great passion for growing as a person and not worrying that much about the money, you might want to delve deeper to see if you can live with this approach.

If you are young and single and expect a social life with the people you work with and you hear, "We are very family oriented here. Most of us are grandparents. We work hard, but don't socialize with each other outside of work," this job may not be a source of social relationships. But, as I discussed in a previous chapter, companies are much more multigenerational than they used to be. You just need to know.

Culture can be a difficult issue. I once placed a fellow who was Jewish. I didn't know that at the time, but he called me seven months after he was on the job. I had placed him with a company that described its "culture" as Christian. It was a good company and a good job for him, so I placed him there. The problem was that people there turned out to be evangelicals and kept trying to convert both him and his wife to Christianity. He got so fed up and uncomfortable with the constant barrage of Bible verses and witnessing that he wanted to leave, and he did. So, company culture can make a big difference.

• **How would you describe my potential peers?** It is good to get an idea of what the boss thinks of all of the people you will be working with. Listen to the metaphors and analogies. I once asked a hiring authority how many people he had working for him and he replied, "'bout half of 'em." If your potential boss describes your potential peers as "slugs," "lazy," "less than competent," or "brilliant," "wonderful," "great," he or she will probably say the same thing about you someday soon if you take the job.

• **If I were to accept this offer, what can I do when I start to be most effective and contribute to alleviating your biggest problem?** Potential employers love to hear this kind of question. It states that you really are concerned about what you can do for them. Therefore, when you are considering an offer, i.e., what the company might be able to do for you, you're saying that you are concerned about what you can do for the company. In other words, keep selling!

• **What is the percentage of turnover in the company?** Do not be surprised if your hiring authority does not really know. The only time your hiring authority is really going to know this is if the turnover in the company is very high. If you find out that the turnover is very high by asking this question, the hiring authority will automatically explain to you why. The reason may make a big difference as to whether you take the job. You would be shocked at the number of times candidates never even think to ask this question.

• **What is the turnover in this department?** Again, you certainly want to find this out. If there is a great deal of turnover, the hiring authority will automatically give you the reasons why. I've known hiring authorities to actually say something like, "Well, some people think I'm very difficult to work for."

The answer to this question may or may not make a difference in your taking the job. However, you at least need to know what you're getting into.

• **How often is the turnover in the job I'm discussing with you?** You may already know this from the interviewing process, but you might want to confirm it. If it seems higher than normal, it is fair to ask "Why?" If the answer is, "We promote out of this position often," it is one thing. If it is, "We can't find anyone to do the job right," you may want to ask more questions.

• **What are the major problems facing the company and this department?** Notice if this is consistent with what you have heard before. Often, in the final stages of the interviewing process, a hiring authority may "come clean" with you about issues in the company or the department that no one wanted to mention before. Up until now they didn't want to discourage you as a candidate, but now they don't want you shocked at some issue the first day you show up for the job.

• **What are the traits you see in me that are good for this job and made you want to hire me?** You need to know how you are perceived.

• **Based on what you know of me, what might my weaknesses be in light of this job?** Ditto to the last answer. Neither one of these answers may be reality. The perception of you and how you really are once you are on the job will be different. You just want to know what the expectations are. Don't worry about the weaknesses, we all have them. Again, you want to get an idea of expectations.

• **Why do you want to hire me? What did I demonstrate to you that the other candidates didn't?** Really listen to this answer. You might have assumed, up until now, why you were being offered the job. You will also learn what you might have done to outdistance the other candidates. This information may come in handy if you need to negotiate regarding salary, benefits, etc. when the time is right. If you ask this question and the answer is, "Well, we had three finalists, any one of you could do the job. I just like you a little better," you may not have much leverage when it is time to negotiate. If you hear, "We looked for six months, could only find two of you that could do the job, and the other person took a job last week. We are exhausted and tired of looking, and we are so glad you are here," you may have some real negotiating strength.

• **Why didn't you hire from within?** You probably already know the answer, but it doesn't hurt to ask again, now that things are getting serious. Don't be surprised if you hear, "We sure came close to promoting from within, and if we don't work things out with you, that is what we might do." A little of your leverage just slipped away.

• **What aspects of the job or the company am I going to be surprised about?** A smile will come across the face of the hiring authority. He or she will think a minute and then either drop a bomb on you with a fact or information that will probably shock you. Or he or she will say something like, "What a nice person I am."

• **What are the worst aspects of the job?** These issues were mentioned somewhere in the interviewing process, but now that things are getting serious you need to make sure you know them.

• **Is the company planning any layoffs or downsizings?** This will be a simple "No" or "Not that I know of," or "Oh, yeah, we go through that every year or so." If you get a funny feeling when you get this answer, be bold and ask, "If there were layoffs or when they come, how will it affect this job?" It is obvious that no one is going to intentionally go to the trouble of hiring any-one and then lay him or her off soon after hiring. But I have seen it . . . even been involved in providing candidates where it happened. They were hired and within a month or so laid off. No one can predict these things . . . or at least will never admit to it.

As mentioned in previous chapters, the business environment is more er-ratic than it has ever been. Your new job is going to only last 2.5 to 3 years any-how. Even if there is a concern about layoffs, the opportunity may be worth the risk.

• **How will my success be measured in this job?** Listen up! You need to know exactly how your success will be measured. If you are in sales, it is ob-vious that you will be measured by the sales you make and the quotas you at-tain. But success in other professional positions is not quite as easy to measure. Also know if and how this measurement will be reflected in salary reviews. Get specifics and write them down. No one will feel more stupid than you if you take a job and get surprised by the way performance and salary reviews are practiced.

• **How is your performance measured? How often? How does that re-late to the job I'm considering?** You may be shocked to find many firms have no formal performance measurement systems. Their attitude is that they already have an incentive system—if you do your job, you get to keep it. The answer to this may be an embarrassment to the hiring authority, but you have to ask it.

If there is a formal performance measurement procedure, you will find it out now. Pay particular attention to find out if salary reviews or incentive bonuses are associated with the tools the company uses. Don't fret if a com-pany doesn't have a formal performance measurement program, just know what theirs is. Get copies of the procedure or performance measurement tools if you can.

• **What happened to the last person in the job?** You need to know this. If the person was fired, you need to know the circumstances. If you learned the answer to this question during the interviewing process, you will want to get clarification now. There is less pressure on you now to sell yourself, so you can delve into this deeply. I have known candidates to track down the person who was fired to get an idea about the situation.

If a person was promoted out of the job, ask to speak to that person. You want to learn as much as you can about what you are getting into. This is a great way to do it.

• **Is the company seeking to grow? How?** Very few organizations are going to tell you that they don't want to grow. But, if you have done your homework, you will know what the track record of growth, or lack of it, has been for the company itself. You have probably also picked up the direction that the company is going in the interviewing process. Some organizations will admit that they don't want to grow, at least, rapidly. If a company says that it wants to grow by acquisition or merger, it may affect your particular position. If it is in the process of being sold, you need to know. Acquiring a company or a merger can create function duplication.

A standard follow-up question to no matter what you were told should be, "So, how might that affect this position?" Listen carefully to the answer. Most of the time, you're going to hear something like, "Oh, it really won't! " You'd better listen to how the person says this more than what he says.

Often, companies need to hire somebody because they need a certain task or job done immediately. They may or may not be thinking, or even care, about what might happen to the position in the near future. They need a job done now, so they hire for it. Most of the time, they aren't thinking about you or the situation down the line. They will worry about that tomorrow. Tomorrow and your future aren't part of their worries. So, just pay attention. You can't predict what might happen and neither can they.

Most people in most companies are overly optimistic about how fast they're going to grow. Growth, or lack of it, may not affect the job you are interviewing for one way or the other. Simply listen to the answer, and then follow your gut.

• **Exactly how much travel is involved with the job?** Usually, if there is an inordinate amount of travel involved in a job, you would have heard about it during the interviewing process. If travel is a big drawback of the position, it is usually brought up in the very beginning of the interviewing process, and you already know about it.

However, if there is travel involved in a particular job, you need to know exactly how much. Get a specific understanding about this in terms that means something to you. For instance, 50% travel can mean a number of things. It can mean a Monday through Friday workweek out of town and then a

Monday through Friday workweek in town. Some people could define it by going out of town Monday evening, being gone Tuesday and Wednesday, and back on Thursday. There may even be a difference between being back on Thursday morning or Thursday evening.

Many times, the travel schedule is required in the first few months and diminishes, somewhat, after the employee knows the territory. So, get a very specific number of days and number of nights, per week or per month, that travel is required. One person's definition of 50% travel is different than another person's. You need to know in terms relative to what you can or can't do.

• **Is there relocation now or down the road?** As with a high degree of travel, if immediate relocation is involved in the position, you will probably learn about it in the initial part of the interviewing process. Relocation is an expensive venture and companies don't do it unless there's real value for them.

Bluntly, and most companies won't admit to this, it is often cheaper to find someone in the local area to do a specific job then is to relocate even a proven employee to where the job is. Unless it's for a very difficult position to sell, most companies are going to try to find a qualified candidate in the city where the job is. Over the past few years, this has not been difficult to do. But, as happened frequently in the late 1990s, there will come a time when companies may have to relocate new employees.

Relocation is a lot more expensive than it used to be, and companies in the last few years haven't had to do it. So, if it is involved now or later, be sure that you are clear about what the company will and won't do regarding relocation. A company might move you but not be responsible or help you out in selling your present home. In some real-estate markets it may be very difficult to do. You need to be aware of the organization's relocation policies and packages, too. Years ago, these kinds of packages were fairly standard. But that is not the case any more.

Relocation in the future for a particular company or position is hard to predict. I've known plenty of organizations over the years that, rather than lay people off, told them that they were going to move their job to a distant city, knowing that the people would not relocate and therefore forcing them to leave the company. It is a very economical way to lay people off without paying severance. Don't be so naive as to think that companies are going to be understanding and kind about this kind of thing. Most organizations have no qualms about "forcing" people to resign by offering to relocate them, knowing they can't, if they think it is in their best interest.

• **How long do you plan to be in your position? With the company?** How someone answers this is as important as what he or she says. Once in a while, a hiring authority will be blunt with you about how long he or she plans to stay in the job. This is good to know, because you may want to move up in the organization also.

Whenever you do, don't take the answer for gospel. As I've tried to establish, a business today is very erratic. Companies, let alone people, have no idea how long they're going to be around. If the average tenure on a job is three years, don't expect somebody to tell you that she's going to be in her position much longer than that.

It is good to know, though, if the hiring authority has plans beyond his or her present position. If you get an answer like, "Well, most of the people in positions in this company say two to three years and then rotate to other departments of the organization," then you realize that you will be faced with the same opportunity. If you get, "I have absolutely no idea. I just take things day to day, month to month, and year to year," then at least you have an idea of how this person feels about her future.

• **Why have people in the past failed to do well at this job?** This is a great question. Often, you will have gotten a sense of how well people did in the job in your interviewing before you get to this point. However, it is a real good idea to ask this question at this point of getting an offer. If you hadn't gotten the real reason about why people have failed before, you will probably get it now.

More often than not, in the beginning of the hiring process, hiring authorities will gloss over the failures that people have had in the particular job they are interviewing for. They don't want to admit that they hired somebody that was incompetnt, or they just think it is better to not say anything negative. Now, however, they want you to take the job. So, they should be in more of a sales mode and willing to share with you the real reason or reasons that people have failed.

Don't be surprised if you hear stories, scenarios, or descriptions of previous employees that you have never had before. The reason you may hear these can be very revealing and may very well end up making a difference in your taking the job. If you hear something like, "The pressure on the person in this position by the comptroller is immense," you may want to investigate exactly what "pressure" means. If it means that nobody can get along with the comptroller, it's one thing. Or if the comptroller is very demanding about the reports that he receives, is yet another. Listen very carefully to the answer that you get from this question. Whatever the hiring authority tells you, he may be saying this same thing about you some day.

• **What are the company's major strengths and weaknesses?** Now that you are strongly being considered by this company and it's trying to hire you, you might hear more than just the party line. Don't necessarily expect something different than you've already heard, but it doesn't hurt to ask. Now that you are being invited to be an insider in the company, you may get a more realistic idea about strengths and weaknesses.

• **What are your personal strengths and weaknesses?** The best time to ask this question is right after you ask the same question about the company. You asked a similar question when you asked this person what it was like to work for her. But now you are more of an insider than you were before, and you might get a more real answer.

Really let this person talk about her strengths and weaknesses. In a way, it is like asking about her, so she will probably open up to you. Listen carefully. The kind of strengths and weaknesses this person will describe will be exactly the kind of person she will look for in others, i.e., you! Take good notes. See if what you hear is consistent with what your potential peers say about this person.

• **Can you explain the organizational structure of the company and of the department?** This is pretty simple and straightforward. You may have been unable to find this out before this interview.

• **What are the trends in your industry?** If you've done your research correctly, you will know the answers to this already. But it doesn't hurt to find out what your potential boss thinks.

• **Does the company have any present or pending legal issues?** You'll probably be one of the few, if not the only, candidates that asks this question. If you've done your homework, you already know most of the legal entanglements that the company may be involved in. This is not only asking about those but also any pending ones. As we've noted, the vast majority of companies in the United States are made of fewer than a hundred people. Major litigation can literally put these businesses in great jeopardy. Now it is rare for most businesses not to be involved in some minor litigation. Let the hiring authority describe what he or she might know.

If the hiring authority does not mention a legal issue that you know could have some major impact on the company, and therefore your new job, if you accept it, now is the time to ask about it. Be sure you understand where the litigation might be before you accept a job. A few things will make you feel so stupid as to show up at your new job and find out that the only thing most of the people in the company can talk about is the pending litigation that will have dire consequences for the company.

• How is the department perceived by the rest of the company? Notice the metaphors that the person uses to describe how the department is perceived. It is likely that whenever description the hiring authority uses, that is the way that he thinks that he is perceived. So, if he says something like, "We are very respected because we provide accurate information, on time," or, "The performance of the department affects everybody in the company, so we're very careful," you probably know what you're getting into. Likewise, if the person says, "We are the most hated department in the company because we say 'no' to everything and everybody," you might know what you're getting into.

• Are there written goals for the department? Who sets them? Even if there are not formal goals for the department, this is a good question to ask. If the department has formal goals for the year, it would be a good idea to ask to see them. If the goals are imposed on the department, you'll find that out. If the department does not have any written goals, you'll find that out too. The sales department with no written or formal goals can't be very effective. The accounting or purchasing department may be a different story.

• How many people have been in this job in the last five years? Where are they now? Listen carefully to this answer. If no one who had been in this job in the last five years was still with the company, you're being told something, and it may not be good. If people are promoted regularly out of this position, it may be good. If there is a high degree of turnover in this job, if you need to know why. If you hear that, "Everyone who has been in this position has been incompetent," watch out! No matter how good you think you are, the same thing may be said about you in the future.

In most situations, there's going to be a mixture of people who got promoted and people who simply left. Keep in mind that most jobs are only going to last two and a half to three years anyhow. High turnover in a job or tremendous stability with people in a job doesn't necessarily make the opportunity good or bad.

If you hear, "Well, I really don't know why people leave this job so often," you need to do further investigation. See the next question.

• **May I speak with the person who has left or is leaving the job?** If the person presently in the job or the person who is leaving the job is still with the company, you should be given access to him or her with no problem. If the person is being replaced and doesn't know it and the search for his or her replacement is confidential, you may not be able to talk to him or her.

If you can't speak to the person who is presently in the job or has been at the position most recently, you will not get tremendous insight into the job. In some instances, the company may not want you to get exposure to the person who is presently in the job. This shouldn't be a deal killer one way or the other. Listen carefully to the circumstances that cause the position to be open.

• **What would be my access to you? Daily, weekly, monthly?** You'll get a really good idea of the manager's style when he or she answers this question. You will also get a sense of how much autonomy you may have in the job. Balance the answer to this question with the answer you got about how much authority you might have. If you have a lot of responsibility but very little authority, and you only see or hear from your boss once a month, you may be in for a real challenge.

Questions to Ask When the Position Involves Management

• **Why are there no internal candidates for this job?** This is the biggest question that you need answered. If you were interviewing for a management position and the company is obviously hiring outside of the current staff, indeed, be even more careful about what you're walking into.

Regardless of whether people would admit it, companies have a tendency to promote from within, even if the people they're promoting aren't as qualified and competent as external candidates might be. The psychology of this practice centers around two things. First of all, internal candidates "know the system." They know the company and all the people in it. The people doing the hiring are familiar with these people, and there's a tendency to think that the people they know, even with their faults, are better than the people they don't know. If they hire externally, they're fearful of whatever drawbacks they might get in a new person. It's just easier to stick with what they know.

The second reason is that companies are afraid that if they don't promote from within, their employees will be disgruntled with the idea that they can't get promoted and leave the organization. Every company wants to appear to all that it gives its employees the opportunity to be promoted. So, it will promote when it thinks it should, rather than interview external candidates.

So, if you were interviewing for a management position, you better get a very clear, deep, and convincing group of reasons as to why no one has been promoted from within. Having been involved in the hiring process for more than three decades, I'm absolutely convinced that ninety-nine out of a hundred times, a company is confined to a less qualified internal candidate than by going outside the organization. But, the known person is better than the unknown person, so it will promote from within when it can, even though it shouldn't.

Well-run companies know this. So, it is likely that you may even be competing with internal candidates. But if you've made it this far in the interviewing process, it is likely that internal candidates are either not qualified or not available.

If you are interviewing for a management position, throughout the whole interviewing process you will get a sense as to whether you were competing with internal candidates. The answer to the above question can be everything from, "We can't find anybody truly qualified to do the job," to "We can't find anybody who wants the job." Don't let your ego lead you to believe that you are going to be the "savior" the company should hire above all of its internal candidates. There may be some very legitimate, reasonable business reasons as to why there are no internal candidates capable of being promoted. You just need to know what they are. You need to constantly ask yourself, "Does this make sense?" Don't dismiss the whole idea of why there are no internal candidates when you hear, "Well, there is nobody qualified to do the job internally."

Because you want a job and good management jobs are hard to find, you will want to accept the reasons that no internal candidates are going to be hired relatively easily. I have filled many management positions over the years that wound up being "no win" situations. Often, they wound up being disasters to the person that I placed. Looking back, both my candidate and I should have seen the problems that eventually arose. There were very good reasons there was no internal candidate: No one wanted the job! Management positions are hired externally all the time. This is not to say that if you're being considered for a management position, it is a good opportunity. There are very good reasons why companies should hire externally. As you can tell, I'm convinced that they could probably hire better candidates externally then they can from promoting internally. But reality is that internal candidates have an advantage.

Just be sure that you ask a lot of questions about why an external candidate is being considered. Don't simply accept the initial "party line." Even though you may want the job—and it may very well be good for you—you must be absolutely comfortable with the answer to this question.

Now, at the time of the offer, is the time to follow up the above question with, "I know that you have said there are no internal candidates for this job, but can you tell me, in detail, why you aren't promoting from within?"

• **How much authority will I have in running the department (the group, the facility, etc.?)** You already may have picked up on a lot of the authority you may have in the interviewing process. But, now you need to get a real, detailed understanding of your authority. Having P & L responsibility usually carries a lot more responsibility than not having it. Don't assume because you think you heard it in the interviewing process. You were focused on selling yourself then, now you are focused on qualifying the job, your expectations for the job, and your ability to do it.

• **I would like to speak to peers about the position that I am interviewing for. Can we arrange that?** Unless the organization that you are interviewing with is replacing somebody confidentially, any firm worth its salt is going to allow you to talk to other managers that are in the same position you are applying for. Make sure you do this if you haven't done so already. (And reread the section above about interviewing in groups and with potential peers.)

You'll get more insights about the company and the job from your potential peers, especially in a management position, than you will from anyone else in the company, even the people you were interviewing with. You'll probably be able to pick up undertones of political issues, personality problems, and organizational challenges by talking to these people. But it is imperative that you do!

If the organization does not want you to talk to other managers, it should raise a big red flag to you. But even if filling the position is confidential and they're replacing someone without their knowledge, a hiring authority should be able to provide you other managers who may talk to you on a confidential basis. Don't underestimate what you'll learn by doing this.

This question is also one of timing. If you asked this question too early in the interviewing process, you will certainly not be accommodated. But once the organization intends to make you an offer, and it has invested in you as a candidate, you have more leverage and are more likely to get audiences you request.

• **Are there any difficult personalities on the staff that I will be supervising?** Pay attention to the hiring authority's initial response to your question. If she hesitates and has to answer the question carefully or pensively, you know that you might have real challenges here. Let the hiring authority describe to you all of the people on the staff that she knows about.

People get really uncomfortable when they're getting a new supervisor. So, you need to be prepared for any difficulties, especially difficult personalities, that you may inherit.

• **Are there any members of the staff or staffs that should be let go?** Oftentimes, if a new manager is being brought on board, people who ought to be fired or moved around are left in their places until the new manager is hired. Upper management will insist that there is enough turmoil going on with hiring a new manager and simply leave the difficult task to the new hire.

Be ready for any kind of answer to this question. If there are really big problems—for instance, a whole department needs to be replaced—you will probably have heard about it in the interviewing process before now. But now it is time to press on this.

If you have to replace the whole staff you inherit, your success will certainly take longer. Normally, you won't have to replace a whole staff. But, unless you are very lucky, you will probably have to replace some of the staff. You should assume that these people should have been let go a long time ago, and their dismissal has been postponed because it is hassle enough to find a new manager. So, listen well.

• **How are the people in the department going to react to an outsider as a manager?** You may have gotten a hint of this answer in the interviewing process. However, the hiring authority that you were talking to, if he or she is like most people, is so interested in the moment, i.e., getting someone hired for the position, he or she doesn't really care what the reaction to a new manager is going to be. He or she will give it lip service, like, "We are very concerned that the present staff not be upset with hiring an outsider." But the truth is, that's going to be your problem and not his or hers. Trust me, if you are in this situation, there's enough emotion throughout the whole staff that it is going to take a number of months for everything to settle down.

No matter what you're told in answering this question, assume the worst. Assume that everyone is going to be really upset, and they're all going to walk out when you show up.

• **May I speak with the staff I will be managing?** Unless the present person is being replaced or the hiring is strictly confidential, you should be allowed to talk to all of the people whom you're going to be managing. You will have a much better understanding of what you're walking into after you do this.

I would recommend always beginning with the administrative or support staff. These people always have a very clear idea of what's going on in a department. People will normally tell the administrative support staff things that they would never tell the supervisor or the higher-ups. These people know most everything that's going on, both positive and negative. Should you take the job, you're going to hear it anyhow, so you might as well start now.

If, for some very strange reason, you are not allowed to talk to the staff that you might be supervising, take that as a big red flag. The opportunity might still be a good one but this is a very bad sign.

• **What are the biggest problems in the department?** The answer to this question will be interesting. If you were told the same things that you hear from the staff you are going to supervise, then you're in real good shape. At least everybody knows what the problems are. Keep in mind that if there were not problems that needed to be solved, they wouldn't need to hire you or anybody else to solve them.

Expect problems. The key here is to find out if everyone from upper management on down agrees with what the problems are. Even if they don't agree, at least you will know what everyone's point of view is.

• What condition is morale in and why? This can be part of the above question. After you've spoken to all the people you will be supervising, you will know what the morale is. The reason you ask this question of upper management is to find out if what they feel and what the subordinates that will be working for you feel are the same. Don't be surprised if they're not.

• Who are the "problem" employees? You're probably going to find this out when you interview everybody on the potential new staff. But it is always better to get upper management's opinion. If you are forewarned about who is going to be your biggest challenge, you might approach them a little differently.

Don't be surprised if you're told that no one is a real problem, but you find out the contrary once you interview the potential staff.

• Who are the "stars" that can help my transition go smoothly? Like the question above, forewarned is forearmed. You'll get a great idea about who can help you and who can hinder you if you interview everyone in the correct way. But it doesn't hurt to have upper management's idea about who will support you the best.

• Are there any of the staff members who are in line for a promotion? Did any of them apply for this job? The first part of this question is asked in order to get an answer to the second part. It's nice to know whom upper management thinks might be good to promote. But it is imperative that you know who of your potential new staff has applied for the job that you are considering.

If you wind up supervising someone who applied for the job that you accept, his or her not getting the job may have a real impact on your relationship with that person. These people, however, can be extremely helpful in your transition as a new manager. They can also be your worst nightmare and sabotage just about everything you do, emphasizing their idea that "You should have hired me for this job."

Your management and people skills are really going to be tested in this situation. Supervising a person who thought that he was qualified to do the job that you got takes a lot of careful communication and interaction. In interviewing this person before you accept the job, it will probably help you to know his disposition. Fifty percent of the time this person is going to feel slighted and leave the company. Just be prepared for it. (Don't be so egotistical as to think that your phenomenal management style is going to keep this from happening.)

• **If I have budgetary responsibility, how large is the budget? Has the department been above or below budget, presently and in the recent past?** You need to know what kind of an economic situation you might be walking into. Hiring authorities may not want to offer this information. In recent economic times, budgets have been slashed and yet performance expectations have been high. If your two predecessors have left or moved on because they couldn't get their job done with the budget they have been given, you need to know. If the department or group has gone over budget, you need to ask the obvious, "Why?"

• **What kind of reports am I going to be responsible for? Are they internal, company reports, or governmental ones?** In these days of Sarbanes-Oxley laws, public companies especially, but private ones, too, are much more careful about most everything financial. Departments such as sales, who traditionally didn't have to be much concerned about "reporting," now have to be very careful about how they report sales the company has made. They can no longer easily "report" sales that aren't real just to make things look good for a while, then go back and amend the reports later.

If you have been in financial positions, you are probably familiar with all of the kinds of governmental reports you are responsible for. But it certainly doesn't hurt to make sure you have a clear idea about what you will be responsible for and what you won't.

• **Does the company plan to make any immediate acquisitions or be acquired or change in any way that might affect the job we are discussing?** Look for hesitancy on the part of the hiring authority when answering this question. You may be privy to information or outright rumors that the company might be sold or be acquired. If so, ask about it. Just be aware that, depending on the level of the position that you are interviewing for, the hiring authority may not know about any plans like these. If you do find out that the company is up for sale or looking to be acquired, think about the kind of position that you are interviewing for and what kind of duplication there might be in another organization. If you are interviewing for an accounting function, for instance, and the company your interviewing with is looking to be acquired, you are certainly aware that your kind of function is at risk.

If you sense that there may be an issue here, it certainly doesn't hurt to just bluntly ask the hiring authority something like, "Look, I really don't want to accept a position and then be involved in a merger or acquisition and have the job I take be at risk. Is there a chance of that happening?" If the hiring authority has any kind of integrity at all and there is some kind of pending event, he or she will tell you.

• **What is the greatest opportunity facing the company? Its greatest challenge?** Asking this question allows the hiring authority to give a balanced answer. The "greatest opportunity" might be nice to know, but what your real interest is in finding out what the "greatest challenge" is. If the greatest challenge is surviving a gigantic lawsuit, you need to know. The answer to this question will most often be fairly benign, but you just might be surprised at any answer you might get. It might be one that could change your whole opinion of the opportunity. *Caveat emptor.*

18 Questions You Must Ask Yourself When You Get an Offer

· ·

The kind of questions that you ask yourself, and others, like a spouse or maybe a mentor, when you get an offer are more important than they have ever been. This is especially true given today's erratic and unpredictable business environment.

Fifteen years ago, maybe even ten years ago, the idea of lifetime employment and career with one firm was still, at least in theory, a business concept. But now, and for the foreseeable future, this idea is a small consideration. You have to interview as though you were going to work for a company for the rest of your natural business life, but, as we've noted, you need to assess an offer with realization that the probability is very high that you will only be there for two to three years.

With that in mind, you need to evaluate an offer based on the short term with the hope of the job lasting for the long term. If and when a company talks to you about the long-term possibilities of promotion opportunities, don't buy into it. If that happens, that is fine. However, you have to judge a job offer based on what it can do for you and your career now and over the next two or three years.

Emotions rule most decisions, especially the ones that have to do with one's job and career. No matter how objective you might be, no matter what kind of formula you come up with, the primary difference between your taking a job and not taking a job comes down to how you feel about it. However, there still has to be some logic, common sense, and reason to the decision. I've developed a ten-question formula to help people decide if an opportunity is good for them. These are simple questions with simple yes or no answers:

1.	Do I like the nature of the work that I will have to perform?	Yes	No
2.	Can I do the job? Is there a good balance of risks/ challenges to the job?	Yes	No
3.	Am I aware of the company's stability or position's stability?	Yes	No
4.	Is the chemistry of the people appropriate?	Yes	No
5.	Is the compensation program fair, reasonable, and commensurate with the job?	Yes	No
6.	Is the opportunity for growth in keeping with my personal goals?	Yes	No
7.	Is the location or territory appropriate?	Yes	No
8.	Is the philosophy of doing business compatible with my personal philosophy?	Yes	No
9.	Does this opportunity build on my previous experience?	Yes	No
10.	Is it likely that this experience would have carryover for my future goals?	Yes	No

My basic guideline is this: If you can answer "yes" to all ten of the questions, that's about as good as you're going to get. If you can answer "yes" to five to seven of the questions, the opportunity may very well be reasonable one, but you need to think about what kind of compromises you may have to make. If you answered, "yes" to less than five of the questions, the opportunity is probably a questionable one.

Now this is about as simple and logical as you can get. The purpose of this approach is to make you think. It is mostly a quantitative exercise and does not take into account the qualitative aspects of how you feel about the entire situation. There is no way to speculate about that for anyone. However, I will tell you that if you only have, say, six yes answers to this exercise and you do not feel emotionally attracted and strong about the opportunity, then you should not take the job because you probably won't be very successful or happy. If you have a total of five yes answers to the survey and feel tremendously passionate, enthusiastic, with a "failure is not an option" attitude toward the opportunity, you may well be able to make it a good one.

These questions do not take into account things such as how long you've been out of work and how many other opportunities you may have available to you. If you have been out of work for six months, and this is the only offer that you ever received, the number of yes answers may not even matter.

Another way to evaluate an offer is the Ben Franklin approach, which means to simply write down the pros and cons, and analyze them. If you have twelve or more reasons as to why you ought to accept the job and only two or three reasons as to why you should not, the decision is obvious. The idea is to make you think about all aspects of the position. The format for this Ben Franklin approach simply looks like this:

Cons	Pros

Forcing yourself to write out the pros and cons and see all the issues can be cathartic. Having your coach helping you out with this exercise is certainly of value. Talking it out with your coach is also of value. Hearing yourself talk about an opportunity and discovering what you think and feel about it will give you a great perspective.

After you consider the two exercises above, you need to address the distinct probability of considering an offer and a job that may only last two and a half to three years. Everyone's hope is that any job will last longer than that, but the reality is that two and a half to three years is going to be more of the average.

So, here are some questions you also should answer.

- **If I get two to three years of experience in this job, how have I enhanced my experience for the future?** Are there certain aspects about the job that stretch you into doing things that you haven't done before? In other words, are you going to expand on the professional experience that you have? Even if the job lasts three years, if you expand your experience into things that you haven't done before, you might be able to leverage all of it down the line.

- **If I get two to three years of experience with this company, will having worked there have been of any value?** There are some firms that are considered "Class A," Fortune 100, "standard-bearer" type of firms. They are the kind of firms that everybody in this particular industry or profession recognizes and respects. There are also some firms that nobody has ever heard of or recognized as pillars of the industry or profession. Is the organization that you are entertaining an offer from the kind of firm that people recognize as quality, and therefore will consider you to be of that same quality by having worked there?

Working for a well-recognized, well-respected organization, even for a two- or three-year period, will sometimes lay a foundation that says, "This person has worked for and was trained by a quality organization, and therefore must be a quality person." That foundation can be the cornerstone that opens up many doors to other organizations even two or three jobs later.

I have placed candidates in positions that might be considered a step back in their careers because the organizations that offered them positions were so well recognized that we knew that we could parlay the experience of having worked there later on. I have always believed that "the cream rises." If you are good, you will be promoted to the level of your competency, provided the opportunities are there. Working with the top people in your profession or industry makes you better.

- **Can this type of organization help me down the line?** I've placed people in startup companies, even though we were told that the company was trying to get its second or third round funding and no one could be sure if they would be around for more than another year or so. It was of value to these candidates to get startup experience.

Now, I certainly wouldn't recommend three startup organizations in a row only lasting a year or two. However, startup experience can be very valuable, especially if you have a very stable, say eight- to ten-year, track record with one or two firms. Startup experience, coupled with traditional experience can give a candidate a broad range of capabilities that can more easily be marketed to an equally broad range of firms in the future.

The same thing can be said for the kind of firm I mentioned in the previous question. The type of firm you go to work for can balance your previous experience. The larger the variety of firms that you might work for within a particular profession, the more you demonstrate flexibility.

• **Is this organization consistent with the things that I've done in the past?** This is a tough question. If you have been out of work for six months and this is the only offer that you have received, it doesn't matter whether the organization is consistent with the things you've done in the past, you probably need to take the job.

However, if you have choices, it is a real good idea to try to "build" your career with consistency. The longer you are with a particular profession or type of industry, the better off you are. I can't tell you the number of candidates I've worked with over the years who spent a couple of years in one industry or profession, and another one and two or three years in another. They became jacks of all trades and masters of none. Not only are they hard to place, but they have a very difficult time reaching higher levels of their profession because they can never get beyond "first or second base" in any one arena.

If you were in the accounting profession or other types where your function may apply to a number of different industries, it may not be detrimental for you to work for different kinds of organizations. But even then, as an accountant or finance person, if you started out in banking, spent three or four years there, then went to manufacturing for five years, and then went into insurance for several years, you won't be a specialist enough for someone to hire you beyond the first- or second-level job. The reason is simple. Beyond the first or second level of competition, for instance, if you were head to head with someone in the banking arena where you spent three or four years and she spent ten years, you probably will not be hired. Likewise, with only several years of insurance experience, you will have a hard time competing with others with ten or twelve years of insurance experience.

We hear from sales candidates all the time who have been in successful sales positions and want to change industries and sell something far beyond the realm of their documented experience. Their attitude is that, "sales are sales"—"if I can sell what I have been selling, I can sell anything." However, they fail to recognize that they are competing with candidates who have significant experience in the arena that they would like to get into. Why would an organization hire a candidate who has been a good salesperson in an area that does not pertain to what it does, when it can hire a candidate with stellar experience in exactly what it does?

Candidates have a hard time understanding this issue. But the truth is, hiring organizations want to hire the best quality candidate they can, with the documentation and track record in what they do (if they can get it). "Good athleticism" does not sell a good athlete, but when a good athlete with the track record playing in a specific position is available, he will be hired. Duh!

So, to build a career, it is better to try to find jobs in professions or industries that are consistent with one another so down the line you appear to be a specialist.

19 Reference Checking Your Next Employer

••

Now that you have an offer or are closer to one, consider this idea. It is rare for a candidate to ever be considered for hire unless his or her references are checked. These are usually previous employers, previous supervisors, or sometimes people with whom the candidate has a personal relationship. They can speak to a candidate's integrity, character, work ethic, previous work performance, etc. This is one of the very many ways that hiring organizations try to protect themselves from making a mistake in hiring.

What is equally as rare is a candidate that thinks to check the "references" of an organization that he or she is thinking about going to work for. It seldom crosses the candidates' mind to pursue just as much due diligence about the organization or the individuals in it, as the organization should pursue about him or her as a candidate.

Most of us work for smaller firms where we not only establish personal relationships with the people we work with, but usually also take on the "identity" of the company. Since companies and the people in them put their best foot forward when interviewing you, as a candidate, they rarely reveal the difficulties, struggles, or problems they have as a company. Just like you, as a candidate, didn't reveal the risks that you bring to being employed, your prospective employer isn't going to intentionally reveal its risks in the interviewing process.

Think about most of the jobs that you have had. Did the company, the job, or the people in the company turn out to be exactly what they appeared to be when you were being recruited by them?

Now there are always problems in any company. If companies didn't have problems, they wouldn't need to hire you or anybody else. All companies have strengths and weaknesses . . . just like the individuals who run them and work there. The challenge for a candidate who is thinking about going to work for the organization is to be aware of all of the problems and issues that a company might have before he or she goes to work there. The problems that the company might have, even if they are gigantic and seemingly insurmountable, are rarely the ones that cause a new employee to feel like he or she made a mistake in accepting the job, if those problems were clearly stated before the candidate goes to work.

Even worse is when the candidate feels that the problems, even if minor, are purposely concealed from him or her in the interviewing process for fear that the candidate would not have accepted the job if he or she knew about the issues.

Most often, candidates are so excited about finding a new job and finding a company that they really like and want to go to work for that they neglect to dig deeper than the surface that people in the company show them during the interviewing process. So if you get close to getting an offer from a company that you really like, give yourself a "gut check" and check the company's references. Here is how to do that:

1. Put in a phone call to one of the people that you might have interviewed with that is not directly responsible for the position you were interviewing for and ask him or her if you can talk to him or her "off the record." This could even be an administrative type of person who isn't even involved in the interviewing process but whom you met while interviewing. Tell that person that you are seriously entertaining an offer from the company, and you would like to know about some of the things "they wouldn't want you to know" before you took the job. Ask the person to be open and honest. You might even ask if there are any serious problems with the company or its people that were not revealed to you. Ask why he works there, and if he knew then what he knows now, would he still accept the job. You can get a tremendous sense of what's going on in the company this way.

2. Call some of the customers or clients that your potentially new company does business with. Find the individual in the customer's or client's

organization who deals directly with your potential employer and ask every question you can think of. Even try to find (although it would be hard) previous customers or clients of your potential employer and talk to them as to why they are no longer customers or clients.

3. Check legal records. Find out if your potential employer or the people are involved in any serious business or personal lawsuits. Minor lawsuits are hard to avoid in business, but the major ones can be devastating to an organization. Acrimonious divorces can destroy a seemingly good small business. Personal bankruptcies or grand jury indictments of officers in a company can represent a whole different set of problems that most firms don't want to talk about.

4. Talk to previous employees. If you're interviewing for a position that was recently vacated, find the person who was in the position and talk to him or her. If she has left the company, she is apt to be more open and blunt with you than if she is still with the firm. But even if she is still employed by the company in a different position, ask her to be blunt about the problems you might encounter. Previous employees who are related to the job you are interviewing for are still good sources of information.

5. Try to get to know, on a personal basis, some of the people you might be working directly with or for. If you get them in a social situation, listen carefully to the way they talk about their company, the people they work with, their customers, their jobs, etc. Check out the attitudes of the people you are thinking about going to work with and for. If everyone's attitude is upbeat and positive about most things, you can bet the company has the same attitude. Beware of the opposite kind of attitude. It can make a company and a job miserable.

6. Professional networking sites such as LinkedIn and Jobster can make it easier for you to find people who have worked for specific companies or specific individuals.

7. Blogs. Although comments about certain companies and individuals might be hard to find, they might be helpful. Knowing what others are saying or have experienced can be very enlightening. Remember, though, that this information may not be true or substantiated. Anyone can write anything in a blog. Be mindful that much of your reference

checking can be a double-edged sword. Many social networkers and bloggers have a strong tendency to be negative and may have only a passing relationship with the people or companies they write about. Consider the sources of information and the context of their comments.

No company or situation is perfect. Don't expect it. You are simply trying to minimize surprises once you go to work. Whatever you discover, put it in the context of the other things about the job and the company. Do your reference checking, but decide what is best for you personally.

. . . As Long as We Are Talking About Reference Checking

It may be a very good idea for you to run a background check on yourself! Sound odd? Well, the truth is that at least once a month in our recruiting company we have at least one problem with background checks that turn up information about the wrong person. That's right: Information, usually negative information, is found and attributed to a candidate and it turns out to be a different person, a bad record, or a mistake. A 2004 study by the U.S. Public Interest Research Group found that 79% of consumer-credit reports contained at least one mistake. This kind of mistake can cost you a job.

So, if you get close to a job offer and you know your references are going to be checked, you better bet that a credit, criminal, and any kind of other check people can think of will also be done. You had better know beforehand what kind of information will be found. If there are mistakes of identity, which is likely with common names, you need to know. If the information is wrong, you need to know. Often companies rely on third-party organizations to do this kind of checking. It is easy to make mistakes.

So, run a credit report on yourself. Google or Yahoo yourself. Find blogs or other kind of online postings that might talk negatively about you or someone with a name like yours. Junk can stay alive in cyberspace forever. You might even check to see if your Social Security number has been used by someone else. We have had a number of candidates who claim their identities were "stolen" off their resumes when they were posted on one of the job boards.

If there are going to be any problems with any kind of background check, you need to know before they happen. You can't control these negative references, but you can mitigate the damage they may cause you.

Epilogue

··

The purpose of this book is to prepare you for doing your best in the interviewing process. At one time, performing *well* during the traditional interviewing process could land you the job. Not any more! The job search climate is more erratic than it has ever been.

The good news is that for the foreseeable future, there are going to be more job opportunities available than there will be people. Estimates range that there will be everywhere from 5 to 12 million more jobs between now and 2015. The 78 million baby boomers will pass the business baton to 48 million GenXers. The United States has been adding more than a hundred thousand jobs a month for the last few years. The Department of Labor says that 4.6 million people start new jobs every month. The GDP has been growing at 3% every year for the last few years, corporate profits are up, and U.S. business has been expanding at 15% per year during the last two years.

The challenging news is that the business climate is more treacherous than it has ever been. Technology has spawned a world economy. Competition has forced companies to expand and contract more rapidly than ever before. The rarity of employee layoffs in the early 1980s is now usual practice in U.S. business.

The idea of career employment is a thing of the past. A "career path" within any company is merely recruitment propaganda. Employers and employees have generational differences in values. A Gallup Organization poll in March 2007 found that 70% of U.S. employees say they feel either "not engaged" or "actively disengaged" at work. The average U.S. CEO only keeps his or her job for five years, according to *Business Briefings* (July, 2007). In 2006, the average 40-year-old worker in the United States had had ten jobs.

The average U.S. company in my opinion, is going to change its complexion every two and a half to three years. The average employee in the United States needs to be prepared to change jobs every two and a half to three years. Although the job opportunities may be more plentiful, the emotional strain of looking for a job is still a fact.

You are going to have to look at each job change as a "step" in your career. Rather than looking at a job with any company as a long-term commitment, you're going to need to ask yourself, "How can I leverage this experience two to three years from now?" Business and companies in the United States are simply going to be more flexible and fluid. The size of every company's workforce will ebb and flow erratically.

For the foreseeable future individuals looking for a job will have a number of opportunities available to them. In order to be able to select the best opportunity for one's career, the job seeker is going to have to perform, not just *well,* but *excellently* in the interviewing process.

Remember, interviewing is a staged, contrived event. A perspective employer is going to ask four simple questions: *Can you do the job? Do we like you? Are you a risk?* and *Can we work the money out?* Now the answers to these questions are much more difficult. You have to really understand the questions and practice the answers.

A successful candidate is not only going to have to know how to answer the qualifying questions of the interviewing process, but also how to ask the right questions to evaluate the career move. He or she not only has to nail the interview questions 100%, but also to ask the right questions to determine his or her own future in the job.

In contrast to traditional hiring, where a career path might have been possible, a candidate has to be conscious of how a new job would "build" on his or her career. The company you are interviewing with is going to change, even if you go to work there. If your next job is only going to last two and a half to three years (. . . and I hope it lasts longer for you), you need to think of the job as a strategic career stepping stone. How can you "sell" this experience to your next employer?

Acing the interview is a must for your career. Practice, Practice, Practice!

Acing the interview is a way of thinking! Practice, Practice, Practice!

Appendix: Some Important Lists for Job Hunters

....

Top Twelve Interview Mistakes Entry-Level Candidates Make

1. **Candidates didn't research the company.** They didn't know the CEO's name, the size of the company, its business, the market cap, the ticker symbol (for public companies), etc.

2. **Candidates didn't sell themselves** or forgot to communicate: "This is what I can do for you, because this is what I have done in school, and for others."

3. **Candidates were nervous, had poor body language, or didn't look the interviewer in the eye.** They obviously didn't practice interviewing or selling themselves. They say things like, "What would you like to know about me?"

4. **Candidates didn't have a real understanding of the position** (i.e., not doing their homework about the job) or didn't even ask about the position's responsibilities.

5. **Candidates were not enthusiastic or did not demonstrate a level of commitment to work, the position, or the industry.**

6. **Candidates didn't share insights into their personal lives that would carry over into their work.**

7. **Candidates didn't know what is on their resume.** For example, when they were asked a question about a part-time or summer job, they didn't remember much about it.

8. **Candidates didn't have thoughtful or inquisitive questions to ask at the end of the interview.**

9. **Candidates were not able to differentiate themselves from other candidates** (i.e., what makes them a better candidate than others?).

10. **Candidates were not able to identify their weaknesses and show how they plan to strengthen them.**

11. **Candidates had an inability to relate what they have studied or what they have done to a business setting.**

12. **Candidates spent too much time getting ready for trick questions,** such as, "Why is a manhole round?" instead of thinking about real, "Why we should hire you?" questions.

Top Ten Mistakes Candidates Make in an Initial Interview

1. **They forget that this is a *selling* situation . . . and don't ask for the job.** A candidate's objective in an initial interview is to sell what he or she can do for the prospective employer. He or she is so unique and so valuable over and above every other candidate, he or she needs to be hired. A candidate has absolutely nothing to decide about until there is a job offer. Success in the initial interview is the first step to that job offer. And a candidate has to constantly be asking *"What do I need to do to get the job?"*

2. **They think that interviewing is a "two-way street."** Most candidates think that the interview should be a give and take on the part of the candidate and the interviewing or hiring authority. An initial interview is a "one-way street." A hiring or interviewing authority is going to have available to them a plethora of initial interviewees for every job to fill. A candidate has to prove him- or herself superior to all of the other candidates before getting to an "equal" exchange with a potential employer.

3. **They focus on what they want in a job.** Most candidates focus on what they want in a job rather than what they can do for a prospective employer. They don't recognize that if they give the hiring authority good enough reasons why they ought to be hired, a hiring authority

can give them plenty of good reasons why they ought to go to work there.

4. **They don't know what they're really selling to an employer.** Most candidates, even if they know they need to sell themselves, don't know what they should be selling. Their attitude is, "Hey, I'm a good person, you'd be lucky to have me . . . When can I go to work?" They forget to sell specific *features, advantages, and benefits* that they can provide the employer.

5. **They cannot articulate or "bridge" their specific abilities for the employer.** Most candidates "know" they're good, and even if they're aware of their specific features, advantages, and benefits, they can't articulate them specifically. In other words, "this is what I've done for others. . . . so, therefore, I will be successful for you." This takes practice and doesn't come naturally.

6. **They have poor communication skills.** It is hard to believe that candidates don't practice looking people in the eye and communicating clearly and concisely what they can do for a company that nobody else can. If they mumble, slouch, don't look people in the eye, and can't speak clearly, they won't get hired. It's not that hard to practice, even if it doesn't come naturally.

7. **Improper or poor dress and/or body language is unprofessional in the interview.** There are still people who dress casually for an interview, slouch or slump in their chairs, have poor eye contact, and do unprofessional things in an interview. Candidates should, at least in an initial interview, dress like a banker and be well groomed. They need to practice sitting up in the chair, leaning forward, looking the interviewing or hiring authority in the eye, and being relaxed yet serious.

8. **They don't research the company or the position they are interviewing for.** I'm always amazed at the number of very well-educated, professional candidates who don't do research on the company or the job they are interviewing for. Cursory research won't do. The people who are getting the jobs usually know more about the company and the people they are interviewing with.

9. **They are unable to articulate what they would like in a new job or company.** I'm not talking about salary, title, etc. I'm talking about people who don't know what their professional goals are, where they would like to be in the future, and what they're striving for personally and professionally. Too often they come across as, "Well . . . I just need a job."

10. **They badmouth their present employer.** Most candidates don't recognize that employers identify with employers. Whatever you say about your present employer or past employers, you will say about them. Your present and past employers have to appear positive.

Other sins: Discussing personal problems in the interview, being late for the interview, not apologizing for being late to the interview, not "closing" the interview properly, not asking what the next steps are going to be, and not asking about the competitive candidates.

Top Five Mistakes Candidates Make in Answering Interview Questions

1. **They don't understand or think about what the employer is asking *from the employer's point of view.*** Candidates don't stop and think, Is the employer asking, "Can I do the job? Do they like me? Am I a risk? (and what kind?) Can we work the money out?" Candidates have to realize from what point of view the employer is acting and answer accordingly.

2. **They answer interviewing questions *from their point of view.*** They try to justify things like being fired, being out of work six months, getting laid off, etc. from their own point of view. They try to explain that they are right, and they were wronged by someone else.

3. **Candidates start answering the question before they clearly understand it.** People are nervous, and in interviewing situation, they start answering a question before they really understand. There's nothing wrong with asking the hiring or interviewing authority to restate a question for you to get a better understanding of it.

4. **Candidates adopt an "I'm not worried about answering questions. I do fine at ad-libbing answers. I think great on my feet!" attitude toward interviewing questions.** This kind of attitude leads to disaster. No matter how well a person thinks on his or her feet, the interviewing process is more sophisticated than it has ever been. Ad lib won't hack it.

5. **Candidates don't practice questioning and answering to the point where they're prepared for just about any interview situation.** Answering questions well takes a lot of practice and preparation. The candidates who prepare well for interviewing questions get the offers.

Top Ten Mistakes That Candidates Make When They Are Invited Back for Subsequent Interviews

1. **Candidates think that because they have been invited back, they're going to get hired.** Subsequent interviews beyond the initial interview are simply steps in the process. Managing the steps is different than an initial interview.

2. **Candidates treat subsequent interviews in the same way that they treated an initial interview.** Although the basic presentation of yourself is the same, subsequent interviews beyond the initial interview need to be "customized" and refined to do them correctly.

3. **They don't get a clear idea of how many other candidates are being moved to the next step and what their backgrounds are.** Interviews beyond the initial interview are like the playoff season in sports. The competition is keener. Candidates have to get a really good idea about how many other candidates are being moved to the next level and what their backgrounds are. Successful candidates will also find out where their perceived weaknesses might be compared to the other candidates. In other words, "How do I stack up to the other people that I'm competing with?"

4. **Candidates don't solicit the help of the initial interviewing authority in "promoting" them to the next step.** Before subsequent interviews, a candidate should meet with, or at least contact by phone,

the initial interviewing authority to find out everything there is to know about the subsequent interviews and the people who will conduct them. The candidate should ask about how many interviews there will be and, more important, whom the interviews will be with. Knowing the background, interviewing style, and as much detail as possible about the people who will be conducting the subsequent interviews is essential.

5. **Candidates are not clear about how the subsequent interviews might differ from the initial interviews.** Asking the initial interviewing or hiring authority questions like, "What will be the main focus of the subsequent interviews? Over and above what I communicated to you in the initial interview, what more will these interviewing authorities want? Based on our initial interview, what are the strengths I should highlight or weaknesses that I should augment in the subsequent interviews?" Get the idea? The candidate can't assume that subsequent interviews are like the initial interviews.

6. **They don't research the company and the position as well as the people doing the subsequent interviewing in even more depth than the initial interview.** Since the candidate now has a better idea of what the company might want in hiring someone, he or she should do more in-depth research about the job, the interviewing and hiring authorities, peers, and anything else that might be pertinent. Know your target!

7. **The candidate doesn't "go the extra mile" in subsequent interviews.** I encourage candidates to develop 30-, 60-, and 90-day plans as to what they would do in the first 90 days of employment and pass them out to the interviewing authorities in subsequent interviews. Some candidates prepare PowerPoint presentations on themselves and their ability to do the job and use them in subsequent interviews. Any kind of activity or effort that will set a candidate apart from the other candidates in subsequent interviews is great.

8. **Candidates relax and forget that it's in the subsequent interviews where most excellent candidates get eliminated.** A good candidate recognizes many tests to interview better and work harder in subsequent interviews than he or she did in the initial interviews.

9. **Candidates neglect to get the support of the subsequent interviewing authorities.** This means asking every interviewing or hiring authority in subsequent interviews if they're going to endorse your being hired. Candidates need to ask every subsequent interviewer after the initial, "What do I need to do to get the job?" and "Will you support my candidacy over the other candidates?" It is crucial that you get "buy in" from the people with whom you interview. You want them to commit to supporting you as a candidate.

10. **Candidates don't realize how crucial subsequent interviews are.** Candidates have to interview better than they did on the initial interviews but also be aware that subsequent interviews are not the final. They are the "playoffs." They need to be taken seriously because they lead to the finals.

Top Ten Mistakes Candidates Make When They Are Told They Are Going to Get an Offer

1. **Candidates think that their search is over and they're going to get hired.** An offer is like any other step in the process of getting hired. It is just a step. This whole process really is not over until you have not only been hired, but have held the job for six to nine months.

2. **Candidates let their guard down and quit selling.** Candidates think that since they're getting an offer, they don't have to keep selling themselves. I have seen lots of offers become much better simply because a candidate realizes that until he or she accepts an offer, he or she needs to keep selling his or her ability to do the job and reasons why he or she ought to be hired.

3. **Candidates think that the negotiations at the time of a final offer need to be adversarial.** Candidates get fearful and scared and approach the final offer stages with an attitude of "fear of loss." They need to approach an offer stage with an attitude of "We're all in this together . . . let's work something out that's valuable to all of us."

4. **Candidates are too anxious to get an offer and don't listen or ask the right kind of questions so that they totally understand the**

offer. Oftentimes, candidates are so anxious to get an offer that they don't really listen to all of it. They don't take good notes or take a logical, reasonable, step-by-step approach to the offer stage.

5. **Candidates are too cautious about an offer and are afraid of making a mistake.** Candidates often are so afraid of making a mistake and accepting a job that they become too cautious about an offer. They start thinking about things to think about and think themselves out of a very good opportunity.

6. **They think that since they're getting an offer (that they might take), they can stop other interviewing cycles.** If candidates recognize that offers are simply steps in the process, they're more likely to get more than one offer. Never quit getting offers until you have one that you have accepted.

7. **Candidates don't take every offer seriously.** Candidates will often go into receiving an offer pretty convinced that they will not accept it for lots of different reasons. I don't recommend doing this. It is important to go after every offer as though it were the last one on earth. Until you hear everything there is to know about an offer, you really don't know enough about it to know whether you accept or reject it. Assume nothing until you have the offer and you know everything about it.

8. **Candidates take too much time to think about an offer.** If a candidate takes more than a day or so to "think about" an offer, any employer in his or her right mind is going to rescind the offer and hire his or her number two candidate. Most employers will assume that, if you tell them that you are going to think about an offer for more than one day, you're going to leverage that offer with another company. They won't like it and will be irritated.

9. **Candidates make assumptions about an offer after they have received it.** Because having to accept/reject an offer can be emotionally stressful, candidates will often be embarrassed and ask further questions after they get an offer. If you don't understand everything there is to know about an offer, act like a good business person and call the hiring authority to get a further explanation.

10. **Candidates set start dates out too far after an offer is accepted.** If an offer is accepted, a candidate wants to be sure that he or she starts the new job just as soon as possible. Any time that elapses between the offer and starting the job beyond two weeks opens up many possibilities for a status change. No company or hiring authority will want to admit that this kind of thing can happen, but I see it regularly. Once you have committed to take the job, start it just as soon as possible. Leave nothing to chance!

Top Five Mistakes Candidates Make When They Think They Have Been Eliminated After an Interview

1. **Candidates don't follow up with the interviewing or hiring authority.** "No" doesn't always mean "no." Just because you think you have been eliminated from contention doesn't mean you shouldn't follow up with the employer, thanking him or her for the time and expressing interest in him or her personally and the company for the future.

2. **Candidates don't let the hiring or interviewing authority know that they would still like to be considered for other opportunities in the company.** Most candidates simply stop selling themselves to a prospective employer. They confuse the job they are interviewing for with being hired. I had one of my candidates a few years back stay in contact with the hiring authority even though he had been rejected for the position he was interviewing for. He was hired by the hiring authority . . . seven years later at a totally different company.

3. **Candidates don't ask the interviewing or hiring authority how they could have done better in the interviewing process.** In other words, what made the difference between the people they pursued and you? What could you have done better? Feedback is the breakfast of champions!

4. **Candidates don't ask the interviewing or hiring authority who else they might know who might need a good employee.** Just because a hiring authority may not hire you doesn't mean he or she

won't like you. If he or she likes you well enough, he or she may not hesitate to refer you to friends who may need an employee.

5. **Candidates don't follow up with the interviewing or hiring authority even weeks or months after the interview.** If you haven't found a job, it certainly doesn't hurt to e-mail or call a hiring authority even weeks or months after the interview. Most hiring authorities love persistence and the willingness to work. Keeping in touch this way certainly can't hurt.

Index

About the Author

••

Tony Beshara is the owner and president of Babich & Associates, which was established in 1952 and is the oldest placement and recruitment service in Texas. He has been in the business of finding jobs for just about every kind of professional since 1973. Tony has personally found more than 6,700 individuals jobs in the more than 30 years that he has been in the placement and recruitment profession. Tony has personally interviewed more than 24,000 people on all professional levels and has worked with more than 21,000 hiring authorities. The twenty-five recruiters at Babich and Associates use the process that he has perfected, and the firm has placed more than 20,000 people using his system. Tony is recognized by the *Fordyce Letter* as the #1 placement and recruitment specialist in the United States.

Tony spent three years teaching on the college level and received his Ph.D. in Higher Education from St. Louis University in 1973, before entering the profession.

Dr. Beshara authored a book titled *The Job Search Solution: The Ultimate System for Finding a Great Job NOW!* He has also created an online course called "The Job Search Solution," a 60-hour program that is loaded with just about everything he has learned since 1973 about finding a job. Tony also hosts a weekly radio show, *The Job Search Solution,* on KVCE 1160 AM, The Voice of Texas, every Thursday from 1 PM to 2 PM. Tony and his beautiful wife of 38 years, Chrissy, live in Dallas and have four grown sons.

For more information on how to manage the emotional aspects of looking for a job, go to: www.tonybeshara.com/emotions

For more information on how to write a resume that works, go to: www.tonybeshara.com/resumes

For more information on how to interview well, go to:
 www.tonybeshara.com/interviewing

For more information on the myths of getting hired in today's marketplace, go to: www.tonybeshara.com/hiringmyths

For more information on job search references, go to: www.tonybeshara.com/references

For more information on getting offers, negotiating, and resigning, go to: www.tonybeshara.com/joboffers

For more information on dealing with discrimination in the interviewing process go to: www.tonybeshara.com/discrimination

For more information on interviewing questions and answers, go to: www.tonybeshara.com/interviewingquestions

For more information on how to get interviews, go to: www.tonybeshara.com/gettinginterviews